Christmas in Calcutta

Christmas in Calcutta
Anglo-Indian Stories and Essays

Robyn Andrews

www.sagepublications.com
Los Angeles • London • New Delhi • Singapore • Washington DC

Copyright © Robyn Andrews, 2014

All rights reserved. No part of this book may be reproduced or utilised in any form or by any means, electronic or mechanical, including photocopying, recording or by any information storage or retrieval system, without permission in writing from the publisher.

First published in 2014 by

SAGE Publications India Pvt Ltd
B1/I-1 Mohan Cooperative Industrial Area
Mathura Road, New Delhi 110 044, India
www.sagepub.in

SAGE Publications Inc
2455 Teller Road
Thousand Oaks, California 91320, USA

SAGE Publications Ltd
1 Oliver's Yard, 55 City Road
London EC1Y 1SP, United Kingdom

SAGE Publications Asia-Pacific Pte Ltd
3 Church Street
#10-04 Samsung Hub
Singapore 049483

Published by Vivek Mehra for SAGE Publications India Pvt Ltd, typeset in 10/13 Palatino Linotype by Diligent Typesetter, Delhi and printed at Saurabh Printers Pvt Ltd, New Delhi.

Library of Congress Cataloging-in-Publication Data

Andrews, Robyn.
 Christmas in Calcutta : Anglo-Indian stories and essays / Robyn Andrews.
  pages cm
 Includes bibliographical references and index.
  1. Anglo-Indians—India—Kolkata—Ethnic identity. 2. Anglo-Indians—India—Kolkata—Social conditions. 3. Anglo-Indians—India—Kolkata—Biography. 4. Christians—India—Kolkata—Biography. 5. Community life—India—Kolkata. 6. Education—Social aspects—India—Kolkata. 7. Kolkata (India)—Social conditions. 8. Kolkata (India)—Ethnic relations. 9. Kolkata (India)—Biography. 10. Kolkata (India)—Religious life and customs. I. Title.
 DS486.C2A77   954'.147—dc23   2013   2013040152

ISBN: 978-81-321-1348-5 (HB)

The SAGE Team: Supriya Das, Shreya Chakraborti, Rajib Chatterjee and Rajinder Kaur

For Anglo-Indians of Calcutta, particularly Keith.

Thank you for choosing a SAGE product! If you have any comment, observation or feedback, I would like to personally hear from you. Please write to me at contactceo@sagepub.in

—Vivek Mehra, Managing Director and CEO, SAGE Publications India Pvt Ltd, New Delhi

Bulk Sales

SAGE India offers special discounts for purchase of books in bulk. We also make available special imprints and excerpts from our books on demand.

For orders and enquiries, write to us at

Marketing Department
SAGE Publications India Pvt Ltd
B1/I-1, Mohan Cooperative Industrial Area
Mathura Road, Post Bag 7
New Delhi 110044, India
E-mail us at marketing@sagepub.in

Get to know more about SAGE, be invited to SAGE events, get on our mailing list. Write today to marketing@sagepub.in

This book is also available as an e-book.

Contents

List of Photos	ix
Foreword by Irwin Allan Sealy	xi
Preface	xv
Acknowledgements	xvii
Introduction	xxi

Part One: Identity

Chapter 1: Angeline: Typically Anglo-Indian 3

Chapter 2: Essay: Culture and Identity 13

Chapter 3: Irene: Questions of Identity 32

Part Two: Faith

Chapter 4: Dulcie: The Kindness of Strangers and an Everyday Faith 51

Chapter 5: Essay: A Christian Community in Changing Times 66

Chapter 6: Jane: God-given Opportunities 85

Part Three: Education

Chapter 7: Peter: The Less the Education, the Fewer the Opportunities 99

Chapter 8: Michael Robertson: Education and the Community 107

Chapter 9: Essay: Reflections on Dilemmas in Education 121

Chapter 10: Philip: With Education Comes Success 138

Part Four: Community Care

Chapter 11: Philomena Eaton: Social Service Convenor
    Extraordinaire   157

Chapter 12: Essay: Community Care and Consolidation   168

Chapter 13: Barry O'Brien: Charismatic Politician   180

Chapter 14: Meryl: Life, Last Days and Care   191

Final Words: Reflections on Research and the Community   206

Bibliography   209
Index   213
About the Author   219

List of Photos

I.1 Robyn, Jane, Rochelle and Carolyn in Front of
Mysore Palace (1997)   xxiv
I.2 New Market a Few Days before Christmas Day (2011)   xxx

2.1 The Changed Face of Elliott Road (2004)   21

3.1 Bow Barracks (2011)   46

5.1 A House Altar (2004)   70
5.2 Bow Barracks: Our Lady of Lourdes Grotto Area Set
Up for Mass (2013)   73

9.1 People Signing with Thumbprints   130
9.2 Young Anglo-Indian Boy Studying in His Home (2003) 134
9.3 Secondary School Student Studying at Her Desk (2003) 135

11.1 Robyn with Philomena Eaton at the World
Anglo-Indian Reunion in Melbourne (2004)   167

Foreword

Calcutta bears a disproportionate burden of colonial history, a burden it once carried with pride. With the transfer of power to Delhi that pride was shaken, and would have passed through a number of stages, from disbelief to the consolations of philosophy. The city's decline is now a hundred years old: for most of the 20th century its past was more attractive than any present it could manufacture, encouraging a culture of regret, if not denial. It was Satyajit Ray's genius to capture, and resist, this backward glance.

If the Bengali is forever looking over his shoulder, the Calcutta Anglo-Indian can be forgiven for stopping in his tracks to turn all the way round. After all, the grey man's burden, and his loss, is a fraction heavier. A community that lost half its numbers overnight at Independence and more than half the remainder over the rest of the century is bound to be disoriented. The present author is only the latest observer to lament the lack of critical mass for those who remain. Only the Jews of Calcutta have disappeared more completely from the local scene.

The marvel then is that those Anglo-Indians who remain preserve such good cheer. The lives of 10 of these are presented in Robyn Andrews' book, told for the most part in their own words. And while many cast a nostalgic look back, they are mostly too busy with the present to regret the loss of those who fled. They range across every station of life, from company secretaries and politicians to slum-dwellers and students: middle-class, rich, poor. Armed with a tape recorder and empathy the author has captured their voices and something of their daily lives. Her gaze is that of an outsider, new to the city and country, but returning repeatedly in the role of a committed participant. Rather than aiming for the imagined neutrality of social science, Robyn Andrews has sensibly allowed her sympathies to be engaged and her own life to colour the picture; she has also steered clear of the jargon that renders much academic work unreadable. She shares her preconceptions and prejudices with the reader and brings to bear in addition certain insights from the Maori experience of her native New Zealand, a slant I would have wished to see widened. Private eye or public anthropology, the result is a gallery of fascinating individuals making the best of the hand dealt them in the city of their ancestors.

Anglo-Indians, as the author notes, are invisible in the national imagination. It is hardly surprising then that scholars looking at the role of English in India should overlook the fact that a community of native speakers exists, even if some of them are actually illiterate. Andrews argues for a zero-illiteracy drive and this goal is not impracticable; parenting, she is willing to hazard, has improved when it comes to the schooling of poor Anglo-Indian children. She also bravely suggests an amendment to the definition of an Anglo-Indian (which the Constitution currently restricts to European lineage through the male line), arguing that there is often good reason to include the maternal line, as the case of the subject called Irene so clearly demonstrates.

Despite destitution at the bottom end of the scale and the steady trickle abroad of emigrants, we are left with a picture that is not disheartening. This has something to do with the author's engagement with the community, whether in old people's homes where lives of incident and interest are winding down or on the campus of Birkmyre hostel where young graduates are gearing up. The story of Philip, whose earnings (at a call centre where he is repeatedly adjudged the best caller) make a quantum difference to his family's quality of life, is a good counter to the author's own doubts as to whether English has brought any professional advantage to the community. Stories such as this should be widely disseminated in the community, and I would urge all principals of Anglo-Indian schools to make them available to their students.

A census of the community is urgently required, as the Anglo-Indian former member of legislative assembly (MLA) for West Bengal, Barry O'Brien, has remarked. I would suggest in addition a vigorous push to collect the oral history of the community through a recording of Anglo-Indian voices by all interested persons, and not just in the city of Calcutta. This would not only preserve individual life stories, but serve as a record of Anglo-Indian speech patterns, slang and every kind of idiom; the results could be housed at the proposed Centre for Anglo-Indian Studies at Calcutta University. Such a collection would be a valuable resource for future study while giving the community, as Robyn Andrews has wisely done, the last word.

Irwin Allan Sealy
Author of *The Trotter-Nama*

Preface

Calcutta is a city I always look forward to returning to. Its sensory intensity gets to me every time: chapattis being dry-fried on *chulas*, heat haze on my calves as I walk past corn being grilled on coal fires, the wafts of toasted flour. However, it's the human interaction, as warm as the climate, which keeps me coming back: the beggar woman who offered me a paan, the child picking a posy of flowers out of rubbish to give to his little friend, complete strangers wishing me Merry Christmas in Park Street during the festive season. In particular though, it's the Anglo-Indian community that draws me back, professionally and personally.

From the many months of field research I've spent in the company of Anglo-Indians in Calcutta I have previously written an ethnographic account as a social anthropology doctoral thesis. I've also written articles for academic journals. My intention with this more expanded work is to reach a wider audience of interested Anglo-Indians and Indians, as well as others interested in the community. I have combined research with storytelling by including memoir pieces, Anglo-Indian life stories (In order to capture the individual characteristics and styles of speaking I have drawn on large sections of interview material with minimal changes in their storytelling. Some of these stories have been presented as interviews and others as biographies.) and short research-based essays. Through this blend of literary styles, with the emphasis on stories, I hope to explore the nuanced lives of Anglo-Indians and the diverse ways of Anglo-Indian being. I draw attention to their place in the life of the nation, arguing against narratives of their near invisibility in the national imagination. Those who already know about Anglo-Indians and are familiar with the stereotypes and the view that they are fading away or losing their identity might be surprised by what they read!

I've organised the book into four parts: identity, faith, education and community care, which are all of concern and significance to the community. Each of these four parts includes an essay outlining the issues, and several life stories that illustrate pertinent facets in the lives of particular Anglo-Indians. None of the 10 life stories I've included are so neat as to illustrate only the issue they're linked to though. And they are not included just to illustrate issues; they also provide a window into what it means to be a contemporary Anglo-Indian living in Calcutta. Stories have a power and a magic that other prose does not. In keeping with this conviction I have included other 'stories' also. In line with the make-up of the four parts of the book, the introduction is also a compilation of separate parts: part one is a narrative, or story, which introduces me as the researcher-cum-storyteller; part two introduces the context and content of the book in essay style, and part three is a story that introduces Calcutta at Christmas time.

A question is regularly asked of me: how I, a Pakeha[1] New Zealand woman, became involved in this research. I always welcome this inquiry as 21st century anthropologists are required to reflect explicitly on their relationship to the research, and to identify biases, prejudices and the expectations they had have, which could impact upon the research. The short answer I've given to that regularly posed query is that my family has supported children from Dr Graham's Homes for many years and I became interested in the community through this sponsorship. Anglo-Indians have a culture of gifting and care for the 'less fortunate' of their community (Caplan, 1996, 1998) and, hence, this response is generally readily accepted. The fuller answer is that a series of events and coincidences have slowly but surely captivated me about India and its people to the point that it's now become something of a magnificent obsession affecting my private and professional life. The following narrative, which describes the early part of this journey, is drawn from memory, my diary, photographs and in places it has been 'corrected' by my daughters' memories.

---

[1]Pakeha is defined variously but refers to non-indigenous New Zealanders, as opposed to, but in relation with, the indigenous Maori.

Acknowledgements

This book is the culmination of more than a decade of research with Calcutta's Anglo-Indian community. The fulfilling and enjoyable experience it became was because of the hallmark hospitality of numerous Anglo-Indians in Calcutta. I am grateful to so many people, many of whom have become firm and cherished friends. The 10 Anglo-Indians: Philomena Eaton, Michael Robertson, Barry O'Brien (former MLA of West Bengal) and other pseudo-named Anglo-Indians, whose life stories are included, took a leap of faith in entrusting their stories to me and I am forever indebted to them. I am also thankful to others who helped me to better understand Calcutta's Anglo-Indians, including Theo Baker, Melvyn Brown, members of Calcutta Anglo Indian Service Society (CAISS) and other Anglo-Indian-focused organisations, MLAs past and present and their families, the Mantosh families, and those exceptional managing committees, staff and residents of various Anglo-Indian homes and hostels in the city.

Without the support from Massey University, New Zealand, this work would not have been possible. As well as providing me with a milieu of scholarship, collegiality and friendship, I received generous funding for several fieldwork trips and was released from teaching for a full semester in order to write.

I have been very fortunate to be part of another group of academics whose research focuses on the community. Over the time I've spent researching for and writing this work there have been opportunities to meet and explore ideas in Melbourne in 2004, Toronto and Calcutta in 2007, Perth in 2010 and in Calcutta again in 2013. I am particularly grateful for the friendship, lively discussions and critiquing from scholars too numerous to mention all by name but including: Rochelle Almeida, Alison Blunt, Jayani Bonnerjee, Adrian Carton, Kathy Cassity, Geraldine Charles, Uther Charlton-Stevens, Rosinka Chaudhuri, Dolores Chew, Glen D'Cruz,

Margaret Deefholts, Mark Faassen, Nigel Foote, Paul Harris, Sheila James, Alan Johnson, Richard Johnson, Michael Ludgrove, Dorothy McMenamin, Vinisha Nero, Deborah Nixon, Anjali Roy, Cheryl-Ann Shivan, Sudarshana Sen, Jayeeta Sharma, Blair Williams, and more recently from Anannya Chakroborty and Catherina Moss who are in the early stages of their own Anglo-Indian-focused research. Included in this group, but requiring special thanks, is Brent Howitt Otto, who, as we worked on other projects in Calcutta discussing observations, made perceptive remarks which influenced portions of this work. I also take this opportunity to acknowledge Lionel Lumb, with his vast experience of journalism, generously provided advice at the final stages of writing. I am extremely appreciative of Lionel's contribution.

The team at SAGE India has been efficient and professional, making it a pleasure to work with them. From the earliest phases I appreciated their enthusiasm and confidence in the work. Comments from reviewers aided me in producing a better finished product. Three pieces included in this work have been published earlier in slightly different forms. I am grateful to the reviewers' comments on earlier versions and acknowledge their previous publications as: 'English in India: Reflections based on fieldwork among Anglo-Indians in Calcutta' in *India Review* (Andrews, 2006b), 'Living and working in Calcutta: Jane's Story' by in *Working Women: Stories of Strife, Struggle and Survival* (Andrews, 2009) and 'Christianity as an Indian Religion: The Anglo-Indian Experience' in *Journal of Contemporary Religion* (Andrews, 2010).

Others closer to home must also be acknowledged: friends who were always interested in what I was doing beyond being polite, and asked to read pieces of work, and colleagues who listened to presentations, read papers and offered insightful and valuable suggestions. Of these, two in particular stand out: first, Noeline Arnott who read each of the stories and essays as they were written and proof read the entire work. Noeline spent a fortnight in Calcutta with me very early in the research and developed an affection for the people she later read about. Second, Henry Barnard, my PhD supervisor and friend. He and his family were travelling companions to India, and Henry maintained an enthusiasm for the work I was engaged in and provided advice that was always of value.

Then there's my family: my adventurous siblings, Peter, David, Kay and Shelley, and my gorgeous daughters, Rochelle, Carolyn, Jane and Heather, all of whom love India. I thank them for the various roles they have played and continue to play: travel companions, encouraging listeners to my latest plans and ideas, and always wonderful company. I also thank my sister-in-law, Colleen, stepson David and sons-in-law Stefan and Rob for their affection, interest and involvement.

Most significant in the production of this work is Keith. He has contributed uniquely and enormously to this book, and my life, academically and personally. Thank you for everything.

Introduction

Serendipity: How I Went to India for a Holiday and Fell into a Research Topic

Twenty-eight December 1996 marked my first day ever in India. My grandfather had left money in his will for all of his grandchildren; mine was spent on five return fares to Madras. We had been planning this trip for more than a year and, finally, we had arrived—a married couple with three daughters: 8-year-old Jane, 10-year-old Carolyn and 16-year-old Rochelle. Bags lying flattened on the floor had been packed, and repacked, for weeks beforehand. We had travelled light—with just two packs between the five of us. I didn't count my worry bag filled with concerns about health, safety, transportation and public toilets. Friends had cautioned me about the trip, 'I know it's your dream but is it fair on your girls?' They were particularly worried about Jane, my frailly built, very fair and pretty eight-year old. A couple of friends even offered to look after the two younger girls while we went. Reassuringly my siblings only encouraged us—and three out of four of them had spent time in the subcontinent during their OE[1] years so they ought to know.

I'd woken early that first morning—too excited, or anxious, to sleep once the room began to lighten. I'd been impatient for the rest of the family to wake up but had reminded myself of the deal I'd made the night before—that they could sleep in. As I lay in the bed waiting for the rest of the family to wake up I heard what I came to recognise as the distinct early morning sound of India: strange bird calls, the occasional voice, traffic sounds beginning, a prolonged swish of the grounds being swept clean of all traces of the day before. These were the sounds I missed months later, back

---

[1] This is a New Zealand colloquialism for 'overseas experience'.

in New Zealand. We'd come to India through a sense of adventure but in those early days we were still affected by warnings of what we might experience.

Over the next few days we ventured out more and more confidently, retreating back to our hotel room only when we needed a break from the heat, the polluted air that irritated our throats and the unfamiliar and sometimes upsetting sights—such as women begging with small children on their hips and children sleeping on the pavements with their parents. Carolyn and Jane took their cues from us; if they could see we were okay, then they were too. Rochelle at 16, and always an independent thinker, was making up her own mind; she often asked for room service meals and slept a lot in the first week. I frequently wondered, but have never confirmed with her, if this was a way of escaping while she got used to so many new experiences—the food, heat, seeing such poverty and being stared at.

I was prepared for much that I encountered: cows wandering along the potholed roads, auto rickshaws vying with motorbikes and yellow taxis, markets where spices were set out in fantastically bright-coloured mini pyramids and the elegant sari-clad women. I would have been surprised if I hadn't noticed these differences from home. I had just completed a Bahelor's in social anthropology at Massey University, studying a host of peoples and cultures, and had used every opportunity in my final year to research and write about aspects of India. I'd read and written about Indian women in the workforce in the gender paper, Hindu religious practices in an Asian philosophy paper and poverty in South Asia in a social inequality paper. I was as prepared as I could be for social and cultural differences; it was the potential for any of us becoming ill that I remained concerned about.

The first time I remember consciously noting the existence of Anglo-Indians occurred early on in this trip. It was New Year's Eve, a few days after our arrival. We were still in Madras and had decided to celebrate the New Year at New Zealand time, which was 4:30 pm local time. In preparation for our hotel room party, we took a taxi to a local supermarket, the most Westernised I have yet been to in India. Two Australian women we had met at the

New Woodlands Hotel had told us about it. They had been there for weeks and one had lived in Madras earlier. While my girls were looking around the shelves and excitedly finding familiar food—Cadbury's chocolate, Coca-Cola and chippies—to take back for our 'party', a sari-clad Indian woman holding the hands of her two young children walked up to us. Bracing myself for another morally fraught exchange with a mother begging for her children beginning with: 'Help us mama, we are very poor', she said instead, 'Good afternoon Madam' and introduced herself. I don't remember her name, or the names of her children, but I clearly remember her pride as she said, 'They are Anglo-Indians. We speak English. Can we talk to you?' She clarified her request, explaining that her children wanted to talk to my girls, which they then did—mostly about where my girls were from, what New Zealand was like and why they were here. Once their gently inquisitorial conversation seemed exhausted, we wished each other a Happy New Year and headed back to the hotel with our treats. Although I never saw them again, little did I realise how deep my connection with this community was going to be. The next day we travelled by the Shatabdi Express to Bangalore. It wasn't until we were back in Madras that we had another Anglo-Indian-related experience.

In the six weeks between our two visits to Madras, we completed a southern Indian triangle: Bangalore and Mysore palaces on the one side, Kerala's waterways and Tamil Nadu's ancient temples on the other two (Photo I.1). Even before we left the subcontinent, we were making plans to come back. People we'd met had repeatedly told us that the south of India was the best part of the country, and we'd certainly become enchanted by most of what we experienced: the frothy yard-long poured coffees, delicately flavoured masala dosas, syrupy sweet *gulabjamuns*, the lushness of rice fields and coconut trees in Kerala, and the extreme friendliness of almost all the people we met. For all that, we were thinking of a North India trip next time, for a different experience of a country of such diversity.

In our last couple of days in Madras, we spent some time with the Australian women we'd met in our hotel earlier. I'd first bumped into one of them in the hotel lobby on the day we arrived in Madras. I might not have noticed her, as she was indistinguishable from many

Photo I.1:
Robyn, Jane, Rochelle and Carolyn in Front of Mysore Palace (1997)

Source: Author.

other Westerners staying at the hotel, except for her companions—three tiny babies in a wide baby carriage. I had been introduced to the mother of the babies and told she was an historian who had carried out research in Madras. Later this encounter was to prove to have a much greater significance than I could ever have imagined at the time of our meeting.

It was a couple of years before I heard Anglo-Indians mentioned again—the next time was in a hotel room in Dunedin, New Zealand, on an icy winter's day where the best option for the afternoon was to watch television. Flicking through the hotel's Sky TV timetable we saw that a newly released Australian-produced programme, *A Calcutta Christmas*, was about to begin. It was said to feature the pre-Christmas activities of a group of 35 Calcuttan Anglo-Indian rest home residents. From the opening of the documentary to the closing scenes (overtly nostalgic postcolonial), we were captivated. I learnt that Anglo-Indians were of mixed descent, culturally more Western than Indian, a community that had originated as a result of more than four centuries of European presence in India. The smoky orange evening light, the yellow pre-aged Ambassador taxis, the bustling Calcutta city scenes transported us back to our earlier trip and fed our hunger for more. The Anglo-Indian factor was unknowingly gathering momentum for me.

I had continued with my studies and as I came closer to submitting my Masters (MA) thesis, we were planning another trip, this time to the north of India, and with company: Henry, my MA supervisor, and his wife Di, with whom we'd become close friends. As we pored over maps working out itinerary options I was especially drawn to the idea of going to Calcutta, perversely, because of its reputation for poverty, pollution and teeming masses. I remembered what McCourt had written of the city in *Angela's Ashes*: 'They're careful the way they step into the lake in the kitchen and they tell one another. Isn't this a disgrace? They keep shaking their heads and saying, God Almighty and Mother of God, this is desperate. That's not Italy they have upstairs, that's Calcutta' (McCourt, 1996: 113–114). A few days there would have to be interesting. We recalled that we had connections there, if we needed to call on them, at the unlikely named Indian institution: Dr Graham's Homes.

Once in Calcutta we stayed in the south of the city, not far, as it happened, from the Anglo-Indian Tollygunge Home featured in the film we'd seen in New Zealand. One afternoon Carolyn (now 14 years old) and I walked down to a local Internet café to check our mail. It was there that I learned that I'd been successful in the PhD scholarship I'd applied for. From then on, travelling as I was with my (now) PhD supervisor, we managed to come up with a topic at every stop—the century-old market in Calcutta, the dhobi-*wallah*s in Udaipur, the English-school-modelled hill station schools and so on.

Carrying out research in India, which at first seemed an unlikely possibility (for all its appeal), soon began to take shape. The scholarship was the opportunity for me, and the whole family, to spend some long stretches of time in India. It wasn't that being there was always easy or fun, but I felt drawn back to the subcontinent all the same. I'd lost both of my parents at a young age, when they were still in their 40s, and as I approached this age myself I was determined to live life to the fullest, taking the opportunities to enrich our lives with a variety of experiences, for both me and the people closest to me. Extended periods of fieldwork in Calcutta, with my family, fitted into the idea of the life I might live, for at least the next few years.

Seven months after coming back from the North India trip, we went back to India for a two-week visit to explore the possibility of research on one of the topics I had considered on the previous trip: Calcutta's New Market. An investigation of the relationships between storeowners and regular shoppers seemed an ideal topic for a social anthropologist—making a purchase in India was never a simple monetary transaction, and New Market had over a hundred years of history. In addition, it had had a recent mysterious fire that the authorities hadn't resolved but conspiracy theories abounded. I hadn't been back in Calcutta long before I realised that this research wasn't going to be as straightforward as I'd naively imagined. The indoor market space that had been bustling and colourful with December crowds the last time we'd visited was now very hot and humid with muddy unwelcoming entrances. It was also relatively empty of shoppers (due, I was told, to the school exams that were imprisoning whole households) and the labyrinthine layout was impossible to navigate on my own. I realised that although many of the shop owners spoke enough English to make a sale, transactional English was their limit, and I had never been a linguist, so how was I going to interview people? The market was a public space so I needed to obtain permission to be there conducting research. My first and only attempt to gain such permission was a frustrating and completely unsuccessful experience in dealing with Calcutta Municipal Corporation (CMC)[2] bureaucrats. Only chai *wallahs* have any chance of getting inside their offices, which were typically open for business only from 11 am to 1 pm and again from 2:30 pm to 4 pm. Disheartened, I emailed Henry for advice. He, always positive, encouraged me to think of ways around it and to be creative about possible angles to adopt.

---

[2] Now renamed the KMC—the Kolkata Municipal Corporation.

My two-week reconnoitre was running out and my research topic was quickly losing definition. I took solace in spending time with a group of people I'd struck up friendships with through a long-term sponsorship relationship with the Calcutta-based administrative centre for Dr Graham's Homes. Just before I'd met and married him, Bruce, my then husband, had been involved with a court case in New Zealand where the will of a Dr Graham's Homes' old boy (possibly an Anglo-Indian) had been contested.[3] After the case, the chair of the New Zealand committee, a Tibetan past-pupil of the Homes, asked the legal counsel involved if they'd consider sponsoring a destitute Calcuttan child to go to the boarding school of Dr Graham's Homes in Kalimpong. This marked the beginning of our sponsorship relationship with the Homes when Bruce, and later our family, sponsored several children, one after another, at the school. At the time we went to Calcutta we were sponsoring Andrea, who was never identified as Anglo-Indian on any of the correspondence we'd had from her or from the school, just as the daughter of 'Mr C. [who] has no permanent job; he sells pens and gets about ₹10–15 [50 cents] per day'. Her case history went on to say that 'Mrs C. is not working. They have one room and share a common toilet, for which rent is ₹80 [per month] and the area they live is a very hazardous one. Besides Andrea and her brother [...] there are two more children'. We had exchanged mail with Andrea and wanted to meet her, but since our visit was during the school term we didn't have the opportunity.

Trying to make progress with the New Market research was excruciatingly slow going, as I told my newfound friends, all Anglo-Indians as it turned out. When I described my frustrating experiences of getting research clearance from the CMC they laughed and asked, 'What did you expect?' I realise now that I may have been able to gain access by paying a bribe. The problem is that I did not then, and still do not, understand the subtleties involved in negotiating in this way.

---

[3] Unfortunately, our marriage broke down a year or so into my PhD programme of study.

The hospitality and support offered to me by these new friends was on my mind when, back in New Zealand, still searching for a New Market angle, I began to read up about the various communities who interacted with the market. Over that time, I read a book by Coralie Younger (1987) in which she proposes a prognosis of decline and eventual demise of the Anglo-Indian community.[4] What I was reading in books and articles about Anglo-Indians was contrary to what I'd experienced in Calcutta: the Anglo-Indians I'd met appeared to be part of a vital, culturally distinct minority community who were still very active in keeping their unique identity alive.

In the end, I centralised Anglo-Indians in my PhD research, focusing particularly on how they were maintaining their identity. I collected all the information I could about their community before taking the family back to Calcutta four months later for a two month fieldwork stint, which turned out to be the first of many. The girls became quite at home there, so much so that I could send them to the market on their own to do my shopping, or down the street to buy delicious hot *laccha* parathas, and they would set out happily for the day together, coming back with stories of their adventures.

While in Madras at the tail end of that first trip we'd had a significant Anglo-Indian encounter, which I had not recognised as such, and there is no way I would have except for a chance remark from another Anglo-Indian researcher six years later. By then I was well into my research and had arranged to meet an Anglo-Indian academic, Glen D'Cruz, in Melbourne to discuss some of my findings. We also chatted about various other Anglo-Indian researchers. Glen mentioned the details of one woman who had published on the community, which were so unique that I realised that she was the woman we'd met at the New Woodlands Hotel in Madras: she was Coralie Younger, the author of the first scholarly work I had read on Anglo-Indians. By the time I made this connection, sadly, she had died. With the recognition of this serendipitous occurrence I realised the significance of others as

---

[4] She also wrote a work that was published posthumously called *Wicked Women of the Raj* (2003).

well—the long-term sponsorship of Anglo-Indian students at Dr Graham's Homes, meeting Anglo-Indians within the first days of that first trip to India, watching the Anglo-Indian film of Tollygunge Homes so soon after it was released, even being notified of scholarship success while in Calcutta—in an Internet café not far from the filmed Rest Home, with my supervisor-to-be. Although I now fail to be surprised at the way Anglo-Indians have become central to my research as well as to all other areas of my life, I draw comfort from the realisation that I was destined from the time I set foot in India to follow the course I have.

Christmas, Calcutta and Research

One Christmas eve, as I walked down Park Street, Calcutta, with its array of Western restaurants and cafes, I noticed a queue of Indians lined up to purchase Christmas cake at Flurys, an iconic Swiss tearoom. On enquiring of one couple who looked distinctly Hindu, 'Why do Indians celebrate Christmas?' the answer came back, 'Why not?'

India is a land of many religions, many festivals. There's the Muslim Ramadan with its days of fasting, Guru Nanak Jayanti celebrating the birthday of the warrior founder of the Sikh religion, Kali Puja revering the feared Hindu goddess with her necklace of skulls, but amongst all of this it would seem fair to say that Christmas day is one that is enjoyed with more of a universal sense of ease. You don't have to be a Christian to join in.

'The season' is a great time for visitors to be in a city that celebrates Christmas so enthusiastically. The churches are decorated both inside and out with life-sized manger sets, guiding stars and strings of coloured lights. The restaurants do an especially brisk trade, with many of the Park Street establishments extending themselves to offer special Christmas menus; for example, we saw turkey kebabs, roast chicken and plum pudding on one menu. (One newspaper later reported that the turkey had been illegally imported.) These central city restaurants are festooned with coloured and twisted streamers, with mini Christmas trees or a Santa

Claus on the tables, and often a two-piece band playing Christmas carols. The markets and malls are busier than ever with shoppers queuing to buy gifts and treats (Photo I.2). New Market's legendary Nahoums, the Jewish family bakery, does a healthy trade in all their Christmas baking but especially their famous marzipan sweets and sugared almonds. Christmas cakes fly out the door from all the other bakeries too, with Kathleens and Flurys being the favourites. There are numerous red-suited, white-masked, gloved and bearded Father Christmases. The image of three such suited gents crossing Park Street together between stopped yellow Ambassador taxis remains with me—even without taking my camera out.

Photo I.2:
New Market a Few Days before Christmas Day (2011)

Source: Author.

For the week or so around Christmas and the first days of the New Year a visitor to the city would not be blamed for thinking this was a Christian city. However, one particular minority group from Calcutta really come into their own at this time. They are the Anglo-Indians who contribute far beyond their numbers to the festive feel to the city. They are a community of Westernised Christian Indians who trace their existence to the arrival of Europeans to India. I discuss their identity in detail in the first essay of this work, so for now I will introduce them only through the definition of the Indian Constitution which states:

> An Anglo-Indian means a person whose father or any of whose other male progenitors in the male line is or was of European descent but who is domiciled within the territory of India and is or was born within such territory of parents habitually resident therein and not established there for temporary purposes only. (Section 366 [2])

Christmas seems to mark an immense coverage of Anglo-Indians by the media. While in Calcutta in Christmas 2007, I saw that a national newspaper, the *Times of India*, ran several stories on Anglo-Indians on the days before Christmas, and one on Christmas Day itself. And in the same month the *India Today* supplementary magazine, *Simply Kolkata*, had photos of and referred to numerous Anglo-Indians entertainers, for example, Rianne Selwyn, Shon Anderson, Cyril Manuel and Shayne Hyrapiet (whose mother is Anglo-Indian) and the bands Colours and Sweet Agitation. Furthermore, in the magazine there was an article on the Bow Barracks' Christmas celebrations—the location is the setting and focus of Anjan Dutt's film *Bow Barracks Forever* (2007). Although particular Anglo-Indians were mentioned here by name, albeit alongside Bengalis and Muslims, there was no mention of their community affiliation.

This small community is responsible for much of the hospitality and entertainment in Park Street, owning some of the restaurants and serving or entertaining in many. I was told that one of the Anglo-Indian restaurant owners regularly organises the decoration of Park Street itself.[5] For Anglo-Indians this season is a favourite

---

[5] In 2012, the recently elected Trinamool party—with Anglo-Indian Derek O'Brien (Member of Parliament) and Chief Minister Mamata Banerjee—was responsible for funding street decorations and Christmas shows in Allen Gardens, Park Street.

time of the year: the children are back from their hill station and other boarding schools, the Anglo-Indian clubs, associations and city schools put on entertainment of dances, dinners and shows. Overseas Anglo-Indians choose this time to come back to Calcutta to visit family and friends, and 'up-country' Anglo-Indians come to Calcutta to visit their relatives. It's a time for shopping at New Market, taking kilos of Christmas cake ingredients to be baked by the family's trusted (but watched over all the same) baker, and making *kulkuls* and *rosa* cookies at home. The community's youngest, oldest and poorest are especially well looked after at this time of the year, with Christmas parties and extra-ration distributions. It's the time of the year that the 'gifting' character of Anglo-Indians is played out enthusiastically: with generous gifts of time and labour from Anglo-Indians in India, and money gifts from those abroad.

In this city of over 8 million, the 30,000[6] or so Anglo-Indians can easily be, and most often are, overlooked for most of the year. At Christmas time though it's difficult not to notice them, even if they are acknowledged by the wider Calcutta population in the same way that a local Olympic sporting hero might be acknowledged only for the duration of an Olympic Games: at Christmas time they are briefly lifted out of the box and dusted off—but even then they are not necessarily recognised completely for what, and who, they are. That Anglo-Indians are often overlooked is evident in most histories of India, as well as in personal histories. One English woman who spent her first 15 years in India makes this comment:

> After I left India in 1945, I more or less blanked out the memory [...] of those others of European descent—the Anglo-Indians—I remembered nothing, except as people from whom we must not catch a 'chi chi' accent or as girls who took the most glamorous partners in dances for servicemen during the Second World War.

[6] Estimations of Calcutta's Anglo-Indian population range from 10,000 people to 30,000 families. There are difficulties obtaining exact numbers of Anglo-Indians as they have not been enumerated as a distinct community, or ethnic category, since 1951. Even when they were, the population statistics were questionably low (Andrews, 2005; Anthony, 1969; McMenamin, 2006). The last census, in 2001, put the number of people in all of West Bengal with English as their mother tongue at 15,000. In 2006, after he obtained his position as Member of the Legislative Assembly, Barry O'Brien said he didn't know how many people he represented.

[They are a] people who are largely absent from the history and literature of the Raj, except for very occasional appearances as crude stereotypes or dismissed in a sentence as having worked on the railways. Yet they had been more numerous than we, British, and we depended on their smooth running of the infrastructure for maintenance of our rule. (From an unpublished essay by Susan Lynn)

As I began my research, what I read about the community indicated that this was a social group who was currently in serious decline with a prognosis of eventual demise (Blunt, 2005; Caplan, 2001; Hawes, 1996; Mills, 1998; Younger, 1987). My first fieldwork trip coincided with the Christmas season and Anglo-Indians were in full swing so it was hard for me to reconcile what I'd read in these pessimistic accounts with what I'd experienced in Calcutta.

Realistically, the numbers (even though they are unspecified) do tell a tale: a huge portion of the population has already migrated and many more leave or marry out of the community each year. Therefore, there has been a significant decline in the numbers of Anglo-Indians on Indian shores. However, this change in spatial dispersal, or geographical residence, doesn't necessarily signal the demise of the community. All social groups experience changes over time. The only ones that don't are those that are extinct. As long as a social group can adapt, they can survive.

Anthropologists, and others, have recorded the changes to some traditional ways of life for various peoples, and have written about challenges made to the 'authenticity' of traditions as a result of tourism and modernisation, for example. They have written of a 'melting-pot' effect: the expectation that with globalisation ethnic groups will lose their distinctiveness. However, in many cases, as researchers from these same disciplines have discovered, there has been a resurgence of tradition, and reclamation of cultural identity; that is, the predicted diminishment and homogenisation just haven't happened. Marshall Sahlins (1993), for example, writes of Eskimo, or Inuit, groups who are able to effectively maintain their traditional diets using such technologies as motorised sleds and helicopters. In addition, their fishing is so much safer and more efficient now that they carry Global Positioning System (GPS) equipment and emergency locator beacons. James Turner

(1997) discusses cultural change in terms of there being an, albeit constrained, continuity between past, present and future cultural practices. Bill Ashcroft (2001) comments on the two-way exchange in practices when different ethnic or social groups live alongside each other, especially in postcolonial contexts. That is, rather than seeing small minority communities as being assimilated by larger ones to the point of extinction, he focuses on the cultural sharing and conversion accruing in *both* directions. These ideas are useful in thinking about Anglo-Indians too; rather than seeing them as a beleaguered minority struggling for cultural survival, let's explore the idea that Indians and Anglo-Indians are sharing their festivals and they are accommodating each other's cultural practices. The reply of 'Why not!' to my question about Indian participation in Christmas traditions captured that sentiment. The Christmas season, then, is an obvious place to begin a discussion of Anglo-Indian presence in Calcutta.

In this work, I will show, through the telling of particular people's lives and the discussion of a set of current issues, that the Anglo-Indians of Calcutta are still a vibrant, culturally distinct community in the 21st century. They are a community that has long had a place in India and they continue to be a significant and influential feature on the Calcutta city landscape.

Research in Calcutta's Anglo-India

In this section, I respond to a question often asked of me: 'How did you carry out the research?' (There is often an additional question enquiring if I've been to India.) The abbreviated response is that as a social anthropologist I use the discipline's hallmark method of participant–observer research. Clifford Geertz refers to this as 'deep hanging out' (1998). Ethnographic fieldwork involves spending lengthy periods of time with the people one has a research interest in, taking part in activities as far as possible and observing all the while. Since I began Anglo-Indian research I have been to Calcutta a dozen times, for durations that range from two weeks to three months but average a bit more than a month per visit. I have also attended the last four Anglo-Indian Reunions in Melbourne in 2004, Toronto in 2007, Perth in 2010 and Calcutta in 2013, and I have spent extended periods of time with Anglo-Indians in Melbourne.

In terms of the techniques I've employed, as well as the more informal *hanging out* (with Anglo-Indian friends, including, more recently, those in Anglo-Indian rest homes), I've interviewed people about particular issues, collected life stories and taken photographs. I've joined in family celebrations such as weddings, wedding anniversaries, christenings and birthdays, and in other life span events such as burial services and memorial services. I've also been involved in the distribution of rations and pensions, accompanying social service groups as they visit poor Anglo-Indians and I've helped out at Christmas parties. I've been fortunate to have been invited to many family dinners and house parties, and attended numerous public Anglo-Indian events. In fact, when I'm in Calcutta I'm often busier socially than when I am at home. An Anglo-Indian man did warn me: 'If you're here for "the season" you'll have something on every night'. I also read everything I can—websites, theses, newsletters and magazines, and I remain in touch (by post, email and social networking sites, and the occasional phone call) with Calcutta friends between visits, and with a number of Anglo-Indians in Melbourne and New Zealand. Several years into my research with Anglo-Indians I partnered with Keith Butler, an Australian-based Anglo-Indian who grew up in Calcutta. Being with him has given me access to a particular Anglo-Indian experience and in those times when we travel to Calcutta together I am able, through him, to engage even more fully in the local Anglo-Indian scene.

I have spent two monsoon Augusts in Calcutta, as well as a hot few weeks in late March, and a couple more in early October. Mostly though, my visits were between early November and late February. Christmas falls during the time of year that is the most pleasant to be in the city: winter, with temperatures in the mid-20 degree Celsius and clear blue skies for weeks on end. As a southern hemisphere university-based researcher, it is also the best time of the year to take research leave as it's least likely to clash with key teaching semesters. Therefore, for many reasons, the Christmas season is my favoured time to be in Calcutta.

Public Anthropology

A key goal of public anthropology is to address important social concerns in an engaging, non-academic manner (Borofsky, 2007). Public anthropology requires an attitude and particular approach to the discipline described by Robert Borofsky (2006), who is regarded as the founder of this approach, in this way:

> Public anthropology demonstrates the ability of anthropology and anthropologists to effectively address problems beyond the discipline—illuminating the larger social issues of our times as well as encouraging broad, public conversations about them with the explicit goal of fostering social change. It affirms our responsibility, as scholars and citizens, to meaningfully contribute to communities beyond the academy—both local and global—that make the study of anthropology possible.

This description corresponds with my aim with the material I present in this work and with my ongoing research with Anglo-Indians in Calcutta. In writing the essays on contemporary social issues, in particular, I have considered seriously the approach mandated by public anthropology. As an anthropologist working closely with members of the community in an ongoing capacity I have a moral obligation to keep faith with my research participants. It is my intention then that Anglo-Indians reading this work will find resonance with their own projects. The inclusion of life stories is another way of presenting material in an accessible way. I consider that it is the combination of essays and life stories that is most effective in making the arguments I do in this book. Through reaching a wide readership I also hope to raise the consciousness of the wider Indian population and mobilise a debate about Anglo-Indians and their place in the life the nation, including their near invisibility in the national imagination.

Life Stories and Their Co-construction

This book includes more life stories than any other genre for a number of reasons. Life stories are an increasingly important vehicle for presenting ethnographic research—partly due, as noted above, to public anthropology's requirement of accessibility to a wider readership.

Another influence in my decision to include detailed life stories were observations I heard at the Anglo-Indian Reunion Symposium held in Melbourne. One of the Anglo-Indian speakers, Australian-based Anglo-Indian academic Glen D'Cruz, said that he felt that texts written about Anglo-Indians (which are usually written by non-Anglo-Indian academics) lack 'the sense of our everyday lived experience'. He said he wanted to see more *stories* of Anglo-Indians, making the point that 'they give material form to our experiences'. He felt that through a range of stories of different people's lives, it is possible to show that Anglo-Indians are not a homogenous group of people. He said that one thing he had difficulty with is that some, especially academic writers, 'try to pigeon-hole us into particular ways of being and ways of life—like saying that they are particularly religious or Catholic and so forth. And this is not actually the case'. He felt that storytelling emphasised the diversity of ways of being Anglo-Indian and that Anglo-Indians have not had a good opportunity to tell their stories. Clearly I agree with him in the value he places on stories.

These comments made me acutely aware of what was being said within the Anglo-Indian community about social scientists' treatment of Anglo-Indians. I determined to be true to my inclination to ensure that my work was alive with the people whose lives I had drawn on in the course of my fieldwork. Anthropological research is carried out through the immersion of the anthropologist in the experiences of people and life of the social groups that they are working with. The texts that are written out of the experience ought to reflect this.[7]

---

[7] There are many anthropological models for this approach, for example, these early contributions from Lila Abu Lughod in *Writing Women's Worlds* (1993), Edith Turner in *The Hands Feel It* (1996) and Barbara Myerhoff in *Number Our Days* (1978). My early exposure to writing of this kind led to my growing sense that much theoretical literature was scholastic pedantry, which only comes to life in momentary flashes when the scholars turned to 'exemplifying' their arguments with anecdotes or case studies of real lives. Simply to describe the lives of one's participants to 'exemplify' concepts struck me as a form of intellectual violation of these people. Surely, it is the lives of people that needed to be communicated?

It is the fine-grained detail of individual lives that is of interest to readers; hence, this is an effective way to convey the different ways that people live their lives. I am presenting stories not primarily to illustrate the issues in the essays (although the work is organised to do that to at least some extent) but rather to offer an alternative and complementary way of understanding the lives of Anglo-Indians in Calcutta and what it has meant, and currently means, to be Anglo-Indian in Calcutta today.

The experience of collecting and constructing the life stories varied between research participants. For one story I conducted just one interview, but for all the others there were a number of interview sessions combined with material gathered in non-interview time spent with them. Of all of the interviews I have recorded over the last 10 years, I selected the 10 *stories* that I judged to be the most illuminating of certain issues. These stories were also diverse enough to provide differing perspectives.

The form the stories are presented in is also varied. This is partly because different stories lent themselves to different ways of telling; I wanted to avoid a set formula in their construction. Tom Barone's *Touching Eternity* (2001) provided a model of telling lives in using a range of discursive features from the presentation of life stories as interviews, biography and more autobiographical monologues.

In all cases I endeavoured to give the stories to the people concerned for their comment, and with just one exception they (or the interviewee's guardian in one case) took the opportunity to have the last word on what is included, omitted, changed or corrected. It was not always easy or comfortable for them to read what I had written and, hence, I am particularly grateful for the ongoing support they provided to me and to this project.

At the beginning of each story, I describe how I came to know the people and briefly discuss the way I collected and wrote the story. I also highlight the links the stories have to sections, or parts, they are positioned within. I have used pseudonyms to protect their privacy for all, except Michael Robertson, Philomena Eaton and Barry O'Brien. It would have been impossible to disguise the identity of these people because they and their works are so well known. As I was writing, I realised that Philomena's life and works have become one of the sub-themes of this work, partly because I spent a lot of time with her—including three Christmas days—but also because she is so involved with her city's Anglo-Indians and is well known and appreciated by them.

Organisation of the Stories and Essays

I am not alone in seeing the rationale for a Christmas focus: the makers of the documentary of the Tollygunge Home for elderly Anglo-Indian men and women did the same. The film *A Calcutta Christmas: Stories of Friendship and Hope* (Delofski, 1998) marks off the days from 1 December until 25 December, Christmas day, interspersing footage showing preparation for the day with footage of conversations with the residents. The structure of this book is similar in that it also combines different styles: the narratives of Anglo-Indian life stories and research-related essays, which include observations, reflections and discussions. I have organised the essays and stories into four parts around four themes: identity, faith, education, and community care and consolidation. In each section, there is a short introduction to the theme, an essay and two or three life stories. Although I have positioned the life narratives as closely as possible to the essay highlighted by the narratives, mostly there is no perfect fit between one life and one theme—people's lives are too complex to fit so neatly.

The themes I cover in the essays are of significance to contemporary Anglo-Indians, and have in fact always been central concerns. In the first essay focusing on identity I describe the community and its origins, discuss the characteristics of Anglo-Indians and the constitutional definition and its implications. From the time of the first Anglo-Indians, identity has been influential in their lives and of significance in terms of their relationship to others in India: both other Indians and non-Indians. Anglo-Indian faith, or specifically their practice of Christianity, is the topic of the second section. Much to my puzzlement, researchers of Anglo-Indians have largely overlooked a detailed exploration of its significance to the community. Because of that omission, I was quite unprepared for its significance to my fieldwork experience and research. Although some of my fieldwork coincided with the Christmas season, the season to celebrate Christianity, I was there at other times as well, and Christianity was *always* important. This essay describes their practice, its significance and the post-Vatican II changes they have to adjust to.

The third section focuses on education—or rather, some of the failings of the education system for Anglo-Indians. Anglo-Indian schools are amongst the most sought after in all of India, and English is the language of prestige, yet the community has within its population illiterate English speakers. In India this is an oxymoronic situation, and for Anglo-Indians it is untenable. There is potential within the community, and through its schools, for this situation to be effectively addressed.

The final section focuses on Anglo-Indian care and the consolidation of their community through this care. Although there are various ways that the community is working to maintain themselves as a distinct community, I argue that it is the practice of providing care, more than anything else, which will mean that the community survives. By caring for their less fortunate they are living by their Christian principles, although there are other models of care in India too: the Sikh concept of *seva*, for example, which refers to a Sikh's voluntary service to the community. How a person enacts this determines their worth, or morality, just as Anglo-Indian service, or care does. Caplan also writes about the moral aspect of gifting and receiving, based on his research in Madras (1998).

Although the beneficiaries of the care are Calcutta residents (and residents of other Indian towns, cities and metros), the providers of care and the providers of the means for caring come from both within the city and abroad. Diasporic Anglo-Indians, individuals as well as organisations regularly send financial aid, which the local Anglo-Indians disperse in one way or another. The effect of the care is consolidation of more than just the Calcutta community of Anglo-Indians: it connects them to each other at a global level. Christmas is the time they do this with the most generosity, and most effectively.

There are 10 life stories in this work; each presents a different way of coming to this point of being Anglo-Indian in 21st century Calcutta. Four are stories of men; one from a very successful businessman, Michael Robertson, who in his 60s still makes a difference to the lives of many young Anglo-Indians and has strong views on the value of education. Another is of a man I have called Peter, a kind-hearted and hardworking family man in his 40s who battles against the educational impoverishment of this background. Then there's the story of Philip who was born and brought up in an extremely impoverished environment, attended Dr Graham's Homes school as a sponsored student and has, at the age of 22, just completed a Bachelor of Commerce. His story provides insights into the life of a 22-year-old Anglo-Indian and of what can be achieved through education. Barry O'Brien's story describes the life he has carved out for himself in modern India. This politician—an MLA for West Bengal at the time of the interview—dwells on his early years and the influences that made him what he is: educationalist, quiz master and politician.

The women's stories include that of Angeline, the first Anglo-Indian I met in Calcutta and whose story captures many of the characteristics I recognise as Anglo-Indian; Irene, a feisty Bow Barracks' resident who arguably shouldn't be included in this work as she's a 'contested' Anglo-Indian; Jane, disabled with polio, who managed against the odds of her early life to live a full and successful life; Dulcie, who, as she waits for a place in a residential home, always positive and thankful recalls happy as well as tough times in her life; Philomena Eaton, who I often refer to privately as 'Saint Philo' for the work she does for the community talks about some of that, but also her early days in Assam; and Meryl, an older Anglo-Indian who, at the time when I recorded her story, was a resident in a Home. At close to 80 years of age, she was looking back at some of the pivotal moments of those years—her own and the community's. Her story ends on a Christmas day, maintaining the book's overarching theme.

The combination of case studies and essays will challenge the 'doxic' (or taken for granted) notions that circulate about the community. By drawing on the vital lives of real individuals, my hope is that there is a change to the lens through which these people of India are viewed. But first, I will give you a taste of one Christmas day spent in Calcutta. This effectively frames the remainder of the book by introducing some of the issues that are discussed in the essays and several of the 'characters' who are more fully drawn later in their life stories.

A Christmas in Calcutta

The Christmas day programme for me and my partner, Keith, was going to be crammed; breakfast with a few local street children, midday Christmas dinner with close Anglo-Indian friends, visits to Anglo-Indian retirement homes and an Anglo-Indian evening house party. This was going to be a day quite different from our usual 'laid-back' New Zealand family Christmases.

Leaving the flat we gave our room boy, Faruk, some Christmas *baksheesh* (tip), which he'd hinted for the day before, when he'd offered a breakfast treat of *puri* and *suji*. Since we had arranged to be out for breakfast, he agreed to make this for us the next day. We got as far as the gate before we heard the words Christmas *baksheesh* again—a more direct request this time, from the Muslim watchman at the gate. We'd be lucky to get a nod out of him any other day of the year. In the spirit of the day, we wished him a happy Christmas and handed over a couple of notes. After all my trips to India I'm still not sure of the best protocol to adopt for tipping and *baksheesh* payments to staff at the places I've stayed. I used to operate a pay-as-you-go scheme, which worked well enough, but it's expensive. Keith (having lived in the city into his early twenties) had more experience than I had of this tipping culture and introduced me to the system of paying up at the end of the stay—the rationale is that this keeps the service at an acceptable level throughout.

We set off again to meet the street children, three boys aged 12–14 years (two of whom were Hindu and one Muslim), who lived near where we were staying. With our own children a long way away, we'd arranged this time together as much for our sakes as for the boys. In Calcutta poverty is endemic; it's not the preserve of either

Anglo-Indians or non-Anglo-Indians. When I'd first started coming to the city I'd met these and other street children and regularly bought food and toiletries for them. With so little shared language, I hadn't been able to get to know much about them. This time though, with Keith who speaks reasonably fluent Hindi, I learnt a bit more. Sunil, for example, had been able to tell me how he'd lost his eye, and the others told us a little about their families.

A few days before we'd suggested we buy new clothes for these three boys as a Christmas gift. That Christmas morning I saw them for the first time after their shopping spree. They told us that they'd been up early and had paid an early morning visit to the local tank to bathe. They seemed happy when I said they looked so much more grown up, and they told us about some reactions from their street friends, one of whom hadn't recognised them (he'd said) and tried to sell them packets of gum—one of the ways the street kids earn a bit of money. All decked out as they were, they now fancied breakfast at the genteel Flurys, but unfortunately there were such long queues that we couldn't oblige them. We hadn't expected such demand for a sit-down breakfast in this Hindu-dominated city on 25 December when most businesses remained open. Instead, we went across the road to another restaurant where the boys ordered huge breakfasts and seemed oblivious of the dietary restraints of their religions.

After breakfast, Keith and I had planned to attend a Catholic mass. Once again, the boys did not allow their own faiths to hold them back and suggested they come to mass with us. Accompanying us certainly wasn't part of any sort of deal we made with them but I was happy for it to happen. We sat through a memorable sermon. The priest chose this day to remind his flock, at length, of their Christian duty to care for their neighbours. The message was clear—in his view, this community was falling short in this area. He reminded us that there are poor amongst us, that India does not provide systematic social services, that it is up to each and every one of us to take some responsibility. I'd spent the last month watching how much Anglo-Indians do to help their less-fortunate neighbours: Week after week I'd witnessed them selflessly giving up their free time as they engaged in organising and running Christmas trees (parties), visiting house-bound people, distributing rations and pensions, cooking snacks and manning stalls to raise funds to do it all again. My experience was at odds with the sermon we were hearing. In comparison with what they did, it was easy for us, as Westerners, to do our bit for our neighbours by dropping some money in an envelope. However, for them the work they did for others never ended.

After mass concluded the boys offered to spend the rest of the day with us—suggesting a movie or a visit to the theme park, Aquatica, as possibilities. However, our arrangements were so that we had to say goodbye, promising to see them another day, very soon. They waved us off as we went off to make phone calls to our children, missing them as we talked to one after the other and heard about their days—it was already mid- to late-afternoon in New Zealand and Australia where they were. After that, we hailed a taxi to take us to Christmas dinner at Philomena's, asking the taxi driver to stop for a few minutes outside the South Park Street cemetery. Keith wanted to pay his respects to his literary hero and fellow Anglo-Indian—Henry Vivien Derozio. The plantings around the tomb were trimmed and the slab looked freshly painted, beautified further with fresh flowers laid on top. Its condition belied its age: Derozio had died in 1831 when he was only 22 years old. I remembered reading that the first Anglo-Indian day (celebrated all over the world now on 2 August or a weekend close to it), in 2002, had included a memorial service at his tomb.

We arrived at Philomena's after her other guests: Vernon Thomas, the author, the photographer Dileep Prakash—who months later produced a beautiful book of Anglo-Indian portraits—and several other well-educated and modestly successful local Anglo-Indians. We were told that Philomena's cook had prepared everything, except the baking, which Philomena had taken responsibility for: fragile cut-out *rosa* cookies, formed and frosted *kulkuls* and Christmas cake. We began our midday feast drinking ginger wine from little cut glass goblets and eating sweet and savoury snacks. Philomena's home has a spacious living area divided by furniture into dining and living areas. The table had been set with cutlery and wine glasses, festive napkins and table decorations, and waiting for us was an entree of sliced tongue and salad vegetables. After saying Grace, we began. Our entree was followed by a main course of roast chicken, a lamb curry, white rice, pickles and vegetables, followed by plum pudding and brandy sauce, all accompanied by a little celebratory wine.

Afterwards we sat around, sated, and talked and joked over Christmas cake and coffee. I had interviewed Philomena a couple of years beforehand, but I learned much more of her life that afternoon. I heard about the 'pound parties' she'd had at home, keeping her parents awake, where everyone brought a pound of some food item—such as 'Polly's dirt' (a fine fried savoury snack so named because it looked like something that had been collected from the bottom of the parrot cage), ice-cream, samosas, cake and cashews. The furniture would then be pushed back, shoes were kicked off for dancing and the records were played, all night long. Then they'd all head off to Mass before finally getting a few hours of sleep. Her favourite dance partner all those years ago was with us that day. They were still great friends and neither had ever married.

Just before we were to leave for our next appointment there was a knock on the door. A young sari-clad woman and her two well-turned-out young children entered shyly. I was introduced to Beatrice and her son and daughter who had come, after an hour-long bus trip, to wish Philomena a happy Christmas. The mother had a quiet air of determination mixed with deference towards Philomena, and to us, as her guests. She could see we were about to leave so she kept her visit short. After a quick cup of tea and cake the trio left, each with a bag of Christmas treats. I was then told her story. Beatrice was Anglo-Indian. She wore a sari because she lived in a Muslim-dominated slum. It did not do to wear Western clothes in such an enclave—she would draw too much unwanted attention to herself. Living with her was the Anglo-Indian father of her children. He, an unemployed alcoholic, was likely to die young because of his drinking. As he wouldn't marry her, his children are not recognised as Anglo-Indian under the Indian Constitution and are disqualified from obtaining benefits. Their situation appeared grim, but I could only hope he does, or did, the right thing to them before dying.

After Beatrice left, we packed parcels of roast meat sandwiches and the delicious Anglo-Indian Christmas baking for distribution to the people we were to visit. Over the course of the next four or five hours, we crisscrossed by car from Wellesley Street to Royd Street, back to Ripon Street and then to Lower Circular Road—this area had all, not so long ago, been Anglo-Indian territory. The first woman we visited that afternoon was paralysed and completely bedridden. She was probably in her early seventies, was in a poor physical state and very weepy. It was obvious that there was little she could do for herself but she told us about her Muslim neighbours who looked after her on a day-to-day basis. Her tiny one-roomed home seemed to be almost a part of their home—they were so close. She sobbed, telling us that she'd had no visits or messages from her family that day, Christmas Day, and said she was waiting to die. She seemed to have cheered up a bit by the time we left—thanks mainly to Philomena's gently humorous way with her. She reminded her, without trivialising her dismal situation, of her belief that the Lord wouldn't give her any burden that she couldn't bear. All we could do was talk with her, give her a bit of money and a parcel of food, and a hug.

We walked up a dusty, dark staircase to visit another woman, Sylvia, where we sat on upholstered chairs with springs poking out of the fabric, dirt and squalor everywhere, with a kitchen that we didn't want to look at too closely. Sylvia had advanced emphysema. She told us that she wasn't quite 70 years, but to us she looked closer to 90, she was so emaciated. Yet, in the soft light her posture and inner grace gave her an elegance that was quite beautiful. Embarrassed that she didn't even have the makings for a cup of tea to offer us, she wanted to share the parcel of food we'd given her. We declined, happier to sit and talk for a while. She told us of her time in London, before she came back to Calcutta, leaving a fiancé behind, to the home she still lived in, to nurse her dying father. She had never married. She spoke in an educated, refined manner, illustrating so well the better days she had obviously seen. For me this was a very distressing visit. The contrast between the way she spoke and held herself and the conditions in which she lived was so marked.

We were running behind schedule when we arrived at our last stop, the Night Shelter in Banerjee Road. This was set up a few years ago by CAISS for homeless elderly Anglo-Indians living on the streets.[8] There might be other options for them: moving into an Anglo-Indian Home such as the Tollygunge Home would be one, but for one reason or another they chose to spend their days independently (a choice many in the west might make too) and their nights in the safety of the shelter. The inhabitants arrive before nightfall, are given a hot nourishing evening meal, have the use of a bathroom, a clean bed and breakfast before they leave again for the day. By the time we arrived, the men and women staying there for the night had gone to bed already. There was no point in us staying so we set off back to Philomena's.

While I'd seen the living conditions of very poor Anglo-Indians before, on this Christmas day the plight of these people seemed particularly poignant. They were living in destitute circumstances so different from what must have been the trappings of their youth, that bygone time when they were deemed, rightly or wrongly, sahibs and memsahibs, when they'd had servants and self-respect, and now this filth and grime, poverty, despair and indignity. What had happened to these people?

By the time we left Philomena's, I no longer felt up to the next event on our programme — a house party at a well-known and politically connected person's home. However, we'd accepted the invitation so after a bit of a rest, feeling rather subdued, we changed into party clothes. Not knowing where it was, we hailed a taxi and gave the driver the address. We alighted in a courtyard where the owners had parked their luxury cars to be loved and cared for by an army of servants. We were received by our hostess, resplendent in sweeping voile, and taken for a grand tour of the mansion, first going up the wide oak winding staircase to the deep pile carpet landing. Before us were hanging several generously framed oil paintings of European landscapes. Our hostess didn't know their provenance, only that they were valuable. The rooms had floor to ceiling family portraits of past nobility, stern bejewelled and caped figures looking out of heavy gilded frames. In one room we met the kindly matriarch of the family, also bedecked and dignified. The bathrooms had gold and marble fittings.

---

[8] I discuss this further in the fourth essay in this work.

We were then taken into the brightly lit gardens and introduced to the other guests. I was relieved to see a number of Anglo-Indians we recognised. Initially, I could hardly keep my eyes on the people I was being introduced to as I took in my surroundings. The backyard had been converted into something between a fairground and a set from *The Arabian Nights*. Children were squealing from the mini Ferris-wheel revolving in one corner, and a steady stream of adults was coming in and out of a faux-snow-covered tent that had been erected in another. Many well-heeled and clad guests sat around a brazier and chatted: about how they'd spent their day, holiday plans, their children's overseas education and employment prospects. There was a fully stocked bar and tables of snacks to tide us over until our buffet dinner, and a disco for the teenagers with a popular city DJ who had been hired for the night; however, the *pièce de résistance* was the ice carving of a bird. Later in the evening, we were introduced to an Indian Maharaja who talked about Anglo-Indians who lived in his region. I couldn't help but notice dandruff sprinkled across the shoulders of his dark suit. His wife came over and dusted it off, explaining that he'd just come out of the faux-snow covered tent and must have rubbed against the snow. He recommended we take a look inside the tent where we found six hookahs—all with different varieties of fruit to smoke, in an eastern ambience created with knotted rugs covering the grass, and piles of large satin-covered pillows to recline against.

We left after midnight, after bidding farewell to these friends who had so generously shared their close family with us. Along with their friends this family does a lot for their community. Driving back, we thought about others in this city that we'd spent time with earlier in the day: the ailing and lonely Anglo-Indian women, the homeless street dwellers, Beatrice and her children. We drove through deserted streets past the city zoo and the Victoria monument. My mind cast back to the film *36 Chowringee Lane*, which also featured a Christmas day scene. The image of Jennifer Kendal, playing the part of the lonely Miss Stoneham, sitting on a wall in front of the Victoria Monument with 'Silent Night' as background music came to mind.

PART ONE

Identity

Scenes such as those portrayed in the film *36 Chowringhee Lane* play on a range of stereotypical images of Anglo-Indians—about who they are and what they aspire to. It showcases Anglo-Indian longing for the family abroad, and provides a negative portrayal of other Indians' feelings about them. The Anglo-Indian apprehension about losing their distinct identity is also highlighted. These are some of the current concerns for Anglo-Indians and in the essay later in this section I discuss these issues in the context of the 1911 drafted definition of who an Anglo-Indian is, and what this means in the 21st century. Also in the essay, I look at Anglo-Indian origins and, based on my fieldwork experiences, interviews and observations, their socio-cultural characteristics.

But first, I introduce my good friend, Angeline. It is appropriate that her story appears as the first Anglo-Indian story in this work; she was the first Anglo-Indian I met and came to know well. My engagement with her and those she introduced me to catalysed the change in my research focus from the New Market to the Anglo-Indians of Calcutta. Her story also belongs first as it illustrates so many of the characteristics I have come to associate with Anglo-Indians, and is a far cry from the portrayal of the pitiable Miss Stoneham. In her working life Angeline was a valued, highly respected secretary, administrator and welfare officer. She was, and still is, full of joy for life—she enjoys socialising; loves her community and practices an everyday Christianity. Her story describes her early life and draws attention to some of the changes that have been seen in the opportunities for Anglo-Indians over the last few decades.

The other life story in this section is Irene's.[1] I've positioned it after the essay as a potentially controversial, counterpoint to the official Anglo-Indian definition. The story of this spirited woman, a *contested* Anglo-Indian from the Bow Street Barracks, does, I contend, belong here as it exemplifies arguments I have made for including a wider application of the constitution definition of who an Anglo-Indian is. The details in her life identify her, culturally, as Anglo-Indian.

---

[1] 'Irene' is a pseudonym.

1

Angeline: Typically Anglo-Indian

On the day I arrived back in Calcutta to begin my PhD fieldwork (which at that stage was still to focus on the New Market) there was a knock on the hotel room door. I opened up to the sight of an older, slightly olive-skinned woman in a knee-length, short-sleeved, pattern print dress caught at the waist with a fabric belt. Her wavy brown hair was cut and styled in a tidy manner, and she wore just enough make-up to highlight her mischievous eyes and ready smile. I couldn't quite place the woman in front of me in my imagination of people who live in India. In her hand was an electric jug and the makings for cups of tea. She welcomed me warmly and introduced herself (in slightly accented English) as the woman who had made my hotel booking, Angeline. She told me she lived downstairs from the hotel I was staying in, as she had done for some 30 odd years. She offered me the use of her jug saying that she knew I'd like to be able to make myself a cup of tea first thing in the mornings, rather than rely on the overly sweet, milky tea offered by the hotel. Her hospitality extended to company and advice anytime I needed it. Such generosity and hospitality is a characteristic I came to associate with her, and with her people. She told me that she was an Anglo-Indian, and it was she who pointed out that I had a strong connection with the Anglo-Indian community, through sponsorship of Anglo-Indian schoolchildren: the children I had previously thought of simply as Indian, with unusually Western names.

As my research topic changed, and I came to know her better I had imagined she might be my Anglo-Indian Nisa[1] or key informant, whose extended life story would form the centrepiece of my research report. Although I did attempt to interview Angeline

---

[1] Referring to Majorie Shostak's ethnographic account of the Kung San people of the Kalahari Desert, which revolved around the life story of Nisa, an older Kung woman, in her *Nisa: The Life and Words of a Kung Woman* (1990).

about her life, we never got more than a quarter of an hour or so on tape before she would say, 'So that's my life', signalling the end of the formal part of my visit. She did not seem to value her life story and could not see how it could be of use or interest for my work. She was always happier to talk about other people's lives. When I look back on the way our interviews invariably progressed, I think her idea of a *good* life story, one I should be interested in, was of a life that involved valiant fights against adversity. She was full of praise for people she knew who had started life with serious physical and/or social disadvantages but had made good (by good she meant becoming educated, in full employment, church-going and happy) through institutional help, combined with their own perseverance, faith and even some form of luck. I have in fact included some stories that meet her criteria in this work, for example, Jane's and Philip's. At first, I interpreted her reluctance to be interviewed about her own life as reasonable caution on her part about talking to someone she hardly knew, but even as I came to know her well this reluctance to talk about herself did not shift. Although the Nisa-like research relationship that I had hoped for didn't eventuate, we did become firm friends and confidantes. She was an invaluable part of my project—without her help I wouldn't have met many of the people I did, nor would I have understood as much about the community as I do. We spent many hours together: going to New Market to buy supplies, visiting a home for the elderly, attending church services and a wedding blessing, as well as spending time chatting in her home, often along with numerous young Anglo-Indians who all called her and treated her as *aunty*. She introduced me to many people and is well known and well regarded in the community. I confided in her at times when I needed advice on social situations, and she offered advice when she thought I needed it!

In one of our interview sessions I asked her about herself—her family of origin, schooling and working life:

> I was born and grew up in Lucknow where my father worked for the railways, he was a railway official. Both my parents are Anglo-Indian. My father's father was a German doctor. My grandmother was Anglo-Indian. And from my mother's side my grandfather is Anglo-Indian and my mother's mother was an Irish woman.

We had a very lovely railway bungalow and in my youth we lived very much in the Western world. In those days the staff that we had working for us always had uniforms. They served at the table, the table was always nicely laid with linens, serviettes, things like that. As children we were treated as children. My mother never beat us (and I don't think beating was really necessary where children are concerned). But she had what we used to call 'the look'. She would give us a glare and we'd know exactly what we had done wrong. As children we used to have our dinners before our parents. We had an early meal, an early supper, then we'd have our baths, get into bed and mother always took time to be with us at prayer time. She brought us up in a religious way, to say our prayers, to know our bible.

We had the best of everything. We were very Westernised in our way of living, the way we spoke, the way we ate and dressed.

Were they, the people on the railways paid quite well?

Well in those days money used to go very far. I mean you will think I am telling you a lie when I tell you my Mum used to get 16 loaves of bread for one rupee. We had sixteen *anna*s to the rupee and it used to be one *anna* a loaf. So if you drew a salary of a few hundreds, you really lived in the lap of luxury. That was the case when I was small.

My mother never, ever worked, she just ran the house. We used to have staff and when I tell you how much my Mum used to pay the staff you won't believe. But we used to have a bearer that used to look after my brother because he was very naughty. He was only in charge of my brother. And we used to have an ayah, what we call an ayah, who's like a nanny, who looked after the three of us, the three girls. Then we had a sweeper who cleaned inside and out and we had a bearer that would serve us at the table. We had a cook and we had a gardener. Because in, the railway houses in those days used to have beautiful gardens and my mother was very keen on gardening. So we had a gardener as well. And I remember mummy used to pay our cook ₹15 a month. And I think the gardener was paid something like ₹7, and the others were paid ₹10 each.

It's not much is it? Did they live on the property?

They lived with us, because the railway houses had outhouses for staff, for the servants. So they had free accommodation. Yes, but that's how much they used to be paid.

Today it's very difficult for us to keep a full time staff member to look after the house. Now, for instance, I have just the one girl who comes for half an hour and cleans my room, because I have no outside garden. I have to pay my girl that comes for half an hour, ₹300 a month. She comes in every day.

What do you call her? An ayah too?

We call them maidservants. An ayah is usually to look after children. My maidservant that comes, she just does the cleaning. She will sweep and mop, and then she will wash up the dishes and then she goes off. She comes at half past one and she goes by 2 o'clock. She has a son. She does a lot of jobs for people. And she has to because she has to maintain her house so she leaves her village at about 5 o'clock in the morning. She lives about two hours away from here. So she comes by train every morning. And she does several jobs, and then she leaves at about 5 o'clock in the evening to go back.

School and Professional Training

Mum and Dad made a lot of sacrifices because there were four of us in the family; one boy who came first, then three girls, and I was the first girl.

The reason she had to make those sacrifices, and Dad too, was because they sent us to boarding schools in Nainital. That's in the north of India. It is very beautiful because it had a lake surrounded by nine hills.

So I say thank you to Mum and Dad. I know that the sacrifices they made to send us to those institutions was tremendous. To educate…, I mean today's education is much more expensive, but even in those days, to send us to boarding schools was very expensive.

We spent all our education there. I went when I was just about eight years old. And I finished my senior Cambridge there. It was an Anglo-Indian school, so an English curriculum. For our second language, we had an option of French or Urdu. It was before the Partition, so in those days Urdu was the language of India at that time.

Oh, is that right?

So I took the Urdu. But my sister took French.

Do you think she regretted that, or doesn't it matter? After Independence it must have been an advantage for you to have an Indian language.

It was an advantage for me. But mind you, as far as we are concerned, we talk in Urdu, English and Bengali. And that's always been an advantage for the Anglo-Indian. I did Urdu because it was easier for me because I was talking the language. We used to talk to the servants in Urdu.

At school we had debating, and we had all the games. There was basketball, hockey, tennis. We played all those games in school. Inter-school matches too. And we took a lot of home science.

And you were taught religious studies as well?

Oh yes. It was a Methodist school so we were taught a lot of religious study then. Actually from childhood we grew up like that. You know, my mother always taught us to pray and things; so we naturally fell in with it quite easily. It wasn't difficult for us.

And from there I went to Ramnee Convent to do my commercial course. In those days we never used to go much to University. It was only if you were going in to become a doctor or a lawyer, or something that needed a degree.

Yes, I see.

But if you were going in for nursing or a secretarial course, you just went up to class 10, in those days it was class 10, which is now equivalent to class 12. It was in the same place. We couldn't take commercial in our school so I had to go to the Convent and then for nine months I did the course in shorthand, bookkeeping and typing. And then I've worked ever since. I came down to Calcutta because they said, you know, Calcutta is more lucrative in its pay for the same sort of job, better salaries and things like that. Which was very important! And I have been here ever since.

So that's been my life.

Views on Life for Anglo-Indians, Including Changes since Independence

Growing up everything for me was English. After we got independence, I found that, which is very natural, we started bending more towards the Indian culture. Not that I could do it. I was too old. I mean I have been brought up in one world, and it was difficult for me all of a sudden to change. But in today's world you will find the children adapt themselves better, which is very good because we are Indian. My nationality is Indian, and, therefore, we should actually learn more about the Indian culture, which they are doing now. Today's Anglo-Indian children are being taught, so they are able to fit in more now with the Indian ways than they previously did.

So you felt that they were quite separate, with the way you were brought up?

Yes, the way I was brought up and the way that we are brought up. Now is very different.

Did you, when you were brought up, have friends who were Anglo-Indians?

Actually when I was brought up there were just two Indian girls in the whole school, who were my friends—that's the boarding school. Whereas now, it has changed completely. We have more Indian students in an English Medium School than we have Anglo-Indians. That is because the Indian now has realised that education is very important. You see before in India, their professions were important to them. You know like farming, carpentry.

Right, like the caste professions?

It was the caste profession which the children followed. But now they don't follow that any more. They all want to be educated, they all want to climb the ladder, which is a very good thing. The Indian wants to learn English so that they can go in for higher studies. You cannot go in for higher studies not knowing a universal language. And they will naturally, having been educated, hold the most important jobs in any firm, or any organisation.

What about the Anglo-Indians who might have the same qualifications?

Well it's like this, I mean in Europe for instance, preference would naturally be given to the Europeans rather than the Anglo-Indians.

Okay, so if an Anglo-Indian lived in a European country you mean?

Yes, it's the same thing over here. I mean you have a tendency of giving your own people the preference. If they are alike in education, qualifications, experience and things like that, you have a tendency and you can't blame them for having that tendency, to employ their own people.

So although you say you are Indian, you know, 'we are all Indian', you feel that perhaps the Indians don't feel quite the same?

Now of course the Indian feels 'this is my country, I am the top dog'. See? It was like the European when the European was in India. You know, then they felt that they were the superior beings, and everybody was below their dignity.

Where did Anglo-Indians fit then?

In the same category as we fit now. In my opinion we were always a second class citizen. Whether it was the European who used the Anglo-Indian because of our English and Western ways. And now it's the other way around. Now the Indian today is very educated. If you look at our colleges you will find there are mostly Indian students who are being educated to accept more responsibility. So this is the difference between the past and the present.

Yes, but one thing remains the same, that you are second....

It will always be that. I don't say that there are not.... Some Anglo-Indians have achieved the top jobs. Many of them have because of their education, experience and knowledge. Before Independence the European gave preference to the Anglo-Indian. All the commercial jobs were all held by Anglo-Indians.

I see, yes.

The telegraph, the railways, all these sort of jobs there were mainly held by Anglo-Indians and that is because of their ability to speak English and to coordinate with the European. At that time, the Indian didn't have the same grasp of English as he has today.

So the Anglo-Indian fitted in better with the Colonial administrators.

At that time, yes.

I see. And your father was with the railways?

My father was an official on the railways and in those days they used to take a lot of trouble with their work. The engine driver would always see that his engine was polished and clean. He took a pride in whatever he was doing. It is sad that today, we don't take pride in things that don't belong to us.

You mean....

Okay, it's the government. Somebody will see to it. Like our buses on the road. Do you see our buses today? You will find government buses are in a worse condition than a private bus. You will notice it on the roads. You will look at them and you will know that this is a private bus and this is a government bus, and you will see the deterioration in the government vehicles. Because they don't belong, you know? They are just something that I have to drive, okay. It's just a job.

Whereas beforehand ... so you are talking pre-Independence?

Pre-Independence, yes. It felt as though it was your own. You took the pride in seeing that your bus was washed down. That it was clean and things like that. You took a personal pride in it.

So Anglo-Indians that might have the same sort of job now, like working on the railways, don't take the same sort of pride?

No they don't, because you see, you see somebody else has the job of cleaning it, even if they don't do it very well. It remains like that and it'll carry on. It's not what it used to be in the years gone by. India has advanced a lot since we have had Independence. We have advanced in many ways. But in some ways it's gone backwards.

The Anglo-Indian now is inter-marrying a lot with the Indians.

Indian Christians, or Indian people?

No, just Indians in general. They have learnt to, and that is because they are meeting them more in offices, in their work sphere, and socially. And very naturally friendships develop which may lead to marriages. Before, you would very seldom have thought of marrying out of our community. Partly because we didn't mix, we didn't even mix with the European much. You know, we kept very much to our own group.

Was that because you couldn't or just didn't?

I think it was to do with the aloofness of the European. They had that sense of superiority. They don't have it now but they used to in those days. And for that reason we kept very much to ourselves as a community, and so we inter-married in our own community.

You have a lot of European in the mix too, haven't you? I mean generally.

But, I can't say I am sorry for the way I have been brought up. I think I like my style of living. I can mix with anybody. Yes, I've been fortunate in knowing all castes and creeds of people. I think I like my style of living, because I like all people.

I got married in 1960 when I was over 30. I have been a very independent sort of a person, which is very bad really, because that's what made me take so long to get married really. It was because I was so independent. I like to do things my own way and I am still very fussy, and it takes me very long to adapt to people.

I worked ever since, and I have enjoyed actually working most for the homes where I have worked for about the last 23 years, a long time. I worked before this as matron-cum-secretary of a hospital in Calcutta. And then I gave that up because I wanted to work for underprivileged children. That was always my ambition: to work for underprivileged children.

You didn't have children yourself?

I never had children of my own.

But you've informally adopted hundreds from what I see!

Yes, over the years I have. And it has been a joy for me. Really. I have enjoyed working for them. I have enjoyed my work. And that is why I think I'm lucky, that now at the age of almost 75,[2] I can

---

[2] Theo is now 86 years old and is still very active in the community, although no longer in paid employment.

still work for them and be happy about it. Yes, I think I get more out of it than I give into it. I do enjoy it very much. I'm very close to the children.

This I can attest to. Her home, accurately observed by her sister, is like Howrah station, with one visitor arriving before another leaves. I doubt that a day would go by without friends, young and old dropping in to see her—for advice, church meetings and whist sessions twice a week. She has served on the Boards of one of the Anglo-Indian homes for the elderly, of East India Charitable Trust (EICT) and is on various church committees. Although she doesn't belong to any social service organisation, she quietly looks after people on a daily basis. She has rehabilitated one elderly Anglo-Indian man and gives him regular employment, and a place to spend hours during the day when he can't be at his other home—the Anglo-Indian night shelter. At Christmas time she puts together packets of treats for street children living near her home.

She said in her interview that she hasn't changed with the times, but that isn't what I see. She gives wise, up-to-date advice to all of her charges, mostly former boarding school students, and they are many. In the 10 years I've known her, there is one family of girls she has been particularly close to. During their boarding school years, she opened her home to them to use as their base during their months of annual winter and Christmas holidays. She lives very centrally, in one large room with an attached bathroom, which doubles as her laundry and general wash area. Her one large room is partitioned into two areas by curtains: one area contains two single beds and storage furniture, the other functions as her kitchen, dining and sitting room. Having these girls to stay requires her to live with them at close quarters, relinquishing her privacy and familiar routines for the sake of others. Since the girls have finished school she's continued to extend this hospitality. She's seen them (emotionally and financially) through their tertiary studies or vocational training, into suitable relationships—which she offers sensible advice on but is far from draconian in implementing—and recently, into their marriages.

2

Essay: Culture and Identity

Introduction

For a community who are often spoken about as being confused about their identity, Anglo-Indians residing in Calcutta, no matter what their educational achievement, are experts on the parameters of their identity. In addition, many can quote, often word perfect, Section 366, Article 2, of the Indian Constitution, which defines who an Anglo-Indian is.

The prime focus of this essay is to review ideas around Anglo-Indian identity. I look first, briefly, at Anglo-Indian origins and cultural characteristics. Based on fieldwork experiences, including those in Toronto at the Seventh Anglo-Indian World Reunion in 2007, I then turn to what I see as the limitations of the official definition and discuss possible solutions, and complications. Most importantly, I argue that the spirit in which this definition was written was to ensure the well-being of the community and I query whether the definition still achieves this aim, and if not, whether a more useful definition could be provided for this community.

Origins, or from Colonised to Globalised

Anglo-Indians may be seen as a product of colonisation. It is through Western expansion of trade and rule in the 16th century that Europeans arrived in India but it was the British who made the most significant and enduring impact. The establishment of the East India Company in the 17th century, and then the British Raj securing a platform to rule the subcontinent kept the British in India for over three centuries. Trade and colonialism were almost exclusively masculine endeavours. In the case of the British in

India, tens of thousands of single males found themselves in India for years at a time, during which many men formed alliances with and married local women. It is from these relationships that the first Anglo-Indians were produced. In the earliest days of their existence these offsprings of British men and Indian women were treated as if they were British. After some time, the British began to distance themselves from Anglo-Indians. One result of this is that Anglo-Indians then came to form a distinct community. Arguably, another factor in the formation of a discrete community was their exclusion from caste-conscious Hindu society.

As both Christopher Hawes (1993, 1996) and Megan Mills (1998), amongst others, have documented, the British varied in their treatment of and attitude towards Anglo-Indians at different times, barring them from some positions but generally giving them preferential employment in subordinate roles in maintaining the infrastructure of British India. They worked in the railways, post and telegraph, customs, nursing and teaching, and in the armed forces. It is a point of pride for many (particularly older) Anglo-Indians that they have a history of unfailing support for the British in any altercation they entered into. In the first War of Independence (also known as the 'Mutiny'), for example, Anglo-Indians fought alongside the British, rather than the Indian groups.

In terms of nomenclature, Anglo-Indians were initially known as Eurasians, with the term 'half-caste' also used occasionally to refer to them. It was not until 1911 when the first census was conducted in India that the name Anglo-Indian became widely accepted and used in the way it is now. In 1935, the current definition was adopted into the Government of India Act, and it became embedded in the Indian Constitution post Independence. Some, particularly postcolonial, scholars refer to them as a *hybrid* community. Their hyphenated name suggests this but I prefer to regard them, after over 300 years, as distinctive in themselves rather than being a 'mixed race and culturally composite community' (Caplan, 2001: 1).

Given Anglo-Indians' background of attachment to Britain, it is understandable that the Indian Independence in 1947 posed a potentially serious threat to them and Anglo-Indians were fearful of reprisals once India gained its independence. These did not, in fact, eventuate; rather they were able to claim a number of benefits, which were written into the Constitution of the newly elected government. The benefits included representation in State Legislative Assemblies where their population warranted it (Article 333), provision of two seats in the Lok Sabha—also known as the House of the People (Article 331)—employment reservations (referred to by Anglo-Indians as *quotas*) in the railway, customs, postal and telegraph services (Article 336) and an allocation of grants for Anglo-Indian schools (Article 337) on the condition that the schools accept at least 40 per cent of non-Anglo-Indian students. These benefits, with the exception of State and National representation, were set up with a formula for their gradual disbandment. Even so, schools continue to be protected by a *dearness allowance* scheme, which subsidises teachers' salaries, and other grants that enable Anglo-Indian students' preferential access to the schools. I elaborate on this in the essay, which focuses on education.

Even though there were benefits rather than reprisals, with the first post-Independence Congress-led government, this did not ameliorate Anglo-Indians' sense of insecurity about their future in India. As the British left India, Anglo-Indians began to do the same, resulting in three major waves of migration (Blunt, 2005; Caplan, 2001; Mahar, 1962). Immediately after 1947 tens of thousands left for England, which they had always considered as some sort of a homeland (Blunt, 2002; Stark, 1926). The second major migratory wave was in the early 1960s coinciding with a move in India to replace English as the national language. The prospect of Hindi replacing English as the national language was a concern to Anglo-Indians as, mostly, they did not speak another Indian language well enough for employment and other purposes. Another reason for the movement at this time can be attributed to the closure of large international companies in the main centres where many Anglo-Indians had employment.[1] The destinations for this second migratory wave were Canada and Australia as immigration to the United Kingdom had become difficult (due to the introduction of

---

[1] This issue was highlighted to me by Anglo-Indians I interviewed (in Melbourne in 2007) about their reasons for coming to Australia, and is noted by Blunt (2005: 156).

controls to regulate immigration [Massey et al., 1998]) and also because Australia had dropped its *whites-only* policy—which had affected all but the fairest Anglo-Indians (Blunt, 2005: 139–174; Massey et al., 1998: 161). The third wave, from the 1970s and continuing, is sometimes referred to in India as the *family reunion* wave (President of the All India Anglo-Indian Association [AIAIA]; personal communication, February 2002). This idea is referred to in migration literature as *family reunification*[2] (Massey et al., 1998: 161; Moch, 2005: 98–99) and is taken into account in the immigration policies of many countries, including New Zealand (Trlin, 1997). The main destinations for this wave of emigrants have been Australia, England, Canada and, to a lesser extent, New Zealand. There are now more Anglo-Indians living out of India than there are in India, and there are people who identify as Anglo-Indians who have never lived in India.

Based on this empirical evidence, and on interviews with Anglo-Indians in Madras, Caplan first identified and named their *culture of emigration* (Caplan, 1995, 2001: 129–141).[3] From my more recent experience with the community in Calcutta, it is evident that there is still a steady stream of Anglo-Indians leaving India, and even more who confidently aspire to. One Anglo-Indian resident who is conducting research on emigration trends in Calcutta believes that another 20 per cent have left the city since the turn of the millennium (personal communication, 2010). This supports the argument of an entrenched culture of migration. It has always been a challenge for Anglo-Indians to get to their preferred destination countries, but the opportunities are now diminishing further as these countries tighten up their immigration policies,[4] but still they leave.

During my research, the deep-rooted nature and significance of migration was reinforced to me in a number of ways during my visits. In addition to individual migration stories there are other indications of this imperative to leave; for example, one area of

---

[2] The term 'chain migration' is also used to express the same idea.

[3] Caplan discusses this issue and suggests that up to a half of the pre-Independence population of Anglo-Indians may have left India (2001: 129–141).

[4] It is not only Anglo-Indians, of course, who are affected by the tightening up of immigration regulations, this affects other Indian groups as well as others, especially those from developing countries, who attempt to migrate.

Calcutta, which is officially named Picnic Garden, is often referred to by Anglo-Indians as *Little Australia*. The area has a large population of Anglo-Indians who have recently moved there (in a process of internal migration) from the central business district (CBD), or the city centre. The explanation given for the name is that if they cannot live in Australia then this is the next best thing—and it is often a stepping-stone to Australia.

Anglo-Indian Cultural Characteristics

In this section, at the risk of simplifying and homogenising a huge diversity of ways of being Anglo-Indian in Calcutta today, I suggest a set of *typical* cultural characteristics. This may seem incongruous for an anthropologist who values the richness and diversity provided by individual stories in this work, but I think it serves a useful purpose as a way to draw a rough sketch or portrait of the community. Anglo-Indians themselves, I believe, would be quick to provide a list of their general characteristics, or at least to dispute others' lists.

I was made aware of this soon after the movie *Bow Barracks Forever* (Dutt, 2007) was released. I was in Calcutta on a fieldwork trip and I had managed to buy a copy of the movie on DVD at the market and view it on my laptop. A few days later, I attended a house party to celebrate a friend's birthday and while sitting around the dinner table I asked what they had thought of it. I was told, in no uncertain terms, that Anglo-Indians had been misrepresented by the movie, that even Bow Barracks Anglo-Indians were not as bad as the director, Anjan Dutt, had portrayed them to be. They were openly angry, saying that Dutt has no idea about how Anglo-Indians live, and that it was a negative and quite inaccurate depiction.[5] They commented that the fighting, the womanising, the *wasters* who had

---

[5] I spoke to one of the real-life characters portrayed in Anjan Dutt's film. He said that Dutt had been hurt and saddened by Anglo-Indian's response to his film, claiming that Dutt had always had a 'soft corner' for Anglo-Indians and appreciated, envied and perhaps even admired the fact they so obviously enjoyed life (personal communication, November 2007).

been deserted by emigrating family and who themselves longed to be in another land were not Anglo-Indians as they knew them. They were particularly offended by the character of Aunty Lobo as an Anglo-Indian woman selling homemade alcohol, saying that they don't even brew alcohol over there. A little later in the evening my host told me that *they* were quintessential Anglo-Indians; that they get on with each other and have a good time together. They said they have great food at the drop of a hat, and anyone who calls in is invited to take potluck with them because there is always more food prepared than is needed. After a dinner where we all sat around and talked and joked together, one of the guests got out his guitar and played songs that they all knew the words to. I was told that this was typical of Anglo-Indians, and reminded by one of them, again, that they, not the Anglo-Indians in the film, were real Anglo-Indians. This characteristic of Anglo-Indians, as being musically talented, was reinforced a few days later when I visited an Anglo-Indian rest home and a committee member there said you could tell a *real* Anglo-Indian by whether or not they could sing certain songs, citing me the example of the song, 'Roll out the Barrel'.

The usual list (found in scholarly works, such as my own PhD thesis) of key characteristics differentiating Anglo-Indians from other communities in India is: having English as their mother tongue, acknowledging their historical link to Europe and being Christians. (The All India Anglo-Indian Association argues that this characteristic is crucial to their identification as Anglo-Indians. I even heard talk of altering the definition to include this dimension.) They frequently dress in Western clothing, especially in all Anglo-Indian company, enjoy (spiced-up) Western food and employ Western eating practices such as using cutlery, and usually have European names. In terms of appearance, Anglo-Indians range from being *fair*[6] to swarthy. Some have *coloured* (blue or green) eyes but most have brown. Some have what was described to me as the *pulled* eyes of north-eastern *tribal* Indians.

I was told by several people, men and women, that one can always tell an Anglo-Indian woman by her *grazed calves*, that is, her

---

[6] To use their term that refers to skin tone, rather than hair colour—which is almost always dark.

slender and shapely lower legs. Other comments that were made to me on many occasions were that Anglo-Indians are the only people in India who have *Indian* in their name, and that they were *people of India*, rather than of a particular region (which most Indians are, for example, Bengalis and Punjabis are people of Bengal and the Punjab, respectively). They are likely to identify themselves as 'Anglo-Indian by community and Indian by nationality.'

Based on my observations and detailed talk with Anglo-Indians I would suggest that some additions be made to any list that might be compiled of Anglo-Indian characteristics: that they are hospitable (I was told by Anglo-Indians that this is attributable to their Indian side), enjoy any opportunity to socialise and are talented singers and dancers. The ability to jive is referred to by D'Cruz (2006: 1) as a quintessential characteristic—one that he said he lacked. The younger ones have taken up the jive, but also dance hip-hop, Bollywood and bhangra. They are more than just Christians; rather, they practice their faith in earnest on a day-to-day basis. All seem to have relatives overseas. They are frequently superstitious. This was really brought home to me recently in my capacity as a judge of Anglo-Indian short stories, when so many included an element of the occult. Laura Bear's (Roychowdhury, 2001) account of her fieldwork experiences is titled *The Jadu House* (the magic, or spirit house)—and discusses this same issue.

In the past, Anglo-Indians' marriage patterns would have been added to the list as they most often married other Anglo-Indians; that is, they were an endogamous community. The situation is different now: with Anglo-Indians more likely to be working, living beside and socialising with other Indians, they are also, increasingly, marrying outside the community. The steady stream of Anglo-Indians migrating from India is also diminishing the pool of traditional partners.

At world reunions, and other places, I am frequently told that Calcutta's Anglo-Indians are different from Anglo-Indians in other parts of the country. For one thing, they say that these *Anglo-Banglos,* as I have heard them referred to affectionately by non-Calcuttan Anglo-Indians, form a more unified and cohesive community than they do in other parts of the country. This is, perhaps, due to having a critical mass of Anglo-Indians that the other Indian metros may not.

Within Calcutta itself, the identity of Anglo-Indians varies, roughly, in accordance with residential area. Given that residential location is used by others to identify Anglo-Indians, I will discuss the stereotypical expectations of the Anglo-Indians in the various areas of Calcutta. This will also serve to contextualise the various life story settings too. For this discussion, there is no better introduction than Keith Butler's description of his fictitious main character, Puttla Butler, who is back in Calcutta in the early years of the millennium looking for Anglo-Indians:

> He had returned to Calcutta after 30 years. He walked the city, looking for Anglos in the usual haunts, ambling down Park Circus, reading the oncoming crowd, his eyes scanning for snooty class Anglos—light eyes, fair skin, grazing calves, nice clothes, then down Elliott Rd watching this time for darker Anglos—lychee nut eyes, coffee skin, slicked back hair, then into Wellesley second lane, searching for once-were-rockers, jivers, Anglo Presley's, slicked back hair, sideburns, collar up, thin leather belts coiled like Brahman holy thread around their waists, then onto Kidderpore and dockyard Anglos living in Muslim *bustees* and shacks....
>
> He then stood at busy intersections, Chowringhee and Dhuromtalla, Shakespeare Sarani and Nehru, Lenin and Alimuddin, with his eyes shut and listened as the crowds streamed past him, his ears straining for the familiar tell-tale lilt of Anglo voices, hoping for a 'Hullo men, got a fag?' or 'Denzil had a scrap with Harold.' but all he heard was buzzing and droning and babbling. (Unpublished manuscript)

Butler's excerpt highlights the demography of central Calcutta where Anglo-Indians lived in the 1970s. His character, Puttla, looked in these areas, to no avail (Photo 2.1). Unlike Puttla, I met many Anglo-Indians in the areas he searched.[7]

---

[7] I am not, of course, in a position to compare the numbers of Anglo-Indians in the streets now, with those 30 years ago. So my idea of 'many' is likely to be very few in comparison to past times. In 2005 as I was completing my thesis I spoke to a friend who had been brought up in Calcutta and now lives in New Zealand. She had recently been to Calcutta for an extended visit and she had made the same observation as Butler through his fictitious character 'Puttla': that in the central city where she had been used to seeing 'crowds of Anglo-Indians'; she could now count them on her fingers.

Figure 2.1:
The Changed Face of Elliott Road (2004)

Source: Author.

Of the central city Anglo-Indians, many live in comfortable homes, which are spacious, light and airy, well-furnished and close to the CBD: in Marquis Street, Elliot Road, Middleton Row, Free School Street and Wellesley Street, for example. These Anglo-Indians generally seem to have reasonable employment, dress and speak in an educated manner, attend inner city churches and schools, and are involved in Anglo-Indian clubs and social service organisations. In most cases, they have lived in the same family home for decades, although they seldom own them.

Over the last decade, well after Butler left the city, many Anglo-Indians from this densely populated central city district have given up their rented homes to purchase apartments further out (as 'Meryl's' sister-in-law had hoped to do, see the last life story in this work). This movement is an example of the trend towards internal migration and of the growth in numbers of middle-class property owners that Caplan also observed in Madras (1998: 24). One of the main areas where Anglo-Indians are resettling is Picnic Gardens, to the east of the city centre, referred to earlier. The parish priest of Our Lady of Velankanni parish in Picnic Gardens put the population there at 1,500 families (personal correspondence, January 2013), and he was soon to test that with a parish census. Here, more than in any other part of Calcutta, Anglo-Indians are really putting down roots and buying their homes, rather than renting them as they have in the past. Ironically, their rationale for naming this area *Little Australia* seems to contradict the idea that roots are being put down.

Another place where Anglo-Indians live, which Butler did not mention, is in the *bustee* (or slum) of Tiljala. In the early 1970s when he left the city many other Anglo-Indians did not know about these people or their plight. Michael Robertson, when I interviewed him for his life story (included in this work in the education section), talked about his shock at the realisation that his people lived in these conditions. Tiljala, also located to the east of the CBD, but closer to the city centre than Picnic Gardens, is the Muslim-dominated *bustee* where hundreds of thousands of people live in mostly tenement-style one-roomed homes. The exact numbers are impossible to calculate due to the nature of such informal settlements.[8] Some of the poorest Anglo-Indians live here and due, in part at least, to Blair and Ellen Williams' philanthropic organisation, Calcutta Tiljala Relief Incorporated (CTR), their situation is now better known.

Whenever I'm in Calcutta I visit Anglo-Indians in Tiljala. Until he died suddenly, I was always accompanied by an Anglo-Indian guide, the blue-eyed Ralph Mulholland, who would direct me from one Anglo-Indian home to another through labyrinthine lanes and pathways. The people I visit live in very small quarters, sometimes with three generations of one family living in one sparse, clean room, sharing facilities for ablutions with a number of other

---

[8] For images of the *bustee*, as well as further discussion, see: http://www.studio-basel.com/Projects/Kolkata/Student-Work/Tiljala.html (accessed on 2 September 2009).

families. Most Tiljala residents are extremely poor, and donations from CTR and other organisations make the difference between regular daily meals and reasonable health, and malnutrition and illness. Others who have regular employment, some in teaching, hospitality or security positions, choose to remain here because the low rental means they can afford luxuries such as televisions and cell phones, and school fees.

Official Definition and Its Implications

Anglo-Indians are the only minority community to be defined in India's Constitution. As already documented in the introduction, the definition reads:

> An Anglo-Indian means a person whose father or any of whose other male progenitors in the male line is or was of European descent but who is domiciled within the territory of India and is or was born within such territory of parents habitually resident therein and not established there for temporary purposes only. (Section 366[2])

At the time that special conditions for Anglo-Indians were being written into the Indian Constitution there also needed to be some way of identifying those who were eligible for the benefits; that is, some proof of Anglo-Indian identity was required. When the definition was redrafted for inclusion in the India Act in 1935, it reflected the history of the community, the marriage patterns and the gendered mores of the times. When it was adopted into the Indian Constitution 12 years later, it was probably safe to assume that by giving males certain privileges, females were therefore provided for.

More than a century after its composition, this gender bias is a problem. It can result in discrimination, which can work against the community in particular ways when it is followed to the letter. Moreover, unfortunately some of the associations and organisations do so, rather than offering the same advantages to children born of Anglo-Indian mothers, assistance is restricted to the children of Anglo-Indian fathers. 'Beatrice' and her children, who I met that Christmas Day, are just one example of the many who may be discriminated against unless social services are flexible in their application of the definition, that is, if they adhere to the spirit, rather than the letter, of the definition. Irene, who you meet in the next story, luckily, had married the father of her daughters so they qualified for assistance available to Anglo-Indians. If the children born of Anglo-Indian mothers can share the same advantages as those born of Anglo-Indian fathers, children such as Beatrice's little son and daughter would stand a better chance of being able to live respectable and fulfilled lives with some choices and dignity. For me the frustrating aspect of this situation is that an out-of-dated piece of man-made legislation may be used to deny this chance to these children. Of significance, also, is that the numerical decline of the community is unnecessarily hastened because the community can only propagate Anglo-Indians via the paternal line.

There are other problems with the constitutional definition and these are being exacerbated with time. The issue of whether or not Anglo-Indians born out of India should refer to themselves as Anglo-Indian is one example. According to the definition they cannot. For all that it was not an issue I heard raised in Calcutta, I am conscious that this, theoretically, could become more of a problem as more Anglo-Indian migrants have families in their adopted countries.

Another difficulty, although with fewer repercussions, is that the definition does not distinguish between domiciled Europeans and the progeny of European men and Indian women. Domiciled Europeans are defined as 'those born in India of parents who were of British and/or European descent who had settled permanently in India' (McMenamin, 2001). Confusingly, it was such people who were originally referred to as Anglo-Indians. The gender-based definition, particularly the fact that women are not mentioned in the definition at all, is also the cause of this confusion.

It seems to me that Anglo-Indians are impoverishing themselves by continuing with this arguably outdated definition. Besides the significant material consequences, there is another type of denial, or violence here too — that of being denied your identity. A deficiency of the definition is that it does not recognise, or take into account, the cultural dimensions of what it means to be Anglo-Indian. This was highlighted to me as I met some bright young people who told me sadly that they weren't able to call themselves Anglo-Indians. This was something they felt aggrieved about. They were talented young people that the community would be proud to have in their numbers, and culturally they were Anglo-Indians: they jived, they were active in their Catholic parishes, their mothers were Anglo-Indians and they felt that they *belonged* to the Anglo-Indian community. In two cases the mothers told me of the painful explanations they had had to make to their children about their exclusion from certain aspects of their community life, for example, not being able to enter an Anglo-Indian essay writing competition in one case. In another case the young boy, upon being told that he couldn't call himself an Anglo-Indian at the time he was preparing for his confirmation, wrestled with the idea of leaving the church and going to the temple with his father instead. At the end, he stayed with his and his mother's church, and continued with his confirmation programme.

Toronto Experiences: September 2007 World Reunion

With my Calcutta fieldwork experiences in mind, I made use of my time at Toronto's World Anglo-Indian Reunion to ask attendees for their views of the current definition. The reaction to this varied. One elderly gentleman said, at a reunion presentation, 'To my mind, the exclusion of maternal ancestry was a continuation of colonial domination of our European connections, apart from the discrimination by gender bias.' He, along with a number of others, thought that a change was already occurring in the definition, or at least in its implementation. And they seemed happy about it. At this reunion, much more than any others I've attended, there was a lot of discussion about the constitutional definition.

Once abroad, of course, the definition has little power in terms of access to advantages. However, the fact that the children of

Anglo-Indians who are born out of India cannot by the official definition be regarded as Anglo-Indian—whether or not their father is Anglo-Indian—may offer an additional explanation for their lack of support for the current definition.

There is evidence of tacit disapproval of the male bias in the Constitution on the part of Anglo-Indians who live overseas who send large sums of money back to India for their less-fortunate community members. People I spoke with were adamant that they wanted the sons and daughters of very poor Anglo-Indian women to receive this aid too—whether or not these children's fathers were Anglo-Indians. Blair and Ellen Williams, the founders of the significant philanthropic fund, CTR, insist that they want to see the children of poor Anglo-Indian women looked after with the money being sent over. Philomena Eaton, the convener of CAISS, whose story is included in this work, assured me that these children are catered for by CAISS.

Back in Calcutta: November–December 2007

The problem as I saw it, especially when I was not actually in India, was reasonably straightforward, as was the solution—a change in the constitutional definition was required. As I went about the city working on other projects with Anglo-Indians, I mentioned to them that I was presenting a paper at a forthcoming conference calling for a change in the definition.[9] The reaction to this idea in India, however, was far from unanimous. There were certainly some Anglo-Indians who saw this as a good idea, essential even, but I encountered those with serious reservations as well. Some of the dissenters' comments included:

> We would lose our identity completely if we do this. The definition has achieved the preservation of a distinct, true, Anglo-Indian identity. (Male, mid-60-year-old Anglo-Indian)

[9] The conference was titled *Researching Anglo-Indians: Indian and Diasporic Contexts*. This international conference was convened by the author and hosted by the Centre of Studies in the Social Sciences, Calcutta (CSSSC) from 19 to 21 December 2007.

We help the type of people you talk about already, so a change to the Constitution isn't necessary. (A member of CAISS)

I don't know what would happen if that came about. (Said in a worried tone by the manager of one of the rest homes)

If we don't follow any code then Anglo-Indians may just disappear. (Member of an Anglo-Indian Rest Home management committee)

The little money we receive for Anglo-Indians would have to go so much further, and there's not enough to go around as it is. (Female social service worker)

Then who would count as Anglo-Indian and who wouldn't? (Male, Anglo-Indian writer)

You can't do that, it's in the Constitution. (Male, hospitality worker)

There would be a dilution effect, and the large fish in our small pond wouldn't like that. (Office-holder of an Anglo-Indian Association)

It won't change; it's not that it can't. (Female social service worker)

It's only the children whose fathers are off the scene, or are down-and-outs, who worry about this. Many of them are very proud to be something other than Anglo-Indian. (Female teacher in an Anglo-Indian school)

Then Sonia Gandhi's children would be Anglo-Indians! Is this something we want? (Male, former Anglo-Indian political leader)

Good things have come from the definition as it stands, for example, Sister Marisa's school for Anglo-Indian 'drop outs'. (Female teacher)

The concerns noted above fall into two main categories—one is around the idea of identity, whereas the other focuses on the ability to access social services. Both are important considerations and are frequently entwined. An Anglo-Indian woman who is involved in social services for Anglo-Indians talked about children of mixed marriages and summed up the connection in this way:

When the father is, say, a Punjabi and the mother is an Anglo-Indian: when kids are doing well, and there's enough money and the father is involved, these kids are happy to say they're Punjabi and they don't need the advantages of Anglo-Indian status. If the kids are doing well then it's not an issue. When the father is not around or they're not proud of their father, *then* it's unfair!

A solution being implemented by some social service groups such as CAISS involves the use of their discretion to provide services to the children of poor Anglo-Indians regardless of whether or not their father is Anglo-Indian. They do not see their role as one of addressing the issue of the definition of Anglo-Indian identity when there is so much work to be done in other ways.

I was perplexed by the objection that the definition cannot be touched because it's in the Constitution, implying that it was, literally, cast in stone, rather than being the man-made product of the times when it was drafted (very close to its present wording, for the purposes of the 1911 national census) 100 years old. It was mainly uncontested older, male, Anglo-Indians who ventured this opinion. A more realistic comment was that although it *can* change, it will not. And this is perhaps because of another of the reasons given, 'that the big fish in this small pond wouldn't want to. And they are the only ones with any real power to do it.'

There were a number of concerns raised about what might happen to the Anglo-Indian community if the definition was changed to include the requirement of an Anglo-Indian mother *or* father. One of the main concerns related to an anticipated dilution effect; suddenly there would be so many more people who would qualify as Anglo-Indian. A more positive way of looking at this scenario is that this potential boost to their numbers would be welcome as it would act to counter the loss of their numbers through migration. This change may be just what is required in order that they maintain a critical mass in India.

Another issue raised about a more inclusive definition is that this could lead to the inclusion of people who are not 'culturally' Anglo-Indian, that is, those who have no connection with the community, such as the children of Sonia Gandhi who would fit the definition if the only change was to make it gender inclusive. The reason that people would like to see the definition changed to include the children of Anglo-Indian women is summed up here by one Calcuttan Anglo-Indian woman who said, referring to Anglo-Indian mothers whose children are denied their identity: 'The thing is, it's the mother who brings up the children, it's her language they speak, and her ways they learn.' It seems to me that it would not be difficult to show that the children of Sonia Gandhi (and others in the same situation) do not live an Anglo-Indian lifestyle, so perhaps some cultural element can be brought into the definition. The AIAIA, for example, was keen to include a phrase making it a requirement that the mother tongue is English.

Arguably, there is no need, after three centuries, to refer any more to European descent in their definition. Would it be enough to simply require that one has an Anglo-Indian mother or father? Britain is no longer referred to as *home*, so the definition could reflect this change in the way the community identifies itself too. What is important is that they are linked to their own people, rather than to Europe.

Although I have experimented privately with various possibilities for rewording or institutionalised reinterpretation, this work belongs with the community. As an anthropologist working from a public anthropology perspective I feel compelled to draw attention to what I perceive as gender-based injustices. My hope is that if members of the community also see the situation in this light, they *will* find a set of words that best reflects who Anglo-Indians are in the 21st century, and/or which ensures that those who need assistance are not discriminated against by being excluded, and those who *feel* they are Anglo-Indian can claim this. While identity could be determined through an Anglo-Indian in *either* paternal *or* maternal lines, perhaps identity could be ascribed through a combination of ways of life, that is, culture, *and* some objectively based 'proof' (i.e., descent), *and* self-identity.

Anglo-Indians are not alone in grappling with issues around defining their identity. Anthropologists such as Barth (1969), Nagel (1998) and Sahlins (1993) have written extensively about the ways in which boundaries are formed, and maintained around ethnicity, especially when there are advantages in doing so. Based on empirical research, various theories have been offered to explain why and how these issues are dealt with. The ways that other groups have approached defining their identity may be worthwhile for Anglo-Indians to consider if they decide to deliberate on their own definition. Drawing an example from my own country may be useful in providing such a comparative model.

New Zealand Maori were colonised by the British, and now live in a bicultural society with the *settler* community. There are no longer any *full* Maori, that is, Maori who do not also have antecedents from another ethnicity. Similar to Anglo-Indians there are benefits and opportunities available for Maori (including funds and scholarships) that are not available to the non-indigenous population. Some proof of indigeneity is required for access to these benefits, but this is generally made up of a combination of whakapapa (genealogy) based on descent from the maternal or paternal line, self-identity and to iwi (tribal) involvement to some level. Maori identity per se does not require iwi involvement; self-identification is enough, along with whakapapa evidence.

Concluding Remarks

The legal definition currently provides tight control over who can and who cannot be acknowledged as Anglo-Indian, with the wording of the definition reflecting the mores of the times in which it was written. However, no matter how the wording reflects this, one can argue that the document would have been written in a particular spirit, which would have been to ensure the well-being of the community, the males and the females. At the times it was written it may not have been unusual to assume that by giving the male certain privileges, females were therefore provided for. A century later the scenario is different. The issues are complex but I think it is essential that this option is discussed by the community. I also see a place for well-wishing academics to be involved in discussing various options; they could, for example, look into the processes involved in creating identity definition models that are used by other communities.

I believe that the central argument can still be made—that the gendered dimension of the constitutional definition is a problem in 21st century India. I believe that India is ready for this change[10] and Anglo-Indians would be doing themselves a service, both individually and as a community, in making it. With a change in the definition, or at least a change in the institutional implementation of the definition, children such as Beatrice's would have easy access to the privileges that Irene's (in the next story) do, rather than live the precarious existence they do at the moment, dependent upon the goodwill of social service providers, rather than assistance being their uncontestable right.

---

[10] An example to illustrate this timeliness was an article in Calcutta in the *Telegraph* newspaper in early December 2007 about females now being able to be bartenders. This change from previous practice was decreed by the Supreme Court of India and the decision was made on the basis of gender equity.

3
Irene: Questions of Identity

I interviewed Irene by mistake: mistaken identity. For all that, the inclusion of her story in this work demonstrates the complexities of identity, and the shortcomings in the constitutional definition of an Anglo-Indian. She is Anglo-Indian except for one significant feature of her genealogy. Whether or not she qualifies as an Anglo-Indian is *contested*[1] as indicated in the first part of her narrative below.

Irene has lived in the Bow Street Barracks for most of her 60 plus years. I met her on my first visit to that locale. I'd been told that it would be worthwhile talking to Anglo-Indians there, although there were Anglo-Indians in other parts of Calcutta who had warned me that the Barracks' Anglo-Indians can be pretty rough.

Prior to recording her life I met with her several times, once over a meal shared by members of both of our families. I also went to a church service with her son and daughter-in-law and met one of her daughters and her very cute granddaughter who, at four years old, sang the same songs that my girls had at that age. Almost every time I met Irene she seemed to have taken on a different persona. On the first occasion she wore a saree,[2] and with her hair tied back would easily pass as a Bengali woman. Other times she wore a salwar kameez, and often she wore trousers and Western tops. She also had a few clothes that she referred to as her tribal clothes—woven or embroidered blouses and jackets. The different personas she projected were, I was to find, reflections of the varied ways she identified herself.

When I interviewed her she was already very busy with daytime teaching and evening tuitions, plus spending time with her daughters

---

[1] This term is one I often heard used in Calcutta when someone wanted to indicate that a person's identity status as an Anglo-Indian was in doubt.

[2] I have used the spelling of 'sari' in other places in the book but in this story I use Irene's preferred spelling, 'saree'. As with many Indian words, there is more than one 'correct' spelling.

and grandchildren—several of whom she tutored. Even so, on a number of late afternoons in that precious time she had between finishing school and beginning tutorials she would make a space for me to interview or visit her. In this way I recorded what she had to tell me of her life, which I've condensed in the following pages. I left an earlier version of this with her for her comments. After doing a fair amount of work on it (correcting grammar and sentence structure in particular)[3] she returned it to me wishing me well with my project.

I've divided this story into two parts: the first addresses her identity, which is important in that it highlights issues about Anglo-Indian identity generally; the second part, the longer text, is a sketch of her life, highlighting the times that she dwelt on in our interviews.

Part One: Identity

When I first interviewed Irene I was still coming to an understanding about who *qualified* as Anglo-Indian and who did not, so I began by trying to get a sense of her identification—both how she identified herself and how others might. I've left this portion in its original (although slightly edited) interview transcription format, hoping it conveys my sense of tip-toeing around a potentially sensitive issue. My questions or comments are in italics, the rest is Irene's.

> My maternal grandfather was a German, and grand mum was a Bengali, not a Hindu.
>
> *Was she a Christian?*

---

[3] To do this myself, or not, is always a dilemma. In this case I ought to have edited it more than I had done. I felt that I had initially offended her by presenting her with her words verbatim. She was determined that that was not the way she spoke. I attempted to reassure her that we all speak differently than we write; but that I was happy with any alterations she wanted to make. So this story is still in her words but tidied up by her. I am grateful to her for putting yet more time towards my research.

Christian, yes, we were all married into Christian families. My mother fell in love with my father after they met in this very same church, which you have visited, the Baptist Church. And my Mum's parents and my Dad's parents didn't want them to get married.

Oh, what was your Dad? Was your Dad a ...?

My Dad had an Indian name.

So was your Dad an Anglo-Indian, or a Christian, Indian Christian?

Daddy was not an Anglo-Indian, but he came from a background where his grandfather, that is, my great-grandfather was a converted Christian. We have our own cemetery and our own church where my grandfather was the pastor of that church. That's on Daddy's side.

When my parents fell in love they had a lot of problems. My Mum would get a good beating, and a lashing, from her family. Her brother used to beat her up also.

Was that was because she was in love with....

Daddy. After getting married Mum was living in at Grandma and Grandpa's place and she underwent a lot of ill treatment there. They tried to take away my little brother from her and they beat her up about many things. Mummy and Daddy had a lot of problems but they stuck it out together.

So your father and mother moved into their parents' (your father's parent's) house. Was that a traditional Bengali house?

Yes, Christian.

So it was run as a joint family house?

No, they never ever lived in a joint family. We had our own garden house. But it was the usual Bengali bungalow, huge with plenty of land, and....

A compound?

Yes. A compound with mango trees, any tree you name was there. We had jackfruit trees, many mango trees, star apple trees and wood apple trees. Just trees, trees and more trees. And of course we had many areas where we kept chickens and goats. I used to spend a lot of time with my grandparents. But they had a dislike for Anglo-Indians.

Oh, did they?

Yes, I would spend time at their house as a little girl, along with my little brother, but I never liked going. But I would go and when I did I would be made to feel uncomfortable because they never, ever liked Mum. My Mum, even until she died, never, ever had any dealings with them.

Why didn't they like her? Did they say?

I really don't know. I don't know why but Bengalis don't care for Anglo-Indians. It might be their way of dressing, or maybe the way they speak.

They would comment on it?

Yes, my grandparents never liked Anglo-Indians. They associate the Anglo-Indians with all sorts of dirty things, and it would make me feel most uncomfortable. So we preferred to be left at home with Mum. When we would go there, in Bengali they would say, 'Ah, Anglo-Indian'; 'she's come from the Anglo-Indian house and they've always got lice in their hair, they have this, they have that, they're so dirty'. They'd say it in Bengali. Whenever I would go over I would be bullied. They would make me sit down and they would look through my hair and find nothing.

So although Irene was not an Anglo-Indian according to the Indian Constitution she was given a tough time by her grandparents because of her Anglo-Indian mother. I had a moment of hesitation about continuing with the interview once I realised she was not, legally, an Anglo-Indian. But how could I stop it at this stage? I continued and I was thankful I had, especially once I had a better understanding of the definition and its potential for injustices inherent through its orthodox implementation. I was later embarrassed to think that I'd even momentarily considered doing something that would maintain the gender-based discrimination. Therefore, I have included her story because she identified herself to me as an Anglo-Indian and practically all of her immediate family members meet the criteria given in the Indian Constitution that defines Anglo-Indians. Her mother, her partners and her children, for example, are all Anglo-Indians by that definition. She had an adopted sister who is also likely to be Anglo-Indian, although there is no way of knowing this for sure. She may have been more accurately described as a domiciled European. Certainly Irene is recognised as Anglo-Indian by her neighbours and she participates in the Anglo-Indian scene.

The next comment she made to me, however, indicated that her identity wasn't straightforward even to her. I'd asked her about her schooling:

> I attended St Paul's Mission School at 5 Scots Lane. My father put me into a school which was run by all the Europeans. And it was a boarding school for all the Anglo-Indian kids who had been left behind, after the British left.
>
> Dad, my Poppa, couldn't pay a big fee. We were not very well off at the time. So Daddy paid only ₹5 a month. The Anglos treated all Indians with contempt—they thought they represented the British during the British Raj. *As Indians,* we were not treated very well at that time.

And was that school, the boarding school, was that an Anglo-Indian school?

> Yes, it was an English medium, senior Cambridge school and all run by Europeans and the Anglo-Indians.

And was it mainly Anglo-Indians and Europeans who went?

> The boarders were only Anglo-Indians and Europeans. They would not take any other Indians in. I feel that we were treated very badly in school. Indians were not treated well in school.

Were you treated as an Indian, or were you treated as an Anglo-Indian?

> I was treated as an Indian in the school.

Why was that? So in your family, your grandparents didn't like Anglo-Indians, but they treated you as an Anglo-Indian? And at school you were treated as an Indian...?

Yes, all the negative parts they tried to bring out of the Anglo-Indians. But then in 1947 it all changed. When we got Independence....

She also told me about going to Indian films with her dad and about the sarees he bought her, much to her mother's annoyance. Her mother never wore sarees, only dresses, and she certainly wouldn't go for Hindi movies.

Part Two: Her Life

Irene had two brothers, who were two and four years older than her, and her family later also took in another child, a girl, when Irene was seven or eight years old. She explained:

> This little girl had European looks but even up to now we don't know whether she was a European. She had been discarded in the medical college hospital [when she was] two or three months old. Her birth mother had left her with the attendants who went around asking the patients if anybody wanted the child. So there was a lady there who said, 'I think I know a family that will take her'. She was referring to my [maternal] grandfather. Because all his children had grown up, Mummy and everyone. And we were just smallies. And my grandfather, and grandmother, agreed to take her. They brought her up until she was about three or four. I can't remember exactly how old. But before they died, they handed her over to my mother and they told her: 'You take very good care of her. Treat her better than you would treat your own daughter.' Now my Mummy was very literal. So Mummy brought her up with me. Both of us grew up together, as two sisters.

This *little sister* was able to board at the same school as Irene attended, making it evident that she was accepted by the school authorities as Anglo-Indian, or perhaps European. Irene talked about her mother dressing them up identically, 'wearing the same clothes, the same shoes, the same bags. We would look identical ... except that her hair was blonde and she was very sweet looking also'. She felt that her mother favoured her sister, which she 'really felt'.

For all that, she looked out for her sister. She recalled, for example, begging her mother to let her sister stay at home and attend day school, because she felt bad about the meagre amount of food she got as a boarder. She also kept a watchful eye on her during her tumultuous years as a popular teenager, even assisting her to see boyfriends against her mother's will. Eventually her sister married an Anglo-Indian boy from Dr Graham's Homes.

Early Working Life

Irene left school after passing out grade nine. From there she worked in retail for a while, at a cosmetics and medical outlet, but eventually, as a way of leaving home, she applied for and was successful in obtaining a teaching position at a Baptist Mission school in Nagaland. She said that the government was initially suspicious of her working with the Angami Nagas but they soon saw that she had genuinely come to teach. She said this was a happy time for her, that she enjoyed the work and the people she worked with. She told me that they're a Christian tribal group and English is widely spoken, so language wasn't a problem. They had trouble recruiting teachers, so they had given her a very warm welcome when she arrived with her father. This was a politically unstable area with a reputation for violent uprisings. During the time Irene was there the political unrest meant that 'there was a curfew after six so you couldn't spend your money on anything. The military was everywhere. You were not allowed to be seen on the road after six. And you had to know the password. If not you would be held up at the nearest Police outpost'. She showed me photographs of the classes of Naga children she taught and the school and residential buildings where she stayed for a year. When she returned home for a holiday after 12 months her parents, who were worried about her safety, refused to allow her to go back, but as she says:

> I didn't stay even then. I got a job in a school in the hills. I was interviewed for the post of a stenographer. I had experience as

stenographer and as a telephone operator so they asked me to come up. So I went up there and it was in February, the year Queen Elizabeth came to Calcutta. I'd never seen snow in my life. That was the first time and I hadn't gone prepared for it. I went part of the way by bus and travelled the latter part on the principal's scooter. I used to wear these short tight skirts and there we were whizzing down the road with snow on either side. Then we reached his wife who was a very sweet person. They had a great fire burning. I stayed with them for a while because they said, 'You'll have to stay here and eat with us because the Mess is closed'. I stayed with them for some time but I didn't like the diet. They used to have potatoes in place of rice etcetera so I was looking forward to eating in the mess.

Although she was hired as a stenographer, it was dictaphone typing that she soon found she was required to do. This was a challenge at first but she said she got used to it and managed to cope with up to 40–50 letters a day. Other duties included organising passports and uniforms for overseas boarders, and *indents* for all the medicines they required.

Relationships: Then We Got Friendly[4]

She was in her early 20s and although she may have had some romantic episodes by this time, it was one that occurred in this setting that made a lasting impression. She begins with a self-identifying comment:

> I was friendly with a nice group who were also Anglo-Indians. These girls were very friendly with me. So we would always go into town and we would get a special [meal] once a week. And there was one master who liked me. He was a PT, a physical training, teacher there. He would always want me to go down and play tennis. And at first I would not go with him. Then we got friendly. We became very, very friendly. I fell in love with him.

---

[4] Getting 'friendly', when referring to the relationship between a male and female, is a euphemism for forming a romantic relationship.

It transpired that this man was married. Once she realised this, she painfully extracted herself from his affections. After this very upsetting episode, she returned to Calcutta.

Then I Came Back to Cal and Met the Man I Married, at Church

She told me about meeting Tommy, the man she married, the father of her girls. He had been keen on her sister, as his whole family was. Her fairness appealed to them. Irene explained, 'His people didn't like me because I was partially an Indian. They didn't want me. They said, "She's an Indian."' Once he saw that he was getting no response from her sister he turned his attention to Irene, which her mother encouraged.

> Mummy had her own reasons. They wanted me to forget that person. So they were in a hurry to make an arrangement, get me married to somebody, so then I would forget the past. They were afraid that perhaps we would contact one another again.
>
> So then Tommy started coming and taking me out on dates. He had a beautiful house across the river, at the Jute Mill in Howrah. He had some quarters there, bachelor quarters, but very nice. Two huge rooms going one into another and a balcony facing the river. He started dating me and then Mummy got angry and said, 'Don't keep her out so late. You're not even engaged to her and we don't approve of you keeping her out so late.' So then he told them he was sorry, and we got friendly, and I don't know what month it was, about six or nine months later, he proposed. He came with a big bouquet of roses on the day he proposed.
>
> I really just went in for it because my parents were insisting and then we agreed so we had to go to the Church for them to announce it. We got engaged in February and we got married in June the same year.

As for his family, she said:

> They were giving objection until the last. Then his elder sister told him to stop me from wearing a saree after I had married him. They

were too much of Anglo-Indian. They were dark but what they were looking for was someone lighter than me in complexion.

I asked how the saree issue was resolved, commenting that I didn't think she wore a saree often:

I wear everything. I wear Naga clothes also. So I just wear anything I feel like wearing. No one's going to tell me what to wear and not to wear. So the day, the eve of the wedding, the last word that my husband-to-be told me was, 'See that you don't wear sarees after we get married'. I said, 'I am not going to stop wearing sarees. So you can consider the wedding off.' So I just went up and I told Daddy about it. I said, 'Daddy, this is the condition he is giving me.' So Daddy told him, 'Even though the wedding is finalised, now it's considered absolutely cancelled. The whole thing is off. That's all there is about it. My daughter wears sarees and she will keep on wearing sarees.' Just imagine, one day before the wedding! Then immediately Tommy came down by bike with his father.

Tommy and his dad backed down on the saree terms, so the wedding was on again and they married the next day. It was 1962, she was 25 that year and Tommy was 10 years older. One of the photos Irene showed me was taken on her wedding day. She wore the most beautiful Spanish-style white lace dress: a fitted bodice attached to a full and very wide skirt. With her fine, slightly swarthy appearance, she could have been marrying in Madrid.

My Husband Was Too Possessive

Tommy's job as an engineer at one of the Howrah Jute Mills provided them with comfortable accommodation overlooking the river. She initially had problems starting a family, but said that the replacement of their motorbike with a car (on their doctor's recommendation) did the trick. They began their family of three healthy daughters quite quickly after that, and Tommy was a fun-loving father to the girls. A point of friction for the young couple was their social life, with Irene finding Tommy's possessiveness difficult at times. She said, for example,

He wouldn't allow me to dance with anyone or allow me to have anything to do with anyone. We would go to a party and he'd say, 'You are not to dance with anybody at the party'. So my whole evening would be spoilt because of it. Yes, I had a lot of trouble with him.

In 1965, three years after they married, they transferred to a different, even more sociable, jute mill. At the time of their transfer their first daughter was 17 months old and Irene was pregnant with their second. Before long she had made many friends and became secretary of the 'Ladies Section', which involved organising barbeques and parties. She enjoyed the company of the other wives and felt that her involvement and popularity was enhancing Tommy's position. After a few years of this, though, and with the girls getting bigger, the socialising wasn't enough for her; she wanted to get a job. He didn't want her to work though, saying, 'An engineer's wife doesn't work.' She agreed to 'let it be' at first but told him that she'd be 'heartily bored'. She said,

> I tried to adjust but I had nothing to do. I had about five servants. I used to play music. I used to dance by myself, as usual. He would go to work and I would be bored with my duties. I said, 'I am getting so bored.' So then I got a job.

A friend of hers was going on leave for three months, so she took this opportunity to try being back in the workforce. She said to him, 'Just let me do these three months at the office as my friend is taking three months leave.' He agreed to her taking this short-term replacement position. Irene explains what happens next:

> So I got the job as a receptionist, typist and telephone operator. But I would not travel by car. I used to go on the bus. Then there would be these bus problems. Sometimes the bus would break down or there'd be a traffic jam, which would make me get home late. So he began distrusting me. So one fine day he took the car and he landed up at my office. And he came in. Now as the receptionist I said, 'This is not your home and it's not mine, so I can't give you that much of time.' I just asked him to wait in the lounge. He got quite hot about all the salesmen talking to me and my having to take calls and give messages.

For the sake of some peace she gave the job up, spending more time at the mill's club with the other wives, playing tennis and badminton while her ayah tended to the children. When she'd moved to the second jute mill she took on a new ayah to help her. This woman is still with her family, now working for her daughters and taking care of her grandchildren. Irene says that she's the only one who knows her whole story.

She told me about the extensive travel she did with her husband, accompanied by their children and the ayah.

> When I went to Kashmir, I took them with me. I had two trips to Kashmir with my husband. You see he was entitled to leave every year. We could go anywhere and the company paid for the trips. He would say, 'Honey, let's make use of that and I'll show you places.' He always used to say, 'Maybe it may turn out that I won't be here sometime to show you places, then you won't be able to say that your husband didn't take you around.' So we were married for about eight years and in those eight years we went all over India.

The time she had with him was a mixture of very happy times along with some unhappy periods. She said it was toughest when he used to drink because he could become very violent. She walked out more than once but always came back for the children. She recounted one occasion:

> One time when he beat me up like that and I left my babies. They were very small. I left them in the cot and I decided to go. I walked a very, very long distance. But when I left the house they were crying. And that was playing in my ears while I was walking. I kept hearing them so I came back. I came back home. When I came back he tried to make up with me, but I told him, 'I don't want to have anything to do with you'.
>
> But, okay, we had to live together. So for the sake of the kids.... I mean if we break up the kids are going to suffer. So that's the reason why I just stuck to him, because of the kids. And his mother and all that: they would have been heartily pleased if we hadn't.

She said that after a while 'we started getting quite fond of one another'. He even made a concession on her working, saying,

'Okay I don't want you to work, but why don't you look around for something that you like.' As a result of this, in 1969 they founded a school for destitute Muslim children, with lessons in the vernacular. She still owns and oversees the running of the school.

Just a year after opening the school Tommy suddenly became ill. He was in his early 40s. She described this time:

> We discovered that he was having blood pressure problems. After a long time I discovered it—he used to hide it from me. The doctor said that he was a dead man walking. He used to say he'd get cramps and then his eyes started getting a little affected....
>
> He used to call me 'honey'. His last three words to me before he died were 'Honey, honey, honey'. These were the last three words. He was in bed and sometime in the night he suddenly he got up. He went into the bathroom. I think he went to wash his face and then the blood rushed to his head and he started bleeding. He bled from the ear. The sink was full of blood. Then he just came to me. He was all red, and he tapped me on my hand. I got up and I put my hands out like this, and he fell on my hands. And he just said, 'Honey, honey, honey', and he went into a coma. And he never became conscious again.
>
> I kept the kids away from him. I didn't allow them to come to the church and see the body. Neither did I allow them to go to the cemetery. They were too small. And this lady [the ayah] who is still working for us, she told them, 'He's up there, he's a star.'

I asked how she managed after that.

> We were allowed to stay in the mill for a little while, but they began to pester me to vacate. But I had no money, Robyn. No money to leave that place even. He'd never let me work for those eight years. So then I was really in a big stew. I was hardly getting any money. I was paying my teachers, and there was no income from there.
>
> Our school was not making money. It was really just social work I was doing there. And they were telling me to vacate, vacate. I said, 'The whole flat's reminding me of him. I don't want to stay here. Every step I take, every noise I hear....' And then slowly but surely they were cutting my supplies out. They cut out my

fridge, the milk. They let it go. I had lights, lights galore, and fans. The lights started fusing. They used to give the bulbs but then they stopped giving me the bulbs. I used to get coal from the company. They stopped the coal too. But the caretaker, he used to knock on the stairs and he would tell me, 'I'm leaving a little coal in a basket for you'. I would send down this girl who's still working with me.

And Mum would send whatever she could. They were not well off themselves. Eventually I couldn't take it anymore. I told the officers at the mill, 'I'm due some money. You will give me at least a little amount and I'll leave and move into my school. I'll partition it.' And so I shifted my kids and went to live in my school.

I was getting a little money for tuitions, one fifty per week. I would leave my girls with [the ayah], but I couldn't pay her. I told her, 'I don't have any money to give you and now you've learnt English so you'll get a job in any other sahib's house.' She said to me in Bengali, 'I'll get a job anywhere. But a person like you I would not find anywhere.'

I said, 'When I do well, and if I come up in the world at any time, you can depend on me. I will never forget this day.' And she has stuck with me. She stuck to me from that time up to now. She knows what I have gone through. Sometimes I used to sit and cry. But I had a lot of pride and I was very scared of taking from anyone because they'd want something in return.

After a while I got two of my girls into a boarding school, just temporarily, so there was just one girl at home with me. They lived well at the school but sometimes they would say, 'Mummy, we feel that you are far, far, far, away from us.' I said, 'Mummy promises you she will take you out of school soon and make you a day-scholar. Just give me some time.

How did you cover the costs?

I got them into the school as ... they were sponsored. They had foreign sponsors.

The girls are Anglo-Indians aren't they?

Yes, yes. Definitely. All the girls are Anglo-Indians.

How I Got Involved with My Son's Father

I have to tell you how I got involved with my son's father. I used to come sometimes and stay with Mummy here [in the Barracks] (Photo 3.1). I'd come over and that boy's [pointing to a photograph of her son] Daddy used to stand on the balcony alone.

Oh, he lived here too, in this place?

He always lived here. This is his house. He said he used to see me standing at the balcony. He had been married before. His marriage didn't last more than four or five years. He married and he had two kids from her—a boy and a girl. And they were very, very small when they broke up. Night and day, he told me this later, she was always fighting with him.

It was after my first husband died that we started getting friendly. We soon got very friendly, both of us. Now he had been married and he was a Roman Catholic. Even if you are divorced you cannot do anything about it if you're a Roman Catholic. So he and I would

Photo 3.1:
Bow Barracks (2011)

Source: Author.

see each other and my mum and my aunts got mad about it and they said, 'You should not be having anything to do with him—he's a married man.' But he had left his wife in the 1960s. Even before I got married their home had broken up. But they said that I had broken up his home. He said when I came into his life there was no one around and he was never ever going back to the wife.

And then one fine day it came to a push and the whole locality ganged up against me, this very same locality. They all came around here and gave us a very bad time. That day my aunts and all tried to break us up. Even my dad was mad because I had got friendly with him.

Now One's a Postgraduate and Two Are Graduates, All because He Helped Me

To escape the pressure from her parents and neighbours, Irene and her youngest daughter moved back to live at her school. But soon after, her young daughter contracted typhoid and almost died. She re-evaluated her situation then and resolved to bring together, under the same roof, all the people she loved most. She moved back to the Barracks, took her other daughters out of boarding school and moved in with this man who cared for and was willing to educate her daughters. The neighbourhood slowly got used to them being there and stopped bothering them about it. Once the girls were old enough, she began taking tuitions to contribute to household costs, and so that her girls could all stay on at school. As she said:

> I wanted to get them a good education. Then my husband told me, 'Why are you educating them so much, honey? They can finish up at the 10th grade. Let them go in for secretarial work.' I said, 'Listen honey, my daughters are coming first and second and third, and they want to carry on. The minute they tell me, "Mamma we don't want to study", then okay, then I'll take them out. But they want to study.' He said, 'Okay, so let it be.' Now one's a post-graduate, two are graduates and all because he helped me.

At the time I interviewed Irene, this man who she said had given her everything had died less than a year before. She was still struggling to get used to his absence and said many times that her years with him had been her happiest. They had had one son who was in his 20s and was recently married, just before I first met him. In the time I have been visiting them he and his wife have had a baby and have come back to live with Irene—providing her with the company she'd been missing. I attended the baby's baptism, or naming ceremony, that was held at the Baptist church where the baby's parents, Irene and her first husband, and Irene's parents had all been married.

Although, as I wrote at the start of this piece, I'd had a momentary doubt recording Irene's story, the more I heard from her, and the more time I spent with her outside of the interview sessions, the more Anglo-Indian she seemed. The language spoken at her home was English (and she was good in Bengali as well), her vocation as a teacher is shared by many Anglo-Indians, she has a very Catholic-looking altar at her home and a showcase. She loves Western music and dancing to it, and says the rosary every day. When I broached the topic of her identity directly, she said she wasn't too bothered about whether or not she was 'legally' an Anglo-Indian or not. She explained that she didn't want anything much materially and her children were recognised as Anglo-Indians, so they'd received assistance when they, and she, had needed them too. So in her view there was no advantage to her in being recognised legally as an Anglo-Indian; hence, sometimes she said she was, and other times she didn't.

While Irene is unperturbed about her legal status as an Anglo-Indian, for other women in similar situations it can make an enormous material difference to their lives and those of their children. Irene's children, however, were recognised as Anglo-Indian thanks to having an Anglo-Indian father, but other Anglo-Indian women who marry non-Anglo-Indians are denied this identity claim. As I have discussed in the essay on identity, this can make a difference to their material well-being, as well as to their life chances and opportunities.

PART TWO

Faith

Faith, specifically Christianity, is central to Anglo-Indian lives. Their Christianity distinguishes them from most other Indians, and shapes many of their practices and values. As I discuss in the essay in this section, I was struck when I first began to spend time with Anglo-Indians by their spirituality and their faith practices that permeate their everyday lives. This is different from what I experience in more western countries, where the churches are only full during festival masses. The stark contrast with India was illustrated on the last evening of my most recent stay in Calcutta when I was warned off going to mass at St Anthony's in Market Street: the church would be too full; it was a Tuesday after all!

Anglo-Indians are, however, facing challenges to their faith practices, particularly the Catholics, who make up the majority population. There are fewer masses being celebrated in English, and more incorporation of *Indian* practices. The essay in this section discusses these issues further.

These two stories in this section, Dulcie's and Jane's, are not the only ones in this work to demonstrate what I saw of the daily practice of faith. Philomena, whose story comes later, is particularly influenced by her faith. She explains that the social work and caring she does so generously for her community, she does because of her faith. As I've noted already, the stories are all too rich and complex not to bubble into other parts; Philomena's is an example of one that could also have been placed in this section of the book. The stories I have included in this part also demonstrate the deeply held belief in a God who is always loving and always present.

Dulcie was cared for by nuns from when she was orphaned at a young age, and at the end of her life she is looking for that type of care again—waiting for placement in a convent-run home. She's had a full life of family, work and plenty of typical Anglo-Indian socialising. Some of the events of her life, however, were tough to hear, and even harder to write up, but a clear trend in her framing of those accounts was her desire to demonstrate that God is always good to her. In the second story, that of Jane's, she is also quite explicit that God has looked after her every step of the way and she believes that without that personal care she wouldn't have the life she now enjoys. Whether it is due to divine intervention or not, she achieved a very good education, which gave her skills that she uses in the life she has today.

4
Dulcie: The Kindness of Strangers and an Everyday Faith

Dulcie came back to Calcutta in 2010 after a 20-year absence from the city. I met her through a friend, Jennifer, who she was staying with while waiting for a placement in a rest home. While she waited, Dulcie and Jennifer were living together very companionably in one windowless room, kitchen and bathroom attached, all with peeling paint, water and mould stains evident everywhere: a place that during monsoons flooded often and marooned the two on their beds where they waited until the waters would subside. Amidst all of this sat Dulcie, well-groomed, a full head of pale grey wavy hair, usually wearing light floral dresses, nail polish and earrings to match. At one stage I noticed she wasn't leaving the house and enquired about that. She said that her one pair of sandals had broken, so now she had no shoes and, hence, couldn't go out onto the street. Dulcie's bearing is gracious, her voice is modulated, her views optimistic. She is grace under pressure if ever I've seen an example of it.

The duo kept abreast of local and world news by reading second hand a daily newspaper. Having no radio or television they filled their days with chatting, reading novels, tackling crossword puzzles, knitting and writing the occasional letter. They were both very hospitable and welcoming to any visitor dropping by. Dulcie was very generous with the interview sessions with me. As a result, I have an enormous amount of material to use. In this account I have focused primarily on two periods of her life, the first period is her school days and the second period, which is ongoing, began after the death of her husband. I've also included some accounts of happy and sociable times before he died. She begins with an introduction to herself, and an insight into her generally very positive outlook.

> I was born in Calcutta in 1930. I've closed 80, so I'm in my 81st year now. It's a lovely age. I could never imagine myself this age and I

don't feel this age yet. I've seen other 80-year-olds and they cannot walk around properly, they're complaining of this ache and that pain. I mean I have a heart problem but I don't give it a thought. I mean why should I worry unnecessarily?

My father, he was in Indian Oil. He was a motor mechanic over there. In those years it was very difficult to get mechanics and, especially, foreigners. My father was English actually. My mother was only 14 when she got married to my father. I think she was of Portuguese descent. I'm not sure. I had a sister who's 10 years older than me and a younger sister. My mother and father died when I was only three years old. My father died first. I really don't know but I believe that he was called to work when he was on a sick leave. In those days he used to crank up these lorries and all, and these Indian Oil trucks are huge. And he went to crank up something and his insides burst. And he started bleeding and he expired. He didn't survive. And then my mother, she died six months later. I don't know if it was because they were still so in love, or what. So we became orphans. I don't really know anything else. There was no one to tell me anything because even my [older] sister, I was never with her. Then I was in school all the time, at Loreto Entally Convent for orphans. At that time they never took any community except Europeans and Anglos. I was there from 3 right up to 16 years old.

These nuns were very good to us; they used to look after us so well. They were my parents. I didn't know anyone else but them. They were very sweet. They would always give me little holy pictures with 'Our Lady, please be a mother to Dulcie' on them. Mostly, I never thought anything at all about parents. The only time I felt that I needed a parent was when these people used to come [to visit other children] with big boxes of sweets and chocolates and this and that, and I'd see them kissing and hugging and all which you miss out on as an orphaned child. And I used to think, 'When is someone going to come and give me something?' That's the only time I missed having parents. I was alone, because my young sister, she could not stay. I don't know what happened; I don't think she could manage very well because it was very cold there.

Cold in the Convent?

No, in Simla. We went to Simla in 1938, before the Second World War started, because the British Army came and they took over our school as their barracks. They had Fort William as their headquarters but they took this place to house the soldiers. It was only the orphans, just about 20 of us, from the whole Convent who were transferred. All the others had gone home or were shared around different schools in Calcutta.

We had a little cottage over there. It was very nice. We stayed there for years. There were others at the school up there too, from other communities: Tibetans and that sort of thing. We wouldn't see them, the day scholars, for three months over the holidays. But we were there rain, hail, and snow.

What did you do in the holidays?

Oh, we used to play around but most of the time we were indoors because of the snow. Some days we used to be snowbound and they'd have to come and dig us out. Summer was lovely though. The nuns used to take us on walks. There was a mountain, which was full of these monkeys, the black-faced monkeys. And there was a sadhu over there. He'd ring the gong and all the monkeys would assemble. And he'd give them food and all. Then we had another place called the Giant's Paintbox. It was a huge mountain and you sat over there and you'd see all the different colours on that mountain.

During the spring season we used to climb trees and all, and I remember we never used to wear shoes because when I was small we didn't have shoes. We used to go round barefoot. And then what happened, there was a lady by the name of Mary Bata, and she came to the Convent and ordered shoes for all of us.

Was she Bata from the Bata shoe company?

I think she and her husband started the company years ago. I mean Bata is quite a big place. It's quite old now, and she died long ago.

We used to be climbing trees and we'd tie the laces together and put them around our neck. And I remember once we were up a chestnut tree and there was a girl supposed to be keeping watch, so as soon as a nun would come she'd let us know. You should have seen the fun. We were all up the tree, about four of us, and you won't believe what happened. This girl on watch was so busy reading she didn't see the nun come. And all of a sudden we heard clap, clap, clap. We were so frightened we all fell. That's how I broke this thumb of mine. It's still bent. We hadn't known where to put the chestnuts but we had these bloomers on so we'd put them into them. Then we fell. You should have seen us, my goodness me, the poor nun. There was she with the tweezers taking all the spines out.

We had quite an eventful childhood actually. We had a lot of fun. The nuns were very lenient with us. Because they said, 'These are our children, we must look after them. God has given us these children.' Nowadays they don't think in that way. Now they are not so lenient either. But then at the same time, you see the nuns can't discipline children as they want. I mean according to the rules you cannot beat a child, you cannot shout at a child. But in our days we got whacked, we'd get nicely kissed on the palms of our hands with a ruler—real smart cracks.

And did you usually deserve it?

Well I suppose so, otherwise they wouldn't have done that. Only there's one thing I remember. We were talking about 'The owl and the pussycat', that they went for the honeymoon. So somebody asked me, 'What is the honeymoon?' So I told them, 'You know there're certain times of the year if you put your tongue out in the night.... You must get up at 12 o'clock and put your tongue out and the honey will fall from the moon. That is a honeymoon.' The nuns were really angry. They said, 'We heard your voice, why were you talking about honeymoons?' You know nuns were very narrow-minded in those days. They said, 'What were you talking about honeymoons for? Do you know what a honeymoon is?' I said, 'Yes, I know all about it.' Oh, I was taken and punished in the dark room. And, who was I talking to? Heather. Both of us we had the dark room treatment.

What's the dark room?

It's a room, you know, it was just a plain room without anything in it. Nothing—no windows, no lights in it. They put us there and it used to frighten us. I think I must have been about 10 then. But, you know, so I had a very adventurous childhood, and mostly I really enjoyed it.

School Work

I used to do people's homework for them because I was quite good in my studies. I used to come first in class. The other girls would say, 'I'll give you this sweet, I give you that sweet', and I'd do my homework and quietly, quietly I'd tell them what to write. But then they used to lick the sweet and I said, 'No more'. So then I would not do those girls' homework after that. I found that they were the losers not I. How they tried to get me to do it. They'd offer to give me chocolate and I still said, 'No'. Because I'm very stubborn like that: once I feel I'm let down that's it, from that tender age.

We came back to Calcutta in 1946, to Entally. They had done it up beautifully, and we used to get lovely food, like for breakfasts we'd get a little loaf of bread each and some tea. We never had cups, we had mugs: those enamel mugs, and enamel plates. And each one was given a duty. Like, this week, we'd see to the mugs, next week we'd be on the washing, or rubbing, or scrubbing. We used to do all that. They were teaching us how to be good hussifs, of course now they say housewives.

In my last year we did a commercial course: book keeping and shorthand and typing. And we did domestic science, but I never learnt how to cook. We were given little caps and some aprons to put on. I don't know how they passed me. They must have said, 'She looks quite sweet in her cap, let's pass her.' I don't know how I passed, but I got distinctions in many things. And I remember one was in English. And actually my spelling is not all that good but still I got a distinction.

Early Working Life

At 16 I'd come home but it wasn't until 1948 (two years later) that my results came out.

Where did you go to then?

To my [older] sister's place in Calcutta. I'd gone to my sister's place, for a holiday earlier actually. By then I really wanted to get a job, but I was too young. In those days bosses would not take you on unless you were 20 or 21 years old.

Oh, that's quite old.

I used to try. I'd have high heels. I'd put my hair up. The bosses would tell me, 'Take off that makeup, put your hair down, take off those shoes, and go back to school.' They would not give me a job. So these nuns got me to teach the little ones in school, and I enjoyed it.

Then after a while my sister took me out and she put me with Mrs Beryl Patel. She used to run a shorthand school, in 83 Park Street, where the Anglo-Indian Association is now. And she got me to teach shorthand. I was so young at that time, only 17 or 18, so what can I teach anyone? I used to get scared because we had boys and girls and we had men over there. They used to come and say, 'Miss, miss, give us a kiss. Miss, miss, give us a kiss.' I used to run and Beryl would say, 'What happened?' I'd say, 'See Miss, I'm going to get a baby tomorrow.' 'Why, what happened?' 'This man caught me and kissed me.' I didn't know what was involved in getting one at that time. Cause one thing with the nuns, they were very narrow-minded, they never taught us these things. I thought if you kissed somebody, finished, you'd had it.

No wonder you were scared.

Then a friend of my sister's got me a job in the Indian Red Cross Society. I knew shorthand typing and they gave me the experience I needed. So that was my first proper job. I think I was about 18. I was getting about ₹50 a month which I'd give to my sister, and she used to give me ₹5 back, and I used to be very happy with that. You know we have a thing called a 'ting-ting' man. He used to come and ring a bell and he'd have a shelf-thing around his neck with all different compartments and you'd have blocks of jaggary, *armsat*, Goa cheese and little hot plums. And they'd be just 12 pice or an *anna* each.

Dulcie worked as a secretary for years in several different companies. At some stage in her career she ran the typing pool, which she remembers as being made up entirely of Anglo-Indian girls, and she made her way up the ladder to being the head girl.

She married her sister's brother-in-law before she was 20 years old. He was a few years older than Dulcie and had worked in the army and had been married before. There were no children from his first marriage, which was to a girl from out of the state, and hadn't lasted long. Dulcie and he had four children: three sons and a daughter. She told me about the parties and fun they had as a family, and with her Anglo-Indian friends around the city.

It was so nice; I mean we had all the foreign people coming over here. It was such an industrial state. Also people worked hard. They played harder, but we worked hard also. I mean the Anglo-Indians had a fantastic time in those days. We had so many Balls we could go to. So many clubs and then we'd go in and out of each other's houses, and work wasn't all that bad for us because, you know, we used to be given transport to and fro, so it saved a lot of your time.

We used to have lovely times actually. I mean I'm thinking of the times that we used to have before now. We used to take our children with us to go wherever we went. I remember once we had won something on the races. I mean I wasn't a race girl but my husband said, 'Come on, come on'. So I said, 'Okay.' There was a horse called Glennuick. I liked the name. I said, 'I'm interested in this horse.' And I bet on that horse. He won, the horse won. And that night we all, the whole family, went to the New Empire.

The movie hall?

Yes, to the movies. We went to the dress circle. We had a box to ourselves and I took the whole lot of them. We went and they had soft drinks, and we had a little gin. We used to like to go there just to have fun. And we used to get a whole lot of *kathi* rolls and all and enjoy ourselves. We could do all that in those days. Now I can't imagine doing that. Nowadays you don't do these sort of things, you know. Now it's mostly Bengalis, they go to the cinema houses. And where do we have the money actually to go to the dress circle and here and there? And even then, even if people have, they don't want to see movies because they want to stay in their houses and watch this TV.

I mean we used to have a lot of fun in those days. My friends used to come over every Friday night and we used to have a party, otherwise we would go to them, because weekends were holidays then. Then on Saturday night, sometimes we are still having a party at 5 in the morning. So we'd go straight to church, to the cooks' Mass. We'd go and then we'd come back and sometimes start the party again. And we used to have *dalpuri*s and *nehari*.[1] On Saturday nights we used to send out for them. My husband grew up with this Muslim fellow who made the best ones around. When they were small they used to play together, play marbles and all with this fellow. Of course he used to teach him. So when he grew up and took over from his father, he remembered my husband. My

---

[1] *Dalpuri*s are deep fried pastries with a savoury lentil filling while *nehari* is spicy meat stew of Muslim origin.

husband sent a big *dechki*[2] and gets it filled with just *kathi*, not the parathas. Just the inside, no parathas. So we had a big dish of this and then the bearer used to make us sausages. You know, these pork sausages in beer, or cider, and *kofta* balls.[3] And you won't believe what a lovely taste it had.

Both she and her husband worked in jobs that enabled them to maintain a home (and several domestic help at any time), educate their children as well as enjoy a very social lifestyle. I skip ahead 40 years now to where Dulcie begins to tell me about her last 20 years. By this time her three sons had all moved to another Indian metro, and her daughter had migrated from India.

My husband had become very sick over here [in Calcutta] and we were alone. Actually we had two beautiful flats over here and we sold those flats so that we could go and help them [her sons]. They had to move every 11 months because they were taking rented flats. So we said we would put money down on two flats so they could settle down. So we bought them two lovely flats. They were right beside each other on the 4th floor. Our intention had always been to be with the children.

That's after he retired?

Yes, he's a bit older than me so even though I was still working he wanted us to move then. He was a heart patient, so he would get very, very upset. He said, 'We're alone over here. All the children are away. Our boys have gone away, the girl is abroad, and should anything happen to me, what'll happen to you? People will come and take over the flats and all and they'd bully you. And your sons won't be here to protect you. Nobody will be here with you.' He said, 'So it's better we go and stay with our sons.' He said, 'Let's go there now!' and because he was getting so excited and agitated I said, 'Okay, let's go.' I didn't want anything happening to him over here. It'd be on my conscience. So then we sold up and went. I mean I should not have agreed with that. I should have kept on arguing. But then, you know, I wanted peace.

---

[2] A metal cooking pot.
[3] *Kathi* is a kebab, paratha is pan-fried pastry rounds and *kofta* is a meatball in a mildly spicy gravy dish.

Then we went there. It was okay there. I mean everything was all right, hunky dory, and so they got the flats. We couldn't take them in our name, because we didn't have jobs to show that we can pay the balance instalments. So you see they had to go in their names. We were mentioned as nominees, but you know what a nominee is? They can change it anytime. As soon as my husband died, because he was very smart in that kind of thing, and I wasn't, behind our backs they went and changed everything. They did that, and I didn't know anything about it. And I don't blame my daughters-in-law, because I didn't rear them, but I brought my children up and I didn't bring them up to do these sorts of underhand tricks. I thought I did a good job. But once they got the flats I think it went to their heads. And then they found that they had no place for Mummy, once Daddy died, there was no place for Mummy.

Dulcie took up work again for five years, until she was well into her 60s. During this time she did stay in one of the flats with her second son, contributing financially to running the household.

I became quite happy with the other boy, the middle boy, because he was not married. But once he got married the wife took him and went and lived with her people. It's a disgrace actually, the boy living with the girl's parents, because they don't believe in that in the Indian community. You live with the boy's parents, not with the girl's parents.

Then my friend sent for me, she said, 'Come to England. Bring your youngest boy too.' This friend is much younger than me. One day, when we were still in Cal [Calcutta], she was in trouble and she came to me in the night and I sort of took her under my wing. I looked after her. Her mother was away in England. She had nobody over here, except her in-laws. She stayed with me for quite some time. She always used to say I'm her adopted mother. So we went to stay there with her.

Did you think of settling there?

I'd liked to have. I loved it in England. Oh, it was so orderly and so nice and clean, and the air so fresh. This was in the nineties. We stayed for about a year but this young boy of mine had a girlfriend, and he came back for that girl. You see she told him, 'If you don't come back, they'll marry me off.' So we both came back so he could be with his girlfriend.

Was she an Anglo-Indian girl?

No, she was a Marwari girl. Eventually my son married her, but secretly. She didn't stay at night, she used to go home. She would tell her parents she was working. My son was doing some business, you know, computer business. He's a graphic designer, and a website manager. He's very good on the computer and he's a wonderful artist. So he was doing this business and he used to give her ₹4,000 every month. So the parents thought she was working. And this carried on for two years. Then he trusted her brother with the secret. The brother goes and tells the mother and father, and that was it.

I think it was because he didn't have as much money as the Marwaris have. The Marwaris are super where business is concerned. And they had already someone in view, a rich fellow. And she couldn't do anything about it because I believe, I'm not sure, but this is what my son told me, he said, 'Mummy I have to give in to them because they're threatening me. I don't know what they'll do, but Mummy, because of you all I have to give in. I wouldn't like anything to happen to any of you all.' He was scared. They took back every photograph, everything that showed they'd been together. They even had the court records changed. I think they must have paid a fantastic amount of money because when we went to check the registry books, my sons' name never appeared anywhere.

After this problem of the marriage and all, I think he went to pieces. Then he met this girl on the rebound and everything went well, and for nine years he kept me. For nine solid years I lived with them. We had no trouble. She was very sweet, and she was getting very fond of me also. But the big one, the big sister-in-law, didn't like that. So she set the two daughters-in-law up against me.

By this time the second boy, he sold the flat and went away. So then I was having a tough time. I didn't have any money either. I'd spent it all on the boys. Then I went and stayed with a friend as her companion. I stayed there for about five years. Then after that I went to stay with my big boy. So whatever it was, I mean, I've had a pretty good life. I've always had someone I could stay with.

But then it went really bad. That big boy started abusing and screaming and shouting and telling me to go. I mean many people have not experienced life as I have experienced it. Because we've come from a very good home, we had a fantastic life and then all of a sudden to be thrown out at night, at 12 o'clock or 1 o'clock at night. And you're going and sleeping under cars.

Why would he do that?

Drunk. You can't help it when a person gets drunk, you know. He doesn't know what he's doing. And I'll tell you, he was such a good child, such a lovely child. Everything was 'Mamma, Mamma'. But once he is drunk. ... I think the wife sets him up. One minute everything's about his mother. I mean naturally, I've brought him up. I've reared him. I've given birth to him. But then when he gets drunk I think she eggs him on to say things. And then he abuses and all sorts. When he's drunk he becomes like a wild animal. And then he throws me out of the house, and how can I go knocking on people's doors at that time of night? But I say the Lord has been very good to me. Something good always happens. Like one night I was sleeping under a car when that car started I got up. I went and sat in the corner. It was dark. There was a dog there that I hadn't seen. The dog moved out and I sat down over there. I wasn't scared, because I'm not scared of animals. You won't believe that dog put his head in my lap.

It must have been a tough time for you though.

I used to feel very, very upset. I mean if I had money I could go to some hotel or something. But I mean I don't have any money. How much we spent on them. They'd all say, 'Mummy we want this, we want that. Mummy we want ₹7,000 or 8,000.' And I'd just take and give it. Because naturally, which mother is going to say no? I mean we work for our kids isn't it? We sacrifice for them.

Is that when you went into a home for a while?

Yes, for quite a while. It was horrible. I was there for two years, but it was a horrible home. It was full of all the menials. People who used to work in the hospitals, cleaning the toilets, cleaning the bedpans: those sorts of people. Most didn't know a word of English. I mean some of them knew a little English; the Goans. There were no Anglo-Indians.

Was it a Christian ...?

It was run by the nuns but they'd cut down our food like anything. We almost never got bread. Only on a Sunday, and of course on

Wednesday after St Anthony's day Mass. Sometimes it would be dry, sometimes there would be butter, sometimes they would mix jam with milk to make it go further. Oh it was so yucky.

Did your boys support you, pay anything....

My son paid ₹2,000 a month for me, the big boy. But he would not come in to see me.

You did well to stay there so long.

I couldn't go anywhere else. I didn't know what to do. I'd written to Jennifer, my friend here. I said, 'Can you put me up?' She said she couldn't because her building's been taken over by the receivers. Then after two years she said I could come. Then as soon as she said I could come, immediately I wrote back and said, 'I'm coming.' I went and booked my ticket.

And now you're looking for a rest home to move into?

Yes, I've decided that I would like to go to St Joseph's. I mean even though St Joseph's is run by nuns too, I think they're a different type of nun altogether. They're Little Sisters of the Poor so they won't look down on any of you. There are other places too. I don't know what they're like. I just know I need a home. I really need a home.

If you could live however you liked what would it be?

Ideally, if I had a choice, I would like a little room of my own, with a little bathroom. Even don't give me a kitchen. I'll bring in gas. I'll cook my own food there, and I'll make my house into a doll's house. I'll put up lovely curtains and I'll have a lovely bed. All I really need though is a bed. I need a cupboard, a table and a chair. And one table where I can cook, you know like roll chapattis and all, make my own chapattis. I'd be totally independent.

I'll go out weekly, or I'd go out when I needed vegetables. And I'd cook mostly veg. I'll make lovely *bhajjies*[4] and now and again I'd make a lovely chicken *vindaloo* or a roast. And you know, I would improve my cooking. I would like to do that. I mean even

---

[4] Fried vegetable balls.

though I'm so old and nobody's going to benefit, but I'm going to have the peace of mind that, yes, I did this, I did that before I died. I'd get my wishes.

Day-to-day Assistance

A couple of people this month have given me money gifts, because we've just had Christmas and New Year. So I was quite all right this month. I've been able to manage beautifully. I've bought all my medicines. I was able to visit the doctor and everything.

And you're getting the pension now, through CAISS[5]?

Yes. I'm down for that. I think you had something to do with it even Robyn.

No, Philomena had you in mind. When she knew you were here.

She's very sweet in that way. We're fortunate with her because the people that really need to give, they don't give. I've noticed that. People who haven't got, they give. That's one thing Robyn, why I don't get from anywhere—it's because everybody thinks I've got money. They just look at my face, and what I look like. I'm used to this. You know they thought I was too glamorous for that other home. One person came and he insisted that I was not an inmate. He thought I was the matron. There everyone goes around with their nightdress on in the day and I could never be like that.

Yes, you always look well-groomed. You've got a lovely top on, you've got nice earrings, and your hair is neat.

I've always been a very dressy person. But you won't believe I don't have a single thing of my own. Everything is given to me. This skirt I've got on is given to me, this thing. The underwear I've got on is given to me. Everything is given to me. Even this nail polish is given to me. Now why should I let it go to waste? If I have the nails I should use it. Whatever I have is given. I owned a lot of clothes before. When I went to UK I bought a whole lot of dresses. I packed

[5] Calcutta Anglo-Indian Service Society is a very effective organisation, which I discuss in some detail in the section on Community Care.

it all, my son took everything of mine. They took my memories also. All my albums, the photographs of my husband. My children when they were small, growing up. I haven't got a single thing.

What happened to them?

My son had them all. He said, 'I'm coming to see you. I'm coming in five days.' He was to bring my case then. Well, where is he? I haven't even heard from him.

Over the years that I've been visiting Jennifer, Dulcie's friend, I've observed the number of people who help her in informal ways. This has now been extended to Dulcie. The most frequent visitor is the tea man who comes up to six times a day and fills up their teacups with sweet milky tea.

We give him one rupee only a day. He's working for the Chinese people [who run a business from the front of the building]. So when he brings them tea, he comes and gives us tea too. Sometimes he'll come with a *naan* roti. He says he doesn't need anything from us, he says, 'I'm giving from my heart.' And he does our shopping for us. If we want bread, butter, eggs, etc., he'll buy them for us even if it gets late and he wants to get home early.

He told me, he said, 'When I needed money she was there for me.' Because one time when Jenny had received some money, and one of his children needed medicines, she gave him ₹150. He said, 'I made a promise to myself that I will look after her. I'll come here and check up on her.'

And what about postage stamps, things like that?

This man posts our letters for us. We give him a little note and he takes it to the office, and he'll bring all the stamps and all we require. One time I just wanted a new pen refill and I gave him ₹10. He gave me back ₹5. He charged ₹5 for the refill. I told him, 'Keep the ₹5 for your tea.' He does a lot for us. Now and again I do give him ₹1–2. I work out what I can afford. And he knows that nobody comes for me over here, as I don't have anyone.

Yes, so he wouldn't earn a lot of money either would he? Who else do you have coming during the day? The bishtiwallah*?*

Yes, he comes at about 4 o'clock and gives us drinking water and the balance he puts in the toilet [into buckets in the bathroom]. I think this man fills his [goatskin] bag from tube well. We strain it in case there's anything in the bag.

And what about the chemist?

He comes. The chemist is across the road. By this man [the tea man] I send him a little note, with the medicines I require. He brings it to me. The chemist comes and brings it. And then if we have it we give him ₹20 and say, 'Buy your children chocolates or something'. Sometimes I don't give him anything. He doesn't expect it. If I need to go to the doctor, that boy from the chemist shop, he comes, he takes me to the doctor, he brings me home. He reads my prescription and he buys me the medicine and brings it. He tells me, 'Aunty, take this medicine.'

Final Words

But nowadays Robyn, I'm very sorry to say it, but everybody's asking what is in your bank first. And if you say nothing, you're shunned. You're really shunned if you have nothing. And I never gave it a thought because we were not brought up, especially women, to speak about money. But now it seems to make the world go round. And it has the loudest voice. It really has the loudest voice. You have money; you're everything. If you don't have money you're nothing. It could be an easier life. And this is what I want now at this age. I want to have peace of mind. I want to have just a few pleasures. I never ever thought I would go through this. I never ever thought. Maybe, I don't know what that is. Maybe the Lord wants me to learn a lot more. He said, 'You have to do all this before you come up here.' So be it. Amen.

Since recording this story over a number of very hospitable and enjoyable interview sessions, Dulcie has made her move into one of the city's residential care homes. I can imagine she will have set up her space there neatly and prettily, and once again have confidence in being fed and cared for and she'll also have the company she craved: other Anglo-Indians.

5

Essay: A Christian Community in Changing Times#

Introduction

Dulcie is not alone in centralising Christianity in her life. Anglo-Indians are a devout people who practice their Christianity throughout the year, but go to extra lengths, with additional joy, at Christmas time. They imbue the central city with their rejoicing, transforming the area convincingly during this time to a recognisably Christian city. The Feast of Christ the King, celebrated on a Sunday in late November, marks the prelude to Advent with a parade so lengthy that it closes Calcutta's central city streets for most of the afternoon. It's not until after New Year that the city settles down again and bothers to consider either its secularity or its dominant religious groups.

Although Anglo-Indians are not the sole contributors to the city's transformation at this time, comprising perhaps just 4 per cent of the city's Christian population,[1] their presence is distinctive. In the Feast of Christ the King parade, it is they who sing their hymns in English, and their schools are well-represented. Although some of my fieldwork coincided with the Christmas season, a season to celebrate Christianity, I was there at other times as well, and Christianity was *always* important. In this book I devote a section to the exploration of what their Christianity means to them. The two stories in this section particularly highlight the importance of their faith.

A version of this essay has been published as 'Christianity as an Indian Religion: The Anglo-Indian Experience' in *Journal of Contemporary Religion* (Andrews, 2010).
[1] This is an approximate calculation based loosely on 2001 national census data on English speakers. That census put the figure at 15,000, which is thought to be too low, so I have used the figure of 20,000 Anglo-Indians in this calculation.

In this essay I do not explore their practice and its significance in as much detail as I did in my thesis, but focus instead on one aspect—the challenge posed by post-Vatican II reformations to their distinct practice of Catholicism. This is a challenge that is quite likely being faced by more than 80 per cent of West Bengal-based Anglo-Indians today, and may be a contributing factor in their still strong inclination to migrate.[2] As a contemporary challenge of significance to them it is important to this public anthropology-informed work also.

Anglo-Indians have, until relatively recently, been well-represented in all tiers of the churches, from cardinals, archbishops, bishops, priests and ministers, and fill a number of educational roles. The public profile of Anglo-Indians is now declining—partially as a result of a decline in the number of Anglo-Indians still in India but also due to the increasing Indianisation of Christianity through the process of syncretism of Christianity with local religious practices. In this essay, I describe some of the changes in practice, particularly in the Catholic Church post-Vatican II, and explore how they are experienced by the Anglo-Indians who remain there. I then focus on an examination of their Christianity, and I look more generally at Christianity in India. What is of particular interest to me in this essay is the effect of the milieu of the, nominally, secular[3] state of India on Christian practices and how this impacts upon Anglo-Indians and raises particular challenges.

A Christian Community

One of my early impressions of Calcutta's Anglo-Indians was their very obvious Christianity. I soon came to see that it is central to

---

[2] The figure, which is likely to be conservative, is based on early indications of a 2011 survey of West Bengals' Anglo-Indians that put Catholics at over 80 per cent of the 430 Anglo-Indians in a preliminary survey sample, combined with Brent H. Otto S. J. and my 2013 survey, which is still under way as I complete this book.

[3] Secularism refers to the separation of the State from the church. Article 44 of the Indian Constitution guarantees this; however, it is arguable that recent governments have overridden this in their wish for Indian unity under Hinduism.

their personal lives and to the life of their community.⁴ They are regular churchgoers, display altars in public areas of their homes, join pilgrimages and, at all social levels, freely discuss their faith. Christianity, for most of the Anglo-Indians I met, is more than a Sunday or Holy Day obligation; rather it is a part of their everyday life. The churches I visited also reflected that attitude to religion — they were often visited by parishioners outside the times of any organised ritual. The pervasiveness of Anglo-Indian Christian practices in their everyday lives was initially a surprise to me because in all the pre-fieldwork reading I had done, I had hardly encountered any reference to this aspect of their community.⁵ As a Roman Catholic, a co-religious of many of the people I was working with, I was well-positioned to make use of participant-observation fieldwork to study further this aspect of their lives, and to draw comparisons with my other experiences of Catholic ritual practice.

Referring to Anglo-Indian Christianity, Allan Sealy, a renowned Anglo-Indian author, claims that Anglo-Indians 'are as pious as any other group in a pious land' (2007). Dumont (1971), a doyen of Indian anthropology, notes that Durkheim's (1965) dichotomy (which understands religion as being separable from other aspects of people's lives) did not apply to India because the so-called *sacred* was so diffused throughout the so-called *profane*. People who have spent time in India would recognise this situation: religion is evident everywhere. In the big cities in particular one is constantly reminded of the presence of a range of faiths by, for example, the sight of tiny shrines set up on taxi dash boards, personal adornment (such as *tika* powder on foreheads, rosaries worn by sufis, small crucifixes adorning Indian Christians), processions and shrines in the streets in recognition of various religious festivals, the fragrance of burning incense, the sound of the regular calls to prayer from the mosques, small

---

⁴ An example of the significance of Christianity to the community includes the recitation of the Lord's Prayer at the beginning the AGMs of the Federation of Anglo-Indian Associations held at the World Reunions.

⁵ While some researchers note that Christianity is important to Anglo-Indians, none elaborate upon it in a way that comprehensively supports this assertion (Blunt, 2005; Caplan, 2001; Mills, 1998).

bells tinkling as Hindu priests begin the day with a blessing and large bells ringing to signal Mass times.

Hindu-ised Christians?

Although Anglo-Indian religiosity may be linked to the centrality of religion to Indians generally, one woman I spoke to in 2002 also drew comparisons with the Anglo-Indian practice of religion *out* of India saying:

> We, Indians, are all spiritual people. We practice different...worship different Gods, but we all do so fervently. People say we do so because we've got nothing. That we pray to have a better life, and if we had the sorts of lives they have in the West then we wouldn't need our religion. They say that, they do! Someone said it to me.

She continued, stating sadly that her brother and sister who have left India 'left for a better life but I don't know that that's what they've got. Materially it's better, yes, but spiritually....' She knows (or strongly suspects) that none of her overseas family practise their faith as ardently as she and her brother and most Anglo-Indians in Calcutta do.

Although this woman was referring to their *attitude* to their practice of Christianity, the more time I spent with Anglo-Indians in India, the more I observed that the way in which they *enacted* certain elements of their faith was different in a number of respects from the way people in most Commonwealth countries enact theirs.

Examples of Anglo-Indian Christian Practice

Altars and Holy Pictures

I soon came to recognise an Anglo-Indian home by the presence of two pieces of furniture: the showcase and the altar; a showcase being a glass-doored cabinet in which the owner displays precious objects such as souvenirs, photos, crockery and trophies, and the altar was usually a small platform mounted on the wall at about head-level with candles, statues of the Virgin Mary and various saints arranged upon it (see Photo 5.1 for an example).[6] The prevalence of statues and pictures of Mary and of other saints led me at first to presume that all of the homes I was visiting were

Photo 5.1:
A House Altar (2004)

Source: Author.

[6] An Anglo-Indian exhibition held in Melbourne's Immigration Museum from December 2004 to February 2005 included a Drawing Room scene featuring a showcase and an altar.

Catholic, but it soon became evident that other denominations were also represented. Housing an altar in the public spaces of homes is not a practice that I was familiar with in New Zealand or in other Western countries. Having also visited the homes of Hindu families in Calcutta, however, I was struck by the similarity in appearance between the shrines in Hindu homes and the altars I was seeing in Anglo-Indian homes. In both cases, they were positioned in prominent, public places, and on the altar, or shrine, there was often a glowing light or candles, and some flowers, and the paintwork on the statues of Christian figures and Hindu gods looked to have come from the same palette.

Namaste

There is a time during Catholic Masses and Church of North India (CNI) services where the priest, or minister, asks for the congregation to give each other a 'sign of peace'. In Catholic churches that I have attended out of India,[7] the usual response is a handshake, or sometimes, between close friends and family, a kiss on the cheek, accompanied by the words 'peace be with you' or 'the peace of God be with you' — that is, the blessing is accompanied by the standard form of non-verbal greeting of these societies. In services I attended with Anglo-Indians in Calcutta, in both Catholic and CNI churches, the universal response at this point was a *namaste* gesture (of hands held palm together at chest level) accompanied by the standard recitation of 'peace be with you'. The *namaste* is not a greeting used in everyday situations among members of the Anglo-Indian community, but it is a reasonably standard greeting used in the wider community, particularly amongst Hindus.[8] Anglo-Indians, therefore, are, in this situation, adopting a Hindu style of greeting rather than using their usual greeting practice.

---

[7] I have attended Catholic services in New Zealand, Australia, Canada, England, Spain, Portugal, France, Italy, Germany, South Africa, Samoa, Rarotonga and Tonga.
[8] Muslims use their own form of greeting.

Rosary and Procession at the Barracks

This final example includes dimensions of both practice and material culture, and draws on my observations at an evening anniversary celebration that I was invited to attend. The celebration is held every year to commemorate the building of a grotto to Our Lady of Lourdes at the Bow Barracks, which is still a predominantly Anglo-Indian residential area. They celebrate the anniversary with an evening rosary and procession, then Mass and supper. It's an event that hundreds of Anglo-Indians, Religious[9] and other Christians from around Calcutta attend.

On this particular February evening, everybody met a little before 6pm in a long narrow gap between buildings, an area that had been converted into a space resembling a chapel (Photo 5.2). The usually dark, relatively deserted area had been transformed with narrow rows of seats and decorated with streamers, and strings of lights and flower heads. The statue of Our Lady of Lourdes had been festooned with garlands of flower heads and lights, and candles were alight at its feet.

The evening commenced with a procession from the grotto, around the residential area and back again to the start. Participants carried candles, which at the end of the procession were added to those in the grotto. The Mass was celebrated followed by a supper of a selection of Indian snacks and sweets.

The evening impressed me as containing elements borrowed from, or at least corresponding with, many non-Anglo-Indian celebrations I have attended in India. The flowers used in the chains were saffron-coloured marigolds and asters: the same as those I had observed in Indian ceremonies and always adorning the relevant statues or effigies (e.g., Gandhi on Republic day, Kali during Kali puja). The use of these flowers in particular seemed to be introducing an identifiably *Indian* element to a traditional Catholic ceremony. I talked about this observation to one Anglo-Indian man who now lives abroad and who was very involved

---

[9] The term 'Religious' refers especially to those who belong to Catholic religious orders, such as priests, brothers and sisters, who have professed the particular vows appropriate to their vocation and order.

Photo 5.2:
Bow Barracks: Our Lady of Lourdes Grotto Area Set Up for Mass (2013)

Source: Author.

with the Church in India (attending church schools and serving as an altar boy through his youth): he said that in his time in India this type of flower (which were known there by their Indian name of *gandhia*) would never have been used—rather they would have been *avoided* because of their link to Hinduism.

Based on these examples, all of which seemed to me to include more than an echo of Hinduism, I suggest that Anglo-Indian Christianity in India is significantly influenced by the milieu in which it exists. Anglo-Indian church services I have attended *out of India* do not contain these *Hindu* elements—there were, for example, no garlands of marigolds, or namastes, in the services that were held as part of the World Reunions in Melbourne or Toronto.

I wondered if the *Hindu* influence on their Christianity was something that Calcuttan Anglo-Indians were aware of, and if so, how they felt about it. To investigate this I gave an early version of this chapter to several Anglo-Indians still residing in Calcutta. One of these, a woman who is currently very involved in the Catholic Church there, said that she thought I had it about right, but said she lamented the changing face of Christianity in Calcutta. Another person I interviewed (2004) was visibly disconcerted at what I had written and said that I was 'pandering to them' (Hindus, and to a lesser extent, Muslims), and that 'they' would love to read of their influence on the practices of Christianity. He wondered aloud if I was trying to 'sell' (perhaps he meant publish?) my work through connecting it with Hinduism. Confusingly he argued that it wasn't only Hinduism that was influencing the way Anglo-Indians practice their faith; Islam also influenced it. Furthermore, he said that he felt that the Catholic Orders of the Jesuits and Salesians[10] were particularly at fault for 'wilfully breaking into and trying to change the Anglo-Indian culture in terms of religion'. He gave as examples the increasingly common practice of asking parishioners to remove their shoes upon entering the church, of raising their open hands skyward in prayer and prostrating themselves in front of the cross—all Indian religious practices.

Robinson, in her work on contemporary Indian Christian Communities, offers an explanation for this trend. She says,

> While a degree of syncretism has always characterized popular Christianity, in recent decades the (Catholic) church has *officially* begun to promote the indigenisation of its modes of worship in certain specific respects. Encouraging seating arrangements on the floor, the harmonization of the architecture of new churches with indigenous forms, the aarti[11] and the ritual use of garlands and *agarbatti* (Indian

---

[10] Salesians are from the Catholic teaching Order of Don Bosco.
[11] *Aarti* is the practice of honouring an event or an image using a flame (often a camphor flame).

incense) are some expressions of the shift. (Robinson, 2003b: 302–303, emphasis in the original)

Susan Bayly, writing about the spread of Islam and Christianity in the south of India, mentions deliberate modifications made to Christian teachings and practices by the early (1700–1900) missionaries and priests in order that they better fit the cultural practices of would-be converts (1989: 241–262).

An interesting comparison is contained in Corinne Dempsey's report of the claim by a Belgium Priest (who had worked for most of his priesthood in Kerala) that Christianity in Kerala has been 'entirely Romanised' (Dempsey, 2001: 18–19, 50). Her findings were that this was not the case; she argues that 'a complete Romanization (or colonization) of domestic traditions is unlikely, as foreign impositions so often become hybridized through indigenous interpretations' (2001: 50). This interpretation concurs with my own findings.

The next section proposes a way of understanding why these changes might be taking place.

The Place of Christianity in India

There are a number of misunderstandings about Christianity in India: one is that there is no appreciable Christianity there at all,[12] another is that the Christianity that is there came from the

[12] This is illustrated by the following excerpt taken from my PhD fieldwork journal:

> One day in Central Calcutta at the beginning of Lent I came across a team of enthusiastic young American missionaries who attended a missionary school in America and were in Calcutta doing a 'practical' stint. I was affronted (on behalf of the hundreds of thousands of Indian Christians) by their arrogance, their lack of knowledge of the extent of Christianity in Calcutta, along with their total lack of interest in finding out anything that would contradict their assumptions (of illiteracy, of education, of ignorance of English, of heathenism, of lack of a sophisticated and coherent worldview). They hung-out inside and outside the trendiest, most Westernised, coffee house on Park Street distributing pamphlets and collecting stories to take back home. I invited them to come to Mass with me [it was Ash Wednesday] to see an example of the extent of Christianity in India; they declined. (Andrews, 2005: 103)

West.[13] Christianity, in my observation, from my experience of spending many months of fieldwork time in Calcutta, including three Christmas seasons (which include full church attendance throughout the Christmas season, decorations in the central shopping districts, markets and malls crammed with Christmas shoppers and queues lining up to buy Christmas cakes), has a firm position in contemporary India.

During the course of my fieldwork I was told numerous times, that 'all Anglo-Indians are Christian, but not all Christians are Anglo-Indians'. Of course, this is the case: of the more than one billion Indians, about 2.34 per cent are Christian,[14] and of those Christians only about 1 per cent are Anglo-Indians. In addition, although this religion is commonly associated with European colonisation, its history predates the earliest moments of colonialism by more than 1,500 years and it is currently the third most popular religion in the subcontinent.[15] The most significant concentrations of Christian populations are in the states of Kerala and Tamil Nadu in the south, the more recently independent state of Goa,[16] and the north-eastern tribal areas of Bihar and Assam (Dempsey and Raj, 2002: 1).

It is the understanding of most Indian Christians and scholars of religion in India that Christianity first came to India through Kerala—directly from Palestine—with the arrival of Saint Thomas

---

[13] It is not only people from Western countries who make this assumption about India and Christianity: while writing this book I was by chance reading a fictional account set in Calcutta (written in 1962 by a Bengali), which presented an opinion of what was thought would happen to Christianity in India once the British left as a result of Indian Independence. A character in the story expressed the view that along with the British, he had expected that India would lose 'Christ, cricket and the cabaret' (Sankar, 2007: 196). Based on my experience of India the prediction was wrong on all counts—there might have been a decline in cabaret (all over the world) but if we think of Bollywood as a kind of replacement then perhaps it lives on in Mumbai. As for cricket: with the addition of the Indian Cricket League now running their multi-million dollar rebel series the relevance of the sport to Indians cannot be overlooked.

[14] According to the 2001 Census of India.

[15] According to the 2001 Census of India.

[16] Goa was a Portuguese colony until 1961 when Indian military force was used to remove them.

(one of Christ's 12 disciples) in 52 AD (Dempsey, 2001; Dempsey and Raj, 2002; Frykenberg, 2008; Mundadan, 1984). St Thomas is believed to have spent time in Kerala before travelling to Tamil Nadu where he died a martyr's death in Madras (now Chennai) in 72 AD. Contemporary Christianity in Kerala comprises a number of different Catholic (Roman and otherwise) and Protestant denominations including, 'Jacobite, Orthodox Syrian, Latin Catholic, Syrian Catholic (including Syro-Malabar rites and Syro-Malankara rites), and Mar Thomite' (Dempsey, 2001: 5). The introduction of Christianity to Goa fits more closely with the 'Christianity came to India with colonialism' model: in the late 16th century, a Western-based version of Catholicism arrived with the Portuguese colonists to be spread by accompanying missionaries (Frykenberg, 2008: 130–132).

Since the arrival of Christianity in India, many different ritual forms of Christianity have developed in reaction to practices already in place. As Narayanan notes in writing about Indian Christians, 'They are multiritualistic in expressing their Christian devotion in the tradition of their forefathers and foremothers. It is a Christian faith that is expressed in the idiom of the larger culture that surrounds them spatially and that preceded them temporally' (Narayanan, 2002: 261).

The development of a *popular* Christian practice that fits with local customs has become the focus of a number of researchers, some of whom have investigated the negotiations between lay Christian *native* rites (which may have their roots in Hinduism) and Church rites (Dempsey and Raj, 2002; Frykenberg, 2008; Fuller, 1992; Robinson, 2003a). The results of such negotiations are sets of syncretised practices, which sometimes privilege official church practice and at other times the native forms. Academic focus on the syncretism of Christianity has, according to Robinson, 'allowed for the idea that Christianity in India is somehow not quite authentic' (Robinson, 2003a: 22). The example most commonly used to argue this concerns caste: In many areas Christians still identify with historical family caste affiliations, even though caste's ideology of purity and pollution is based on ideas relating to one's proximity to Hindu gods. As such, articulations of caste affiliation are interpreted as a challenge to *genuine* Christian belief.

Of the publications focusing on popular Christianity in India, there is very little relating directly to Christianity in Calcutta, or West Bengal. Dempsey and Raj's *Popular Christianity* (2002), for example, comprises a collection of essays focusing on popular practices in various parts of India (most notably Kerala and Tamil Nadu), but nothing from this region. Frykenberg (2008), who writes from an historic perspective, is a partial exception: while he acknowledges the influence of the East India Company in providing converts to Calcutta's Christian community, he discusses Calcutta only briefly, and not in terms of contemporary practice. In addition, he overlooks the influence of Anglo-Indians completely.

Anglo-Indians and Christianity

Although the British brought Christianity in the form of the Protestant denominations, the majority of Anglo-Indians in India now are Catholic.[17] The reasons I was given for this are: (a) that it was the Church of England Anglo-Indians who were the wealthier ones; therefore more of them were able to migrate from India; (b) in mixed denomination marriages between a Catholic and a Protestant, any children the couple may have are brought up as Catholics (Sen, 1988); (c) Catholic families are more likely to have bigger families. All of these factors are thought to augment the trend of Catholics out-numbering non-Catholics. Given this situation, I focus the remainder of the essay on the changes that have occurred in the Roman Catholic Church,[18] the reasons for the changes and their impact on Anglo-Indians.

---

[17] This claim is based both on the survey data—referred to in an earlier footnote in this chapter—and on the unanimous views of Anglo-Indians I have spoken to in and out of India over the time I have been involved in Anglo-Indian research.

[18] According to Anglican ministers I have discussed this with, the changes I outline in the remainder of this chapter have parallels in the Church of England—which the CNI is affiliated with.

Post-Vatican II Inculturation

Turning now to documents issued by the Vatican itself it is apparent that, as Robinson (Robinson, 2003b) and Bayly (1989) suggest, there *is* a concerted effort on the part of the Catholic Church to modify its practices to better fit with local customs and traditions. The *Instruction* for *Inculturation and the Roman Liturgy* issued from Vatican City in 1994, for example, includes in its frontispiece the following:

> Inculturation signifies an intimate transformation
> of the authentic cultural values
> by their integration into Christianity
> and the implantation of Christianity into different human cultures.
> ...
> By inculturation the church makes the Gospel
> incarnate in different cultures
> and at the same time introduces peoples,
> together with their cultures,
> into her own community.
> ...
> Coming into contact with different cultures,
> the church must welcome
> all that can be reconciled with the Gospel
> in the tradition of a people
> to bring to it the riches of Christ
> and to be enriched in turn
> by the many different forms of wisdom
> of the nations of the earth.
>
> (Congr. for Divine Worship and the Discipline of the Sacraments, frontispiece. Format of the original)

The rationale for the practice of inculturation is two-fold: to make the gospel relevant to as many people as possible by drawing on cultural forms familiar to them, and, to broaden the community of the church through the inclusion of many cultures, that is, to make it a truly 'catholic' church (Congr. for Divine Worship and the Discipline of the Sacraments n. 4–8) (sacraments, 1995).

Angrosino defines inculturation as 'encounters whose outcome is a convergence that does not replace either of the cultures from which it arose. Both parties to the inculturative exchange undergo internal transformation, but neither loses its autonomous identity' (1994: 825). The areas of liturgical inculturation may include language, music and singing, gesture and posture, involvement in popular devotion, art, altar design and *liturgical furnishings, vessels, vestments, and colours*' (Congr. for Divine Worship and the Discipline of the Sacraments n. 43).[19] Angrosino maintains that there are various methods of inculturation and uses, as it happens, the case of the 'sign of peace' to exemplify one method, which he refers to as *dynamic equivalence* (which involves 'the replacement of an element of the Roman form with something in the local culture that has equal meaning or value' [1994: 825]). He notes that while in America the typical *sign* is the handshake, in Zaire it is the ritual washing from a common bowl that is used, as it is this that symbolises the church as a forgiving community (Angrosino, 1994).

It seems that India, at least for the purposes of the Church, was thought of as part of the *Asian continent* and was primarily regarded as a mission territory, along with other Asian countries such as China in which the *local* customs needed to be incorporated into the fabric of the Church (Pontifical Council for Culture n. 20) (Culture, 1995). These *local* customs were regarded as being sufficiently different from Western, or Roman, customs for inculturation to be required.

The process for making changes was, and still is, strictly controlled by the Vatican. In India it is the Conference of Bishops that confers and makes decisions about which social and cultural elements would be beneficial to be incorporated into practice. These are then recommended to the Vatican where final decisions are made. The local Bishops and congregations are then notified of what changes, or incorporations, are to be actioned (Congr. for Divine Worship and the Discipline of the Sacraments n. Instruction n. 63–69). The decision-making at the various levels and the local-level implementation are required to be carried out with the understanding that the 'innovations should only be made when the good of the Church genuinely and certainly requires them; care

---

[19] I was told by a Kolkata-based Catholic priest, that the parts of the Mass which may be adapted to reflect local customs and symbolism are restricted to the 'entrance processional, the offertory, communion, and recessional'.

must be taken that any new forms adopted should in some way grow organically from forms already existing' (Ecumenical Council n. 23) (Council, 1963).

Whether or not, or to what extent, India's Anglo-Indian community's cultural values were taken into consideration in the move towards inculturation in India is not documented. In an attempt to ascertain some sense of this I interviewed a Calcutta-based Bengali priest in 2008. He explained that '[Anglo-Indians] may react against the Indian way but they're in the midst of the majority, therefore they don't have much say'. He continued,

> By and large Anglo-Indians don't accept these changes. It's in regard to their mindset: they inherited the mindset of the British. For them anything that goes in line with the British will be more acceptable than Indian ways. Anglo-Indians are fragmented now: they are in small numbers and don't have much cohesion.

This Bengali priest explained that for West Bengal the most significant changes to the Mass and other ritualised services occurred in the 1970s with translations of services into local vernacular, and the production of a local *Book of Blessings*. This incorporated local traditions such as the 'use of symbols through dance and music' for example, through incorporation of songs by Rabindranath Tagore, the Bengali Nobel laureate. He said that in Calcutta the most recent influences on practice were from the Adivasi (north-eastern tribal) traditions, and added that he didn't imagine that Anglo-Indians would attend an Adivasi service, although other non-tribal Indian Christians would. He opined that in some cases practices had 'gone beyond Vatican II' and some restrictions would soon be implemented, for example, 'dancing during liturgical celebrations' would not be allowed.

In terms of the implementation of changes, the emphasis in Vatican documents is on *gradual* change and full preparation of the congregations in order for the changes to be accepted, that is, to avoid 'the danger of rejection' (Council, 1963, n. 23) of changes. For all that the instructions emphasise prudence it is noted that there are many instances of congregations not being ready for inculturation (Angrosino, 1994; Vatican, 1994). My observations and correspondence with Anglo-Indians concur with this: in general, they do not welcome the changes, as suggested by the priest, and indicated in the following quote: 'Anglo Indians have adjusted well to 'some inculturation' [...] but definitely do not like the dancing and aarti at Mass!!' (Email communication from a Calcuttan Anglo-Indian parishioner, August 2008). Mark Tully and Gillian Wright (2002: 102–103), writing about Christianity in Goa, includes the excerpt below from an interview with a priest, which also indicates support for the status quo:

> We want to acknowledge the Indian in our church, but the West won't go away. Next week the Pilar fathers will be celebrating a public Mass on Indian Independence day, and it will include Hindu rituals like *aarti* and the smearing of *kumkum* on the forehead. Our people will take that provided it's just once in a while, but basically, Christians here outwardly still want to be Westernized. We must become an Indian church, and we must be seen to become one, otherwise the rest of the country will not accept us, but we mustn't go too fast or else the passengers will get off the bus.

This sentiment is likely to apply more to Anglo-Indians than to any other group in India as they are more likely to want to hold on to the Western nature of their church given that it lines up with their own cultural predispositions. In the words of another Anglo-Indian after reading an earlier version of this text, 'This is why I live somewhere else (Australia). I never particularly saw Christ as Anglo-Saxon, but I cannot imagine Him as a depiction of Krishna either.'

Impact on Anglo-Indians

It is significant that the history of Anglo-Indians spans the time that the Catholic Church was in its most static period. From the time of the Reform of Trent in the 16th century the church *brought order into chaos* by centralising to Rome with the result that there was a unity of rites and books and strict regulation of liturgical initiative, which included language of the Mass, art and music, and even the festivals observed. It wasn't until after the 1960s that Vatican

II 'opened the windows again'[20] and allowed for local variation on the Latin liturgical rites.[21] The timing of this is significant for Anglo-Indians as, by the late 1960s, they were rapidly declining in numbers. It has been a point of pride for an Anglo-Indian family to supply the Church with a family member for the priesthood (or other religious) with the result that there were many Anglo-Indian priests serving in parishes, brothers and nuns serving as teachers in the local schools, as well as bishops, and at least one cardinal in Calcutta alone. Corresponding with the declining numbers of parishioners, there were likely to be fewer Anglo-Indians going into these vocations. It should not be surprising then if they were over-ruled (or not even consulted) on decisions about inculturation of *local* practices. It can be no more than an exercise in speculation to suggest what might have occurred had Anglo-Indian Religious remained in their former numbers throughout this post-Vatican II and post-Independence period. Would Anglo-Indian clergy, on behalf of their community, have been able to stem the flow of Indianisation within the Church? Probably not, given that Anglo-Indians were already so outnumbered by Indian Christians. As it was, Anglo-Indians had begun their rapid exodus just at the time that their influence may, possibly, have prevented some of the official inculturation of local practices into Church practice. Which begs another question: Would it have made a difference to the flow of Anglo-Indians from India if the Church had not begun to adopt these practices?

Concluding Comments

Popular Christianity in India has led the changes that the Catholic Church is now adopting. The Vatican's inculturation policies are catching up with what is already happening in India after

---

[20] In the words of New Zealand parish priest who I discussed this essay with as I wrote it.

[21] Angrosino (1994) notes that there is a level of *noblesse oblige* demonstrated by the church in 'allowing for' adaptation (in this he makes a similar criticism of the Church as Hage does in relation to the State in allowing privileges, for example, citizenship to migrants [Hage, 2004]).

2,000 years of *negotiations* between the cultures of lay and Church Christians. This official indigenisation to *local* practices, however, presents particular difficulties for a community such as the Anglo-Indians, in that their culture is generally quite different from that of other Indian Christians. That is, the fact that Anglo-Indian practices have been closer to Western forms of Christianity means that the kind of indigenisation referred to here moves these practices *away* from those that they feel comfortable with, that is, those that are close to their own. The risk is that they may come to feel, or come to be, estranged from their churches and faith practices, which have central importance to them. So while it should not be surprising that in the subcontinent there may be an official move to more Indian, in particular Hindu, forms of practice, an effect for Anglo-Indians is that this is one more area of their lives in which their traditionally more Western ways are being eroded, providing them one more reason to contemplate leaving India.

6

Jane: God-given Opportunities#

I could have positioned Jane's story within either the Faith or the Education section as these are two significant pillars of her life. Given her social and physical circumstances, without education she would have had little chance to have made what she has of her life. However, she wouldn't attribute so much credit to education; it's *the Lord* who would get full credit. Her faith has given her remarkable strength and endurance, as you can read.

The first time I saw Jane was just before midday in Kyd Street, central Calcutta. My attention had been drawn to a black-haired woman who was taking some time to emerge from her taxi. She was elbowing her way out of her seat while the driver stood patiently waiting. Once she worked her way to the edge of the seat she took the crutches he held for her, thanked him and then used the crutches to support herself as she got out. She made her way across the busy, potholed street close to where she was meeting us for lunch. The fact that the street was uneven certainly didn't help, but it wasn't enough to stop her. Life for Jane, as I was to discover, was very much like that street: bumpy, uneven, but never enough to stop her.

I met Jane through a woman who Jane and many other Anglo-Indians call 'Aunty'. One day when I visited her she was meeting Jane for lunch and suggested I join them. We lunched at a Chinese restaurant where I sat next to Jane and soon learned that this tiny Anglo-Indian woman in her mid-30s was intelligent, articulate and very independent. I was delighted to meet her, not least because she contradicted some negative stereotyping I had come across.[1]

A similar version of Jane's life story was first published as 'Living and Working in Calcutta: Jane's Story' by SAGE Publications in *Working Women: Stories of Strife, Struggle and Survival* (Andrews, 2009).

[1] Anglo-Indian women are negatively depicted in literature and film as being promiscuous, dishonest and living the high life without thinking of the future, for example, see Nirad Chaudhuri's *The Continent of Circe* (1967) and the Merchant Ivory film *Cotton Mary* (1999). Megan Mills discusses Anglo-Indian stereotypes in her works (1996, 1998).

She exudes life and energy and optimism. She has a very good job as secretarial assistant to a high-profile man with considerable public influence, and she is highly regarded by him. She lives in a flat she owns and is able to take an overseas holiday most years. Given the circumstances of her early life, it is remarkable that she is able to live such a life.

After that initial lunchtime meeting, when I told Jane about my research and she agreed that I could record her life story, I arranged to see her again a few days later at her flat. To get there I took a taxi from my accommodation in central Calcutta—getting into the taxi only after throwing off the unwelcome *assistance*[2] of a Bengali gentleman by assuring him that I was quite capable of getting where I wanted to on my own. This prelude to visiting Jane highlighted the necessity for a woman, especially one with the disabilities she has, to have secure living arrangements and be confident about transportation.

On the evening of the first interview session Jane answered my knock on her door with a smile and the affectionate, typically Anglo-Indian, kiss on each cheek as she welcomed me in. Her flat was spacious and light and brightened with Christmas decorations—a Christmas tree on a table in one corner and the strings of Christmas cards testimony to her many friends. After sitting down and briefly chatting about our days since we last met, we settled into the work; she told me about her life and I taped her story. Although I have not included all of her story here, the details of her early life and her enormous faith, effort and determination are obvious and account, to a large extent, for the life she leads today.

Jane was struck by polio when she was a child but this was only one of a number of blows that she has had to contend with. I will let her tell her story from those times as she did in our interviews.

---

[2] He was very keen to get into the taxi with me, saying he would make sure I got to my destination. I was suspicious of his real intentions and felt much safer without his assistance.

It Was Difficult for My Parents to Take Care of Me because I Have Polio

> When I was one year old suddenly I contracted polio. My parents didn't give me the vaccine. But there were five of us in the family.

You were the youngest?

> I am in the middle (of four sisters and one brother) so it was very difficult for my parents to take care of me because I had polio, and they are from a very, very poor family.
>
> They were facing a lot of problems and during our childhood my parents separated. They have both remarried. So, looking at all this poverty they wanted to discard me as a handicapped child. My mother thought that 'in the future how am I going to support this girl when I also have others to take care of?' So then she took me to a lady who works [as a welfare officer at a hill station boarding school]. I never saw my parents again.

But I Had Another Disadvantage: To Be Born a Girl Is Like a Sin

Being born into an extremely poor family was her first disadvantage; contracting polio was another and as she says:

> My main problem is that I had polio, but also it's because I'm a girl child. We face discrimination from there itself. To be a girl is a big boon[3] here in India and being handicapped. People think that it's because your parents have sinned, and that the sin has fallen on the child. That's why people don't want to take such a child out into society or expose them to friends and family.

So they looked at your polio...?

> Yes.

---

[3] I presume Jane is being ironic in saying this.

Looked at the effect of that, and say that that's a result of their sin. Is that what you mean?

Yes, sort of. They feel like that in the Indian society.

Is that a Hindu belief?

It's more a Hindu belief, yes. So that's why ... for me to come out and walk on the streets.... They look at me and people think, 'How could she walk on the streets like that?'[4] And this lady, the welfare officer, said, 'Okay if this case is genuine, and if it's so that her parents don't want her, maybe the school could try to take care of her.'

But I Always Say that God Has Been So Good to Me

Did you have to be Anglo-Indian to go to the school?

No.

Did your family have to be Christian?

My parents are Roman Catholic, but [admission] was based on the situation, not on being Christian. So because I had polio, and I was in a critical condition; I was very thin, and very weak. It was a blessing in disguise. You can see children like that being used here, by their mothers, to beg. They even break their bones to put them on their hips and then take them around to beg. But I always say that God has been so good to me.

---

[4] Later in the interview she added:

>And, literally, people they just stop me on the street as though, 'My God, how can you just walk on the street? How can you...?
>*Is this in India? [She's visited 13 other countries in the world.] Who are the people who stop and...?*
>Mostly Hindus.
>*Is it children?*
>No, the parents. Because most of them have handicapped children in their homes. So they feel that I am a living example to them. Some of them are so positive, and some of them just want to know how I have progressed in life.

When they took me to the school I was very weak and really needed some attention. I was loved by all of them. They did exercises for me. They made special parallel bars so that I could practice walking, and I had massages every day. I would always cry because my legs used to pain quite a lot. But they really took good care of me, gave me vitamin pills and every day I used to have exercises. I didn't much like to do the exercises. Of course, as I started growing up I realised that I have to do things for myself and have to try to be optimistic in life and see what I can do with these legs.

I'm also a human being and I have feelings and it's not easy when you have parents, and yet you don't have them at the same time. Here in India, to get an education is very difficult. My mother approached that same lady and said, 'Maybe this handicapped girl would like somebody to help her, so why don't you take my elder daughter into the school as well?' And so my elder sister was admitted into the school with me.

How much older is she?

She's one year older to me. But the sad part was, as we started growing up, she never recognised me as her sister because I was handicapped and excelled in the class.

I was always a fun-loving kid. I loved to get attention and ... so what if I'm handicapped? I've got my hands. I've got my brains. But the growing up was not easy, because being a child you want to play, run and swim, do it all, try to take part in all the activities in the school. But I just had to sit and look at them and I really felt that I was missing something in life. The girls would get parcels and letters from their parents, and I have this younger sister who used to write to me only.

She used to write to you when you were at school?

Yes. They studied in a Catholic school here in Cal. As we started growing up we were taught about Christianity, and that was a very important aspect in my life then. I said to the Lord, 'If I don't have anyone, at least I have you.' And that was a big source of inspiration to me. I came to the understanding that He was asking, 'What are you going to do in this dark world?' And it was then that I really gave my life to the Lord and said, 'You take over my life. You have brought me to this world and now it's up to you to break me, mould me and make me into what you want.' So after I gave my life to the Lord I really felt that things started moving positively for me.

How old were you then?

I was eight years old.

Quite young.

Yeah, I was quite young.

If I'm Going to Sit Back and Just Cry over My Polio It's Not Going to Help

I always felt that if I'm going to sit back and just cry over my polio it's not going to help. So I tried to take part in as many events as I could in my school and I discovered my singing, drawing, and handicraft talents—stitching and sewing. So I really felt that I should put more emphasis on that and give some more importance to that. We had singing competitions and dramas that I used to take part in. My school friends never, ever treated me like a handicap and that was really one plus point for me. They'd say, 'Come on Jane, let's go here' or 'let's go there'. So I thought, 'Yeah, why not?'

How did you get around? Did you use crutches?

Yes, from the age of three I started using crutches and callipers. And since we have three months of holiday during the wintertime, my school would pay for me to go to a very big Christian medical college in South India to have full physiotherapy, muscle assessment and to see if I was improving. But the doctors made me aware that callipers and crutches would always be a part of my life. So I knew from an early age that there was no chance of improvement. Since I was slowly growing, I had to have new callipers and crutch measurements, and I would be there for practically all the winter holidays. Every year I had to go back and forth.

Initially I did feel a bit lonely because I was just a child. I didn't know the patients because they were changing all the time. I spoke English so I would talk to all the medical students and sometimes one would say, 'Why don't you come and sing to us? Bring the guitar, and we can have a singsong. Or read the Bible and pray with us. I'm sure the patients would love that.'

They Say It Is Very Difficult to Get One Certificate—I Had Seven!

Jane completed her secondary schooling and then was given the option of staying on at the school while she completed further training as a secretary.

> I did a secretarial course through the Pitman's Board in London. They say it's very difficult to get one certificate. And it was a correspondence course so the question paper comes from England. When I got the results, I had seven certificates and I did the highest examination! I got a first class advanced certificate and I did all the other examinations. So that really gave me a big boost and I thought, 'This is something for me to go out with into the dark world'. And what occurred to me was that especially because I'm from a poor background, I really had my mind set on working for poor people. So I thought if I take this secretarial training I could sit in an office and do some correspondence and be a secretary, and that became my aim in life. So after I did my training at school I came back down to Calcutta. This was a shock to me at first, to be living in such a vast and crowded cosmopolitan city after the calm and serenity of the school in Darjeeling district—which is up close to the Himalayas.

But I Had One Problem, and That Was Transport

> It was Aunty who helped me to find a place to stay as a paying guest. It was not easy. I think she must have been turned down quite a lot of times because nobody wants the risk of taking care of a handicapped person. But finally she did get a nice Anglo-Indian family and I stayed there for three years.

> *As a boarder, a paying guest?*

> As a paying guest, yes. It means you pay for the month, and they give you just one bed, and maybe some food. It depends on their household situation. So there were times when I had to depend on the shop food.

When I came down to Calcutta I had to look for work. Even though I knew that finding employment was not going to be easy, because of my disability, I had to support myself financially to survive. I went for many interviews to all these NGOs [non-governmental organizations], because these are the ones who are supporting poor people. They would ask if I was willing to sit for a test. I always said, 'Of course'. I didn't want to be taken because I'm handicapped. I knew I had the ability. I have a sharp brain and definitely I can pick up the skills. I can pick up things very fast. I did sit for a lot of examinations and they would say, 'Yes, you've got the job' immediately. But I had one problem, and that was transport. I can't depend on the buses or even waiting for a taxi. It's too hard for me. Also, it's expensive, and it's difficult to get a taxi every day to come and go. So I asked these companies, 'What about giving me transport?' 'Oh, I'm very sorry, we don't give transport to staff.' I said, 'But you have to make an exception. You are the ones who are helping people in need. We are the ones in need. I mean you have to make an exception somewhere.' So opportunities would arise, but then not materialise because they couldn't offer me transport. I had to turn down a number of offers of work because they weren't in a position to offer me transport to and from my residence.

I was starting to feel really rejected but then an opportunity came up—for me to go back and do a year's 'service' at my old school. This turned out to be a blessing in disguise because just as I was about to finish the year I heard about a job with an international Christian NGO. I was excited but half expecting that even if I was successful it would meet with the same fate of 'no transport'. It took some of the seniors at school to talk me into applying, and then I was selected.

And this time I managed to get through to the organisation about transport. They said, 'We will give you transport but we will take a part of your salary—₹60.' So I joined this organisation and I was there for 19 years. I really feel that it's so rewarding when you give your whole life for the cause of poor people. Especially when I didn't get it from my parents. This organisation offered help to deprived and poverty-stricken people of our country but it also offered hope to people like me, for my self-improvement. I have since left this NGO and have joined another religious firm, to date, holding a prestigious post for the top-most boss.

I asked Jane about the flat she lived in. It is a beautiful, spacious, well-maintained and well-furnished home: one of the most pleasant homes I visited in Calcutta, or anywhere else for that matter.

The difference between this and her earlier accommodation must have been striking. I can only speculate about how it affected her well-being and ability to work. While she may have been pleased to leave her previous shared accommodation each day to go to work, the lack of comfort and privacy must have begun to take a toll on her, physically, mentally and emotionally.

> A handicapped friend from Holland bought this flat for me as a gift. He saw that I was going through such a bad time. I was staying as a paying guest at first but then I moved into a hostel. It's not always easy to be a paying guest. You have to be very obligated to the person you stay with.
>
> *Did they not trust you in the house?*
>
> No, it's not that. It's just that they feel it's not nice that a girl stays alone over there, especially when she's like this. Or they think people will take advantage of you. In that protective way. Wherever I've stayed, they have always been very loving to me. And they were all Anglo-Indian people. But for the last six years before I got this flat I stayed in the hostel which is just outside my office gate. It was quite difficult for me because I had to climb three floors every day. It was a real olden-day building. I had to share this room about the size of my bathroom with three old people.

It's Been So Wonderful Just to Feel That I Have a Place of My Own

She told me of the visit to Calcutta made by her Dutch director.

> He was interested in me because I was handicapped. He would always try to help me and he would take me out to clubs and parties. One time the Dutch director's friend paid us a visit and when he came to see me he said, 'Jane, where are you living? I'm really interested to get to know you better because you and I have something in common. We both have polio'.

Jane offered to show him where she had been living for the last six years, sharing the little room with three others who were all over 60 years old.

I said, 'I am living in that room.' And he said, 'I can't believe it. I can't see how you can climb up all those steps.' I said, 'It's so difficult to get accommodation in Calcutta and even if you get the accommodation, it's so expensive.'

So this friend didn't even really know me, and he's got his own family abroad. But when I was away in Norway that year he said to my Dutch director, 'I am so upset about Jane living in that condition I want to buy her a flat. No matter what the cost is I just want to buy her a flat.' So my director said, 'What are you saying? It's so expensive.' But he responded, 'I just want to see that this girl gets rehabilitated and she has something of her own.'

So he bought a flat and gave it to Jane. Accommodation in Calcutta has become expensive, which has led to many Anglo-Indians who once lived in the central areas moving to outlying regions. Jane's flat is comparatively close to the central part of the town and is very conveniently located to her place of work.

And now I'm living here from 1996. Friends keep visiting me and it's been so wonderful just to feel that I have a place of my own. I didn't have even a spoon to my name when I was in that hostel. I just had this one suitcase with all my clothes for the office. In the hostel, they just gave us one bed and a small table and a chair—for ₹400 per month. It wasn't much, but at the same time....

You didn't get much for it either?

They put on the water pump only three times a day and if I missed the water in the morning.... Because the next two times it would get turned on I was in the office. So if I missed that one....

I would fill up on water first, because there were the other three who had to fill the water also, and they just put it on for one hour, and so we had a lot of problems. If I come back from work very late and I wanted to eat something hot or drink some hot beverage, I couldn't because they wouldn't allow us to keep a stove. They were very strict and at the same time accommodation is so difficult, so I really....

How did you eat then, how did you manage?

They gave us the food. They brought it in a tiffin carrier and they kept it on the table. But when I came back at nine o'clock or later it was so cold. It was all I had so I had to eat that cold tasteless food.

You Should Try to Be Optimistic and Go out and Reach Your Goals and Try to Touch Others' Lives

Besides making her way through each busy day and becoming an extremely valuable employee, she does all she can for others, especially those she identifies with. I asked her about the organisations she works with.

> Mostly, I'm involved with the handicapped, because I myself have a handicap. I really like to help these type of children. There is this centre started by one lady from England who got the calling from God to work for these children. Because there's so many handicapped kids on the streets and everywhere in India but nobody to take care of them. So she started this home and my devotion to them is, well.... Just because I am a handicap I feel that, okay, I didn't get love from my parents so I know what it is for them to just be lying and crawling around without getting any affection, except from the servants who just like treat them like dolls. They just lift them up and dump them somewhere else and you know I really feel sad about that.
>
> So this is one of the organisations I work for, and I take a lot of visitors over there and they donate quite a lot. And even if they don't, they go back and they collect money to send to the children. The other one I work with is a place for the juvenile children and their mothers who have been thrown in prison because of no fault of theirs. These women they sleep on the pavements and sometimes a man just wants to have a fling or sex or they want to have some fun with women so they go and they take them to the backyard or somewhere. And they rape these mothers, then the mother gets pregnant and then for no reason they are put into prison. Then they give birth and have the child. They literally are growing up in the jail. So a missionary from Norway started a centre for these type of women.

This Is Amazing, That Somebody from Another Country Does This!

> So this man from Norway already knew that there's so much poverty here they don't have enough time and money to look to somebody else's needs like. So many are poor and they are just scraping to

look after themselves, and if they take on somebody else it's a burden to them. So it had to come from an outside source, to see the need for these types of children. I go and visit them quite often. I take visitors over there and, but you know they are such talented children. I mean you just have to give them a little push and they sing, dance, draw, they do so many different things and they make beautiful embroidery, art and everything. Once in a year they have an exhibition. They get a lot of sales and whatever money they get, it goes back to the girls because then they need to be taken care of.

Jane does all she does out of a deep sense of compassion for others. She, more than most, knows about the impediments that can be part of one's lot. Her life could have been very different from what it is and she does what she can to make a positive difference to others. She is appreciative of what she sees as the primary source of all that is good in her life.

> God has taken away my legs but He's given me 10 gifts in their place, and I really feel like.... I can be so proud of my achievements and what I have done today for people, and many people have said that I have been a great example to them.
>
> It's just that I'm very positive and I always feel that if you sit and brood over things that will not help. You should try to be optimistic and go out and reach your goals and try to touch others' lives. And I know that God is with me and He's really using me through my singing or through even just talking to people. That is a strong testimony for Him as well. I have been so lucky because my friends have sponsored me abroad eight times to Norway and Holland, and I have travelled to 13 countries in the world. I even studied in Norway for one year. Where could you get all these opportunities if it were not for the love of God?

Jane's story is so varied and complex. One cannot but marvel at its path: its highways, its dips, its dead ends. But always there seems to be a beacon at the end of the road: a benefactor, a kind word, a solution to a problem. How does Jane see it all? Her final comment to me was to implore readers 'not to look at the disability but at the ability instead'.

PART THREE

Education

Education in modern India is a commodity. Schools have become a business and learning English is the currency to social and financial success. Anglo-Indian schools and teachers have always been in the vanguard of Indian education. It is not chance that the 18th century Eurasian teacher Henry Derozio ranks alongside social reformers such as Raja Ram Mohan Roy or that the first Anglo-Indian member of Parliament (MP), Frank Anthony, started the Frank Anthony Schools across India. Even though there is evidence of other educational initiatives, Anglo-Indian schools still hold sway across the length and breadth of the subcontinent.

From the earliest days of the European missionaries arriving in India, and then the Christian teaching orders—the Irish Christian Brothers and the Jesuits for example—English medium faith-based schools have proliferated and served the Indian student population. Once the railways began to snake around the countryside, the railway towns built schools for local railway families, who were mostly Anglo-Indians. Most towns had both a Catholic and a Protestant church, and both would have a school attached to it. In addition, in association with the railways, to meet the need for older children to be well educated while parents were moved from one railway town to another were the boarding schools such as the one Angeline attended in Nainital. There they received an excellent education, with many going on to take vocational training such as the Teachers Training Certificate (or TTC)—so that they could get back into the school system, then as teachers. After Independence the schools kept going, the profile of the students changing from being an Anglo-Indian majority in the classes to a majority of non-Anglo-Indians. Reminders of Anglo-Indian teachers are ever present. Inaugurating the most recent World Anglo-Indian Reunion in Calcutta, Amit Mitra, Finance and Excise Minister for West Bengal, extolled the virtues of the legendary Mr Clifford Hicks and how that Anglo-Indian virtuoso inspired him to greater heights. It would be fascinating to know how many Indians have been educated at Anglo-Indian schools over the years and how they made their mark in life.

In this section, I look at the impact of receiving, or not receiving, an education. Jane's story provides a bridge into this section. Although she doesn't particularly attribute her success to her education there's little question that it has made all the difference to the options available to her. The first story in this section is Peter's who describes himself as an uneducated man. He is candid about the repercussions of this for himself and his family. Michael Robertson's story comes next—not only has he received a good education and has a successful career, but he is passionate about what an education can do for the people of his community. In the essay I focus on the anomaly, in the Indian context, of all being English speakers but having poorly educated people amongst them. I also discuss ways that educationallydisadvantaged Anglo-Indians might be assisted further in order to make the most of the educational capital of their community. Finally, in this section, I have the story of Philip—22 years old—who, in his own unique way, shows what can be achieved by taking advantage of opportunities.

7

Peter: The Less the Education, the Fewer the Opportunities

The first time I met Peter it was Ash Wednesday 2002. I had asked my friend, the welfare officer at Dr Graham's Homes at the time, if she could arrange for me to meet a family who had children at the school. Within a few days I received an invitation for lunch with the D'Cruz family who had one son at the school. I readily accepted. The D'Cruz family lived more than an hour's journey from where I was staying; hence, Mr D'Cruz, or Peter as I came to know him, said he'd collect me. He and his daughter arrived half an hour early on the arranged day with a taxi to get us to Sealdah station. I heard later that they had come to collect me from the station by the auto rickshaw service that made the trip part of the way, then by foot for the last kilometre.

Peter is in his early 40s, and looks a bit like a slim Michael Caine. He was dressed that day in a well-pressed pale cotton shirt, dark belted trousers and sandals. His daughter, Lisa, was dressed in a fine white embroidered salwar kameez. Her long dark hair caught in a ponytail with a tortoiseshell clasp and tiny nose stud gave her a distinctly Indian look. She was 16 years old and quite beautiful. I was perplexed about her attire though—wearing white clothing seemed impractical, and I could not understand the 'Indian' rather than Anglo-Indian style of dressing.

I insisted on paying for the taxi when we arrived at the station. My friend had told me that she never has so much as a cup of tea when she visits people applying for their children to go to the school—in most cases the reason they want a place for their children is that they are too poor to afford any schooling, so even this most basic hospitality would be a financial burden. I did not want to inflict this on these people, especially when I was the one who had requested this meeting. Once out of the taxi we fought our way through the crowds to the ticket office, then, keeping my eyes fixed on their backs I followed them to a carriage on the Diamond Harbour-bound train. Only once we were seated did I have a chance to talk to my hosts properly.

Peter told me that he sometimes worked on these trains, and that his wife was at home cooking lunch for me. So much for my resolve not to be a burden: I wondered when it would be best to give them the money I had for them. The welfare officer said this would be welcome, and suggested I put it in an envelope to give to them. Their son was also at home waiting to meet me; he had just one more week before school started again and then he wouldn't see his family for months. Lisa was at a boarding school in the city and she was due back there in a week as well. She talked about the subjects she was studying and exams she was soon to sit. She told me, and Peter confirmed, that she had been working hard over the break to prepare herself.

Forty-five minutes and numerous scheduled stops later we had arrived at their station. A four rupee cycle-rickshaw trip brought us to their home. I had lost my sense of direction as soon as we had turned into one, then another, of the narrow and unevenly surfaced lanes. We passed small children sitting on concrete-block doorsteps right on the edge of the lane, and numerous shops that were no bigger than a wardrobe, with the owner perched cross-legged on the waist-high counter. There was a certain economy of movement about this arrangement—he could reach all of his stock from this sitting position.

I had spent over a month in the city by this time, mainly in the central city areas, as well as visited friends in Lake Gardens several times, but there was something quite different about this area. It took me a number of headscarf sightings before I realised that we were now in a Muslim-dominated area, whereas everywhere else I had been had been predominantly Hindu. There were mostly children and men in the lanes, but the occasional woman I saw was covered from head to toe. Lisa told me later that she had to dress modestly in this orthodox area, which explained the salwar kameez.

We dismounted from the rickshaw at a gate, stepped over a concrete ledge and walked along a narrow path to a curtained doorway, and stepped inside. I was introduced to Maya: a sweet-faced woman in a sari who greeted me shyly, wiping her floured hands as she stood up from her crouching position in the corner of the room. A 180-degree visual sweep of the room and I had taken in the sum of their home and contents: one large double bed, a dressing table, a wardrobe, a showcase and beside it a small desk tucked in a corner with a lamp strung above. On the pale blue washed walls was a picture of 'The Last Supper' with two little cards of Mother Teresa pinned to it and a red light above. There was a statue of the Virgin Mary, plastic flowers and a carved box on an eye-level-high altar beside it. A few feet above the corner where Maya had been crouching was a deep curtained shelf that they used for storage. Below that was a set of stacked storage baskets and beside it their cooker. This was where Maya had been busy working when we had arrived — cooking a tomato dish for our lunch.

We sat on their firm bed to eat, around a pretty patterned table cloth with all the dishes she had prepared displayed on it — along with the tomato dish were serving dishes of matter paneer, *gobi* and *aloo* (cauliflower and potato curry) and a vegetable I didn't recognise (perhaps okra or 'lady's fingers'), a salad, rice with peas and the softest and flakiest parathas. This feast was served warm, and all cooked on a single-burner kerosene stove with a cut-out tin can surrounding three of its sides to protect it from draughts. I had brought my own bottled water and excused my drinking it rather than what they'd offered, explaining that I had a weak stomach. I was always cautious about water but didn't want to offend them.

After lunch Peter made me a glass of delicious hot sweet milky coffee. That was the first of many coffees he made me. After that initial meeting, I visited Peter and his family on many occasions, frequently being invited to share a meal, and a good part of the day with them.

I wanted to record Peter's life story as part of my project. He consented but I never managed to get much on tape because of his shyness about being more formally interviewed. He was happy to talk about his life — but only on auto-rickshaw trips, or when we were sitting around over a meal with his family or when he walked me back after spending time with his family. I have pieced together some of what I had learned of his life to write this account, which he has approved.

He was born and brought up in a poor, very congested, inner suburb of Calcutta. The third of four sons, his schooling finished in the middle of second grade. He refers to himself as 'an uneducated man'. The truth of this was revealed to me on one of my visits that coincided with his and Maya's wedding anniversary. I arrived at their home and gave him and Maya an anniversary card. Initially, to my puzzlement, Peter pocketed the card unopened. Later, when Lisa arrived home he passed it to her to read to them. The explanation offered by him was that he could not read, due to his curtailed education. He explained further, telling me that his mother decided that he should stay at home and cook for the family instead of going to school. His mother was a schoolteacher, so perhaps she thought she could educate him at home, but that never happened. When he told me this he became visibly upset. I was unprepared for this and regretted causing him the embarrassment he obviously felt. I was reminded of Bourgois' (Bourgois, 1996) fieldwork incident when he inadvertently drew attention to the illiteracy of one of the key players in his research, 'Ray', a crack house owner who was also illiterate. The incident nearly jeopardised Bourgois' whole project as a result of humiliating a key player in his research. Although my fieldwork incident was not as dramatic, it marked an important realisation about illiteracy within this community.

Some of Peter's early childhood memories include delivering lunch to his elder brothers at their school. From early on he had the responsibility of preparing the evening meal in time for his mother's return after her day of classroom teaching followed by private tuitions. His father was a driver[1] in Calcutta but Peter referred to him so infrequently in his discussions that I am left with the feeling of little family involvement or influence from him. His mother, on the other hand, was described by various family members as 'ferocious'. The job his father had was eventually taken over by one of the older brothers. Another brother was able to spend time overseas continuing his education. There

---

[1] In some countries the term 'chauffeur' might be used where Anglo-Indians and Indians refer to 'drivers'.

is no question that Peter is bitter that his two elder brothers were given opportunities that he was denied. He attributes his present situation to parental partiality.

He and Maya married while they were both in their teenage years. Maya is from a Muslim family. Peter says he 'converted her' to Christianity and to 'being Anglo-Indian'.

Peter and his family have moved since my first visit and now live not far from the place they grew up. Like many very poor Anglo-Indians, they still live in an almost exclusively Muslim area. They are the only Christians in the vicinity and the only English speakers—a mother tongue for Peter, an adopted one for Maya. They now live on the fourth floor of an old apartment block. A maze of narrow lanes must be negotiated to find their building. In places the space between buildings is so narrow and shadowed that it feels like an internal passageway. Peter says you can jump from one building to the next where the buildings are of the same height; something that is handy to know if you are a keen kite-flyer (as many Anglo-Indians are). Going up to their floor there is no stairway lighting—even in the middle of the day it took a good few seconds for my eyes to adjust to the dimness. On the way up to their home, we passed rooms that were being used for various forms of light industry and manufacturing. A group of women were sewing caps and t-shirts; leather was in various stages of treatment and in one small poorly ventilated room a group of six or seven young boys, aged from what looked like about 7 to 13, were stitching leather wallets and bags for export.

Peter pays ₹100 (a little over US$2.50) per month for a home that is quite central and bigger than their last home. Water is delivered and paid for as they need it, and power, used primarily to run the ceiling fan, costs about ₹40 per month. They have access to a fridge in which they can store a little meat and fish.

Peter gave me the impression that he feels very isolated and alone where they live. He said that he doesn't talk to anyone, and that he stays in the house except when he comes and goes from work, and Maya locks herself in when he is away. Where they now live is more central and larger, plus they have their own bathroom, but a trade-off has been that they are no longer very close to a railway station.

Peter's mode of earning a living for himself and his family is through selling infant's t-shirts. It is very insecure, in terms of both the money he makes and his physical safety. At one stage he owned a sewing machine, which he used to sew the t-shirts but now buys them for ₹10 (US$0.33) from a local 'Mohammedan' (to use Peter's expression) woman, and sells them for ₹15 (US$0.50). He had to sell the machine several years ago when Lisa became sick and he needed the money to cover the medical treatment.

Peter makes an average of ₹40–50 (US$1.50–1.70) per day (from the sale of 8–10 t-shirts). This leaves him absolutely on the breadline. In the past he restricted his sales to people on trains or on station platforms. When he lived close to a railway station, he didn't need to spend any of his income on transport. Now that he lives further away from easy access to a station, he sells on the roadside and in public parks, as well as on the trains.

Two incidents give an indication of the precariousness of his life. As if it's not tough enough that he spends all day making barely enough for his family to survive, there are days when even doing a day's work is interrupted. One day, for example, Peter was selling wares on the trains during a license inspection. To trade on the trains vendors require a license—yet another cost. As his license needed renewing, he and others in the same situation were taken to a lock-up for the day. They had no food or water for the entire day, were fined and eventually allowed to leave. He arrived home late, and upset.

On another occasion when I was visiting, Peter was again late in arriving home. The later it became, the more Maya fretted for him. While we waited for his return, I was told of an incident that had led to his late return the previous week: He was selling in an open, public garden area when he noticed a girl on a bridge close to him. He guessed she was about the same age as his daughter and it looked to him as if she was about to jump off into the deep water below. He called out to her and ran and grabbed her before she could jump. He caught her from behind and held her there as a group gathered around them. What began as a spontaneous, life-saving gesture rapidly came to be seen in a different light by some members of the group. They accused him of behaving inappropriately with her. The police were called; interviews were conducted with the girl, Peter and witnesses from the park. The girl's parents were contacted. All this while he was being held by the police. Eventually his version of events was believed and he was allowed to return home. He arrived back late, and distressed, with very little to show for his long day away. He relies on public transport to get to and from wherever he is working. If he is late in returning home he has no way to contact his family as they don't have a telephone and are unlikely ever to afford one.

The precariousness of his life has made him determined that his children are not left in the same situation. He said to me on numerous occasions that his lack of education is his downfall. He told me that he had wanted to emigrate to find a better life somewhere, anywhere, else. After saving and spending ₹800 in getting a passport issued, he is reconciled to the fact that he will never ever use it because even though he would work hard, as he says, 'no country will take an uneducated man'. He knows it is too late for him but it is not too late for his children. His ambition for years has been for his children to gain a good education, including a degree and professional training and then to 'find a nice job'. Then he will stop working. Maya echoed his sentiments when she said, 'What we don't have we want our children to have.'

The sense I had of him is that he is a man who assesses himself and finds that he is lacking in a significant aspect for Anglo-Indians, that of education, which he, accurately, links to employment prospects. He can see that it is too late to improve himself educationally, so he does what he can to improve the lives of those closest to him, and through them, his sense of selfhood will be enhanced. He has transferred his aspirations to his children and provides whatever he can to improve their chances of achieving what he cannot. Both he and Maya take a keen interest in their work and their grades, while showering them with love and affirmation. It is only through his children's success (which he measures largely by their educational achievement and, through that, their employment and material comfort) that he can augment his own being. If his children are successful, he will be more generous in assessing himself.

Their dream for their children is becoming a reality: when I revisited them in November 2009 Lisa had completed her TTC and is completing a Bachelor's degree by distance-learning while she works at an Anglo-Indian school full time as a teacher. She is engaged to a Bengali boy who has his own small electronics business. Peter and Maya's son, who seemed to have grown half a metre in the couple of years since I saw him last, was in his last year of a computer engineering degree at one of the best universities in Calcutta. He is affectionately good-humoured with his parents and, like his sister, has well-developed social skills with which to engage a visiting anthropologist.

Peter and Maya have every reason to feel proud of the job they have done as parents: they have managed to provide for their children what they themselves had missed out on. Besides actively encouraging their education, they have supported them emotionally. Their children are now well placed educationally, vocationally and socially to lead lives of dignity and options. I will be interested to follow them into their adult lives as I keep in touch with Peter and Maya.

In the next story, Michael Robertson makes a plea based on the experiences of people such as Peter and Maya and their family. He sees the remedy to poverty and its accompanying indignities in achieving a good education, just as Peter does.

8

Michael Robertson: Education and the Community

When I spent Christmas in Calcutta in 2007 I saw Michael Robertson twice—and on both occasions he took a central role in the events occurring. The first time was on a balmy December evening at the Calcutta Racecourse where, in his role as chairperson of Dr Graham's Homes' board, he introduced to the several thousand guests the 'Children's City' choir—a group of 30–40 Homes' students who had come down from Kalimpong in the Himalayas for their annual fund-raising concert. They sang a range of songs, from Western show themes to Bollywood, from old medley favourites to Indian nationalist anthems. The next time was at Calcutta's St Paul's Cathedral, once again with the choir, this time for a performance of hymns and Christmas Carols, which began in the light of a single candle in the darkened church with a spine-tingling boy soprano rendition of the carol, 'Once in Royal David's City'.

I had interviewed him four years back; he was then in his 50s, looking fit and prosperous in an impeccably cut suit, a full head of grey hair and a tan that he could well have acquired in the Mediterranean. My initial short interview was in the offices of Dr Graham's Homes where he'd come to attend to some school business. As I waited in the high-ceilinged office for him to finish his business with Kelvin, one of the Homes' committee members, I noticed that Kelvin had adopted an uncharacteristically deferential manner with this well-spoken slightly older man. Michael was enthusiastically but impatiently running an idea past him: 'We could set up a florist shop for the floriculture graduates, or a bigger concern, a Himalayan Products' shop.' Impatiently dismissing Kelvin's worry that 'the CMC would need to grant building consent, and that will be a problem', Michael countered with 'I have a building contractor company. We can do it. A little shop on the premises and a cool-store room for the flowers. Perhaps here in Birkmyre [hostel] somewhere'. If anyone can do it, he can. This is the man who got Calcutta's Vedic Village, an ayurvedic retreat, a wellness centre, up and running in a little over nine months.

Finished with Kelvin, but still fired up, he met with me and in the little time he had, gave me a quick rundown of his views on a number of issues: His embarrassment at older Anglo-Indians who hold on to their British past; of the Dr Graham's Homes' graduates who are *not* typical of Calcutta Anglo-Indians having been brought up in the hills; of his own and the O'Briens' success 'in business, in India—which is the real test'. And of the Anglo-Indians who he believes will be gone in just another generation, using his own daughter as an illustration: 'She has no links to Anglo-Indians. She's completely assimilated. Her cohorts are her Indian Uni friends.'

He offered to meet again for a proper interview to talk about Calcutta's Anglo-Indians, in a few days' time at his offices. He also suggested that I talk to Barry O'Brien,[1] 'who wants to be the next Anglo-Indian leader. Find out what it is he wants to be the leader of', he suggested, before graciously dismissing me.

The following Monday I made my way to his central city offices. He greeted me warmly and showed me into a tiny modern office, which seemed to double as the board room squeezing in a glass-topped table, six chairs and an air-conditioning unit—the latter essential but creating a noisy background for recording an interview. He was extremely generous with his time—giving me two hours, along with the always-appreciated Anglo-Indian hospitality of coffees and biscuits.

He discussed a range of issues, but what I focus on here is what he was most passionate about: Anglo-Indian welfare through education. He began by telling me of his own background, which I also include here. For this story, I use interview transcript pieced together into a first person narrative. I've used pullout quotes as subheadings to break up the narrative and to highlight significant themes. Michael takes up the story from here:

---

[1] He became West Bengal's Anglo-Indian MLA from 2006 to 2011. At Michael's advice, I did interview Barry and his story is also featured in this work.

Dad always involved himself in social causes. He was a trustee of his old school, St James, for 40 years. That's a long service and he was also a trustee of the girls' school, Pratt Memorial. There were the two schools, Pratt and St James with the Church between. We lived just close to them in Lower Circular Road. So you know we involved ourselves in the church community around us. In fact my grandmother, for as long as she was in India, went to St James' Church every single day of her life till she went back to the UK. They supported the church a lot and we went to St James too, my older brother and I. And my sister who's four years younger than me went to the Pratt. We finished our senior year there, which was class eleven in those days. Nowadays it's ten plus two. Then I went on to college—St Xavier's in Calcutta. Around the time I was going, in the 1960s, we felt certain changes happening around us.

Up until then our lives had been quite isolated: We came from an Anglican background, were taught in the church school, which was an English medium school, an Anglo-Indian school. And then Sunday school was compulsory for us too, every Sunday. We were taught music, Western music. I used to play the piano, my brother used to play the violin. So we were brought up with a generally English background. So we were very isolated from what was India.

My Anglo-Indian Friends Had Gone

At that time Anglo-Indians were an insulated group; the friends of my parents were largely Anglo-Indian, or British. And perhaps many Anglo-Indians didn't get the kind of exposure that I got. But in the late 1950s and early 1960s emigration proceeded so fast and suddenly young people like me, who were twelve and thirteen or so, found they had no friends. All my Anglo-Indian friends had gone. They'd all gone. All the families that had been our friends, the ones that met every Sunday or weekends, who used to mix and go out together, my parents' friends, they all disappeared.

It must have been very tough on my parents and a tough decision to stay back in India. Now my father always took a stand that he had a good job, and he wasn't prepared to start all over again. He was perfectly happy where he was and so when his brothers and sisters and their friends also went off... And they didn't have it easy outside there remember. They didn't have it easy. Some had no money at all and they had to re-establish themselves. You know, all these great success stories that used to come back were often quite coloured. I think my father was intelligent enough to see the reality. But it was the ones who stayed behind who had to justify their decision.

There Was a Different India outside Your Home

Now having lost those friends I started seriously mixing with other communities. We used to visit each other's houses. We started talking in each other's languages and you got to know that there was a different India outside your home. It was a real revelation. I think it was a new understanding. And obviously you then tend to go the other way: You get very Indian. I started wearing Indian clothing. I started growing my hair.

Now I lost my mother when I'd just started college. I was just 17 when she died. My father was a very strict parent as long as we were in school. The day I entered college, he let go off the reins. He felt I was an adult I guess. He said I had to lead my own life. And I was a good guy in the sense that I was a very good student. I used to study hard. I never needed any threats or anything to do my work. I was a model student in many ways. My brother wasn't; he was a bit of a rebel. He didn't go to college and eventually he went off to Australia and married an Anglo-Indian girl and they settled there, and never came back. I was the one who was very different in the family. My father accepted it very well I must say. I think it was because of the fact that I had stayed behind in India. I mean he understood that I had to find my own identity. And he respected my friends and the people around me. He was well respected too.

I took on the role of taking care of the family when my mother died. I used to manage the finances. I used to manage the house. I used to manage the servants and everything. I was only 17 and my sister was only 14 or 13 at the time. I have another sister too, and she was fairly young when mum died.

Outside I was getting influenced a lot by the politics of the day, which was also changing in India. It was the late 1960s and early 1970s. It was a time of political turbulence around the world in fact, if you think about it. Young people were definitely gravitating to a rebellious outlook.

My three years in college were fairly turbulent, but again I had to study hard. It was also very difficult being in college. Exams got delayed because of the political situation. You sometimes had to walk into an exam with your shirt open because you knew your paper could be grabbed away from you and torn up, and then you'd have to re-sit the exam. That was always on our mind; that protestors might rush into the classroom and tear up your paper. So you used to find a position at the back of the class where you'd get more warning, you see. You'd stick it into the front of your shirt if they came in. So that's the way we had to study. I mean those were tough, tough times. One or two of my friends completely joined in. They took it to extremes, and were killed. Killed! So we grew up in a politically conscious environment. Very political.

The Week I Left College I Got a Job

I was very lucky that the week I left college I got a job, and that was at the height of the recession. Jobs were very difficult to come by. I joined a company called Andrew Yule, which was a managing agency house, a multi-product company. It was into tea and paper and engineering and welding and lubricants and it was huge. We used to manage a lot of companies. I joined that company straight out from college. I was just 20. And I had to cut my hair reasonably short. Even into the 1980s I had very long hair.

I had a BSc Honours in Physics and joined up as a management trainee and eventually finished 23 years later with that company as a general manager. I had planned to do my Master of Business Administration (MBA) but what happened was that as a result of the delays in my examinations I lost a whole year for entering. And I'd got a job, whereas many of my friends in college couldn't get a job. After a year in the company I had planned to go back and do my MBA. But the new term came and I had to take the decision and I decided to stay back with the company. My father was furious at that time because he wanted me to get that qualification. But I promised him that I would continue my studies. I said I would do it once I was further along in the company. He was not convinced. He wasn't at all convinced but, you know, I was over 21 by then. I had to decide my own career and I took a decision, and it was right in the long term. I did very well. And I mean I still haven't given up studying. I pick up a management book every day and I do something to keep up to date, because if you're not up to date today you're lost.

So I stayed on with Andrew Yule and it grew very fast. Then I got an opportunity to go to the UK to study at Leeds University for a year under the Colombo Plan. I was able to make quite an impact when I came back. I convinced the company that it had to privatise. I played a very key role in its transition from a private company to a public sector company.

In fact, I met my wife at Andrew Yule a few years later. Marguerite was working there, although she left for another job soon after we married. She had a bachelor's degree in microbiology and a master's in chemistry, first class, from Bombay University. So she's very well educated.

There Was This Meeting of Anglo-Indians

When I was only about 22 years old I knew I had to find my own identity, but it was very much away from the community. I never had anything to do with my community. I didn't even know anybody from the community and I sort of rejected it. I was staying as far away from it as I possibly could. But one day my father said to me there's this meeting of Anglo-Indians, and he said they were young Anglo Indians trying to find their way in a new sort of direction, and would I attend the meeting. So I went to this meeting with him. It was there that I met some people who thought like me; very intelligent young people, including Philomena Eaton.

They were mostly older than me by about 10 years, but what they were saying was very much in the language that I felt very strongly about: That the community had to have its own identity in this new context. That education was a very strong issue in terms of the community and its protection. That employment was important.

Anglo-Indian Children Have to Be Protected in the System

What happened around that time too was that because my father was so interested in children's education, from an administrative point, and he was on the boards of schools, I started looking at his interest.

I always say that India should recognise the fact that Anglo-Indians have the right to teach in English and nobody else has and, therefore, you know, the Anglo-Indian children have to be protected in the system in which the education is generated. Now all these schools call themselves Anglo-Indian schools. Now this gets into a very sensitive area which I have considered all my life and I think I will go to the grave being strong about. People are a little scared of me because I make this point very, very strongly: the West Bengal government gives huge sums of money under the DA, the dearness allowance. It's a grant given to a minority to protect their interests. And they give it to schools, to teachers who teach in Anglo-Indians schools. Okay? So almost 30 per cent of the salary, or 40 per cent of the salaries of teachers in these schools were paid for by the government because they were teaching Anglo-Indian children. This is a unique thing in the Constitution of India.

If you want to know more you've got to read [Frank] Anthony's book because it covers all these points in great detail. Now the right to teach English, for example, is protected in the Constitution (because Anthony was one of the writers of the Constitution). So my argument is that if you have the right to teach English only because of this community, you have to ensure that this community is educated. And even if you have to subsidise that education for Anglo-Indians at each and every school, then you have to do it.

The Anglo-Indian schools are the top schools in Calcutta. People line up to get admitted. They'd pay anything to get into these schools. And they do. There's a lot of talk of corruption, unfortunately. And if these schools have survived because of the Anglo-Indian community then they've got to protect Anglo-Indians in that system.

The Community Is Becoming Backward

The community has been becoming backward; Dr Graham's Homes is an example of how much in backwardness the community has gone. And I recognised this problem only after this meeting with these people that my dad had told me about. It had been a genteel, a wealthy community at one point of time, and slowly, because of migration and the loss of jobs, they started moving into slums. Like Tiljala. Tiljala shocked me. I was shocked that I was living in the city and I had no knowledge of the circumstances of our people in Tiljala.

Anglo-Indian Week

I was one of the proponents of something called the Anglo-Indian week and in 1973 we put on a great show. I was the secretary of that week. At 22 I was very young, and I remember that I took on the whole of the design because of my greater knowledge etc. Many of the functions which we still run, we ran then, for instance: the crowning of the Anglo-Indian queen, the football match, and we brought in all the folks from the old age homes and we gave them a huge party. They still continue that even today. I mean those little slogans, those names for the old folks at home, 'handful of happiness', things like that are still done even today. And then there was the Derozio elocution contest named after Henry Derozio, the Anglo-Indian poet. Well I devised the Derozio elocution contest because I believed that elocution had moved poetry to language. That Derozio contest still continues today.

We had a song and balloons and that sort of thing, and we had a seminar where we talked of issues. As a consequence of that I became the secretary of the Anglo-Indian Association. Now that gave me my first exposure to the community leadership of Frank Anthony.

I Used to Train Boys and Girls around My Table

I used to work very hard for the community at that time, you know. I used to train boys and girls around my table in physics and chemistry and maths because those are the weak subjects.

Hindi was a weak subject too but we had Hindi teachers to do that. But since my strength was physics and chemistry, I used to offer for anybody who came. I said, 'You come and learn with me.' And there were many; Barry O'Brien was one of them. He'll tell you that. I then started getting recognised in the school community and I got on my first board position at the age of 23. I was invited on the St Paul's Mission Board, then on my school board, St James, at the age of 24. Then St Thomas' Kidderpore, St Thomas' Howrah and Julian Day School. That was all around the same time. So you know at a very young age I started understanding the intricacies of education.

But then I began to get very unpopular because I started saying, 'Why aren't Anglo-Indians protected in these schools? Why is it that they drop out after year 8 or 9 or 10? Why is it that we can't give special coaching in Hindi and keep the kids in school? Why is it that they don't have their textbooks and exercise books on time?' Because, you know, the school can subsidise these books because they've got to keep these kids in school to get recognised as an Anglo-Indian school! But I felt that all of this was generally hidden from the government. We were talking numbers but we were talking numbers at nursery, first, second, third classes. And when it came to 11 and 12, there were no children. They had all dropped out.

For the Community to Survive It's Got to Put Education First

So I questioned as to why we were not getting Anglo-Indians passing in grades 8, 9 and 10, and I said, 'If these children come in at nursery levels. They're admitted at the right age, which is three or four. They come in knowing English. Then what happens?' This is the same thing I do even in Dr Graham's Homes. I challenge my principal. I challenge everybody, my teachers, everybody. I said, 'Why are these children dropping out?'

I believe that for the community to survive it's got to put education first. The kids have to be educated. And they've got to be educated correctly. They've got to get into school at the right age because it's a tough curriculum today in India, and it's very competitive. They've got to be supported by special coaching classes because the paying students have private tuitions and private tuitions are rammed into the schools. It's shocking but it's true.

So these kids, to be equal to any of the other children, have got to be given those tuitions and I feel it's the responsibility of all Anglo-Indian schools, who are minting money in education, to provide this service to the community. And I don't hesitate to say it. Unfortunately I'm not on any boards at the moment, though I still have a very strong say when it comes to education and I have the power of the press behind me. I have a lot of friends in the press. And I don't hesitate to make the point when I have to. If the community's to survive it's got to be education first.

I believe very strongly that education is going to be the survival of the community and nothing else. I tell these boys in Birkmyre [Hostel], I say, 'You have to go through college.' Once they're through college, whatever it is they study, they will find a job. But they have that base to go forward. If they come to me as a graduate I can get them jobs. They've got good personalities; they talk well, so you know....

We scrub them up and you put them in front of somebody and they can lick the pants off anybody else. If they're clever then they can. But the school has to support them. What happens to a child who comes into class today? The cost of books is so expensive. Now that's something I recognised in the seventies. And what I do is I get my friends in the entertainment world and we to get together at a concert in December and we raise money. That money is distributed to as many Anglo-Indian children as possible to provide them with exercise books from day one. I also used to attack teachers who humiliated these children in classrooms because they didn't have their books. I said, 'It's not their fault.' And the principals who made the children stand outside the classroom because they didn't have their books. I said, 'They're losing in education', and I was not liked for saying these things. It didn't suit the image of the school, you know.

Through Education They'll Definitely Better Themselves

They'll take great pride in themselves, I hope. Through education they'll definitely better themselves. I'll give you an example of two boys in Dr Graham's Homes: it was prize day and I noticed that these kids were getting very good marks with a lot of prizes. Later I was wandering about the campus I met them and I said, 'You get to 80 per cent in class 12 and I'll send you abroad to study.' That was a challenge which they got very excited about. No kids from Dr Graham's school had ever been abroad to study. I looked at it; it was about £30,000 per year which I said we could drum up. And I said if we send them out for two years they'll be able to survive. It was just after I had come back from the UK and I knew what the costs were.

Two years later both of them came to me. Colin was definitely the cleverer of the two boys. They'd excelled, both had done great in their exams, both had applied for colleges in the UK and both had been accepted. But education had jumped to seven thousand pounds a year and we could therefore only support one. Sadly it was the second boy, Shane. Shane did very well to pursue it and also to find subsidies through friends in the UK. So he managed: he got through, and he went on to study hospitality management. He's been in the US for three years and is doing exceeding well. I've got to say, it was paid for by a person in Calcutta for him to get to the UK. Some people are very generous that way. You get friends who just say, 'I'll do it'. And he went, but the other boy was devastated. He said, 'I'll not study', and it took another committee member of mine to talk to him. I mean, you know, he was so rude to us. He still tries to avoid talking to me. But I said, 'You get into St Xavier's College, do an economics honours.' St Xavier's has one of the highest standards that you can get. 'You do your economics' honours, postgraduate, and I'll see that you go.' It was a tough time getting him to go into college because he really didn't want to go. But eventually he did and then I encouraged him to study Japanese and sit for an exam in a scholarship scheme. He passed that exam with a first and secured an electronics engineering scholarship in Japan. He's currently studying in Japan and probably he will come back here a very rich man.

I don't know if Shane will come back, but if he does he'd come back to a top job. He went on to work in some big hotels in America. But I hope these kids will come back. They've got brothers and sisters who they can encourage to also study. But what it did for Dr Graham's Homes! It really stimulated them. The children started recognising that if they worked hard and they went to college that they could succeed, like those kids.

I've Sent Four of Them to Japan

I've sent four of them to Japan now. One was a girl who went to Japan to study floriculture. She's completed and she's back here. And what I'm trying to do now is trying to get her to recruit a lot of the boys and girls who have not done so well in class and train them to work with her in the wedding planning industry. Now you know people laugh sometimes when I suggest these things, but there's a market for it. It will take you way ahead of anything else you could do. You've got to think of new industries. You can't only think of the old ways of working. I'm thinking that as a wedding planner, there's a huge market in this country. You know, you have to design everything from the invitations right down to the last detail. There's big money in it. The music industry is also a huge business. And the television industry is huge business today. You know communications has just taken off, so there are huge opportunities in these industries.

This is why I brought the kids to Calcutta to see all this. When they come down for the children's city concert I show them around. For that first concert I also sent a personal invitation to literally everyone I knew, and there were two and a half thousand people there eventually. It was brilliant. I was able to showcase the kids' talent. I picked up four and a half lakhs for that function.[2] I got it sponsored from friends and we finally got four and a half lakhs. But I also got people interested in helping these kids out. I mean, you know people then started recognising, 'Hey, these kids have talent. They can sing beautifully.'

It's important to get these breaks. They need to make their futures here because, first of all, the doors are closed. Most countries have closed their doors. It's not easy to get into Australia and it's not easy to get to New Zealand. So you know I don't think all that migration will happen anymore. So that's another reason why they've got to be good here. They've got to be good here and they've got to find their feet. This is something I think they've got to recognise, that they cannot count on leaving.

So They'll Integrate

They're going to be mixing with Bengali kids anyway, and many are going to inter-marry, so they'll integrate. They've got to appreciate that there's still a lot of prejudice in this country. Really there's an enormous amount of prejudice. More than 50 years on from Independence there is tremendous prejudice against the community. Let's not wipe away that fact if a girl wanted to marry into another Indian community, there's always resistance. There's resistance not from us but from the other community, which is very strong. So there's a tremendous problem with that. Many of our girls get hurt; badly hurt because of that, and that's why perhaps their parents feel it's better to get them away, get them out of the country. There's less prejudice outside this country.

[2] A lakh is ₹100,000, which is approximately US$9,500.

Michael has himself followed the advice he enthusiastically gives to young Anglo-Indians, and has made a full and comfortable life in Calcutta. He has a high profile in the city and is well respected—both within the community and more generally. He regularly makes it into the press with his latest career moves—in 1997 as the new manager and chief executive officer of the Tollygunge Club, and then there was another peak of press interviews when he left that position five years later and took up his current role as chief executive officer of Vedic Village. In 2003, when I interviewed him, the construction was all but completed and the village was to be opened just a few weeks later. I had no doubt that it was ready on the day.

When I returned in late 2009 I spent an evening with Michael and Marguerite at the Bengal Club. There they filled me in with what had happened since I recorded the interview with Michael. The biggest and most exciting news was that Priyanca had married a young Anglo-Indian man, a captain in the Army, earlier in the year. They married at St Paul's, marking its first military and Anglican wedding in 45 years. Michael said it was a very happy day, and a real celebration for the family, as well as for Anglo-Indians. Priyanca's new husband shares her long-held love of equestrian sports and they have settled down in Jaipur. Before she married she completed postgraduate studies in England. She now works in Jaipur as a teacher of special needs children.

Marguerite has recently taken voluntary retirement but has involved herself in two other jobs, both voluntary: two days a week she spends time at St Joseph's Rest Home where she carries out menial duties, including clipping resident's toenails. In a socially hierarchical society such as India's, especially with its Hindu milieu emphasising bodily purity, this is a remarkable act of charity. Her other job involves one day a week folding old newspapers and magazines into little bags from which medicines are dispensed from the various outposts of Mother Teresa's order.

Michael was as busy, and gracious, as ever—finding time to read and comment on what I've presented here. Much of his working life is currently spent on Vedic Village concerns. The enterprise has become known as one of India's premier spa resorts and is soon to be incorporated into an international luxury hotel chain. He is still on the Dr Graham's Homes board, completing 15 years as their chairperson. He assured me that his belief in the importance of education hadn't changed since I'd interviewed him; in fact, he thinks the problems for Anglo-Indian are even more complex now, and he is convinced that a good education is the only way forward for his community. He was happy to say that there were currently over 70 Dr Graham's Homes' old boys and girls studying at tertiary level, one of whom is enrolled in an MBA programme.

After the essay in which I explore some of the ideas Michael talked about, we meet Phillip, a young man who is enacting exactly what Michael believes to be the way forward. And the results are impressive.

9
Essay: Reflections on Dilemmas in Education[#]

Introduction

One wintry December Sunday, on an early fieldwork trip, I spent the morning in the rooms used by an Anglo-Indian social service organisation assisting and observing older, frail, Anglo-Indians collect their rations and pensions. As they lined up and collected their envelope of money and heavy bags of food, I noticed, to my surprise, that many of the recipients were signing for their pension with a thumbprint instead of a signature. This was during my second prolonged fieldwork trip to the city and came as a complete surprise to me because by this time I had assimilated the 'doxic' or taken-for-granted notion: that in India a person who was able to speak English must be literate. The idea of an illiterate English speaker in the Indian context seemed like an oxymoron, so completely taken for granted is the idea that fluency in English is equivalent to literacy.

By this time I had met Peter but the anniversary card incident hadn't yet occurred. Even when it did I thought of it as an isolated incident for some time. However, because Peter had referred to himself as *an uneducated man* so many times, and I knew of his dire financial situation and prospects, he was in my mind when I interviewed Michael Robinson. Peter's situation was an extreme version of what Michael was trying to protect the next generation of Anglo-Indians from becoming. Peter and Michael's life stories exemplify the different life chances available to those with and without educational capital (and all the other forms of capital that

---

[#] A version of this chapter has been published as 'English in India: Reflections Based on Fieldwork among Anglo-Indians in Calcutta', in *India Review* by Routledge (Andrews, 2006b).

follow, or accompany it). Philip's story, next, demonstrates what someone who is making the most of those life chances can achieve. In this essay, I look for ways that more Anglo-Indians might have this success, which includes teasing out several of Michael's ideas.

The paradoxical situation of illiterate English speakers is just one of the ironies that characterise Anglo-Indians' relationship with the Indian education system and the English language. Another is that though Anglo-Indians founded many of the elite schools in India and continue to be significantly involved in their administration and teaching, thus contributing to the lives of privileged Indians, it is widely accepted that Anglo-Indians are the most disadvantaged students in these schools (Gilbert, 1996; Lobo, 1996a, 1996b). Yet another is that, even though English is the most highly valued language in India (in practice if not in theory), the fact that it is Anglo-Indians' native tongue seems to bring them no advantage.

In this essay, as with others in this book, I address these paradoxes and ironies as an anthropologist committed to public anthropology. Public anthropology, Borofsky (2006) says, is explicitly concerned with fostering social change. It is easy, in thinking about this dimension of public anthropology, to think that only those forms of anthropology that call for radical change can be counted as being in the spirit of this goal. In actual fact, I would suggest, it is the modest challenges to the status quo that are more likely to succeed. The policy prescription I conclude with in this essay might seem *trivial* to some but in actual fact would, if implemented, have very significant impact on the lives of individuals. Public anthropology should be concerned with issues of social justice and equity. It should not be a surprise that some very small steps can achieve real progress in relation to those goals.

In addition to Peter, Michael and Philip's life stories, in this essay I draw on additional short case studies to highlight the particular social situation of illiterate and poorly educated English speakers. Peter's experiences highlight this particularly poignantly. On the other hand, Philip's story (and that of Jane's, placed earlier on this book) illustrates the way that lives can be completely turned around through the advantages of education.

One of the goals of this essay is to promote a move towards recognising English as just another language of the land. Through this recognition, the expectations of literacy on those for whom it is a 'mother tongue' may come into line with expectations made of other vernacular language speakers. This may seem to be a contradiction of my aims, but it would, in important ways, take some of the pressure of unresourced expectations from Anglo-Indians.

Anglo-Indians and the Education System

Anglo-Indians have been at the forefront of English-medium education in India and many are still involved in education at the highest levels. The converse is also the case. Anglo-Indians at the highest political levels are, or have been, involved with education. The last three MLAs for West Bengal, for example, were all teachers, principals or were owners of schools. Early indications from a recent survey of West Bengal's Anglo-Indians put teaching as the highest occupation group.[1]

They are generally considered an educated community based at least in part on their history. Briefly, an elite system of schools, modelled on the British system, was set up for the Anglo-Indian offsprings of European (mainly British) men.[2] The first school, for example, was set up in Madras in 1673 for children of British or Portuguese heritage to learn, in English, 'about English history and customs, so the company could "insure the continuation" of British customs and attitudes and to "provide trained recruits" for the East India Company' (Gilbert, 1996).

The schools were initially established for two main purposes: to educate and evangelise. Education was necessary so that Anglo-Indians could take up subordinate positions in the East India Company (which ran India's infrastructure for a century before the British government took over the role of administration of the

---

[1] This represents a shift from the time they were known as a community that worked on the railways; in fact, one researcher referred to them as the 'railways caste' (Bear, 2007).

[2] Lobo's *A Comparative Study of Educational Disadvantage within the Anglo-Indian Community* provides a comprehensive, and very readable, history of Anglo-Indian schools in India. Its focus is the exploration of reasons for Anglo-Indians not achieving in their own schools.

Indian Empire in 1858) and, later, in British India's government services. As Anglo-Indian scholar Ann Lobo argues, Christian missionaries considered 'the Anglo-Indian population as the ideal entry point' (Lobo, 1994: 34). The first schools were associated with churches and it is still the case today that most Anglo-Indian schools are affiliated with a church. They are referred to variously as Christian schools, English-medium schools and, of course, as Anglo-Indian schools.

The place of Anglo-Indian schools in the Indian education system was strengthened, when in 1835, Macauley (who at the time held responsibility for the education budget in India) presented to the government his now famous *Minute* in relation to the establishment of English-medium schools. One of his recommendations suggests that:

> It is possible to make natives of this country thoroughly good English scholars, and that to this end our efforts ought to be directed. It is impossible for us, with our limited means, to attempt to educate the body of the people. We must at present do our best to form a class who may be interpreters between us and the millions whom we govern; a class of persons, Indian in blood and colour, but English in taste, in opinions, in morals, and in intellect. To that class we may leave it to refine the vernacular dialects of the country, to enrich those dialects with terms of science borrowed from the Western nomenclature, and to render them by degrees fit vehicles for conveying knowledge to the great mass of the population. (Young, 1952: 729)

Although Macaulay's *Minute* is directed at the Indian population, Anglo-Indians were also seen as a class between the *Indian masses* and the British.

Anglo-Indian schools are part of the system of elite schools in India.[3] They have been prone to criticism, from some quarters, as

---

[3] I became aware that these are the preferred schools (for the English-medium education and the extra-curricular activities they offer) during periods of fieldwork through talking to Anglo-Indians and non-Anglo-Indians. This is supported by A. A. D'Souza who stated that '[t]he intrinsic quality and worth of Anglo-Indian education is today acknowledged by all sections of the Indian people, and in recent official Education Reports, these schools have been held up as models for other Indian schools' (1976: viii). I was interested to see that even the most cursory Internet search at the time I was writing this indicates that Anglo-Indian schools are listed amongst the top schools of India.

colonial institutions (Raman, 1996). Nevertheless, wealthy non-Anglo-Indians also compete for places in these schools.[4] As long ago as in 1969, Frank Anthony, an MP and president-in-chief, at the time, of the AIAIA wrote:

> The community, today, through its schools is in the educational vanguard. Anglo-Indian teachers are the best qualified to purvey education through the medium of English. The demand for entry into the Anglo-Indian schools remains clamant and insatiable. The long and increasing waiting lists of applicants to Anglo-Indian schools have to be seen to be believed. Ironically the most clamorous in the queue are the most raucous among the Hindu chauvinists. (Anthony, 1969: xii)

Given the Anglo-Indian involvement in English-medium schools, it was surprising to find a wide range in levels of educational achievement and, particularly unanticipated, to discover illiterate Anglo-Indians. Even without a knowledge of their background in education it seemed to me from early on in my research to be a widespread assumption that anyone who speaks English fluently is educated and, of course, literate. Therefore, finding illiterate people in this English-speaking community was unexpected.

English: A Language of Prestige?

In reading about the use and place of the English language in India, I soon became aware that the ability to speak English carries prestige, and that it is taken for granted in India that a speaker of English is an educated person and so, of course, literate (Green, 1998; Mee, 2001; Mishra, 2000; Raman, 1996). At the time of Independence, English was regarded as the language of the elites. It was the language of the government and the national language in a country where local dialects are most commonly used in the local regions. It is also the language of the constitution. The Indian Administrative Service (IAS) insists on its members being fluent in English and much of

---

[4] Lobo claims that '[t]hese schools are much sought after by wealthy non Anglo-Indian Indians, who want their children to acquire fluency in English' (1994: 33).

its business is carried out in English. The idea of English being the language of the elites is still pervasive and the acquisition of English language still aspired to.[5]

The fact that English is both necessary and desired is played out on an everyday basis. Small-scale local businesses, for example, may get by without English-speaking staff but larger businesses with international dealings will not, as invariably business transactions are carried out in English. The fact that many Anglo-Indian women in Calcutta are employed as tutors in conversational English language for the wives of Bengali businessmen is an indication of the desire for the English language.

Assumptions about literacy, education and being an English speaker are not restricted to non-academic circles. The following statements are indicative of the perceptions about English speakers. They deal in different ways with the issue of the place of English in the lives of Indians. Literary critic Jon Mee cites Aijaz Ahmad's observation that proper English exists solely in the elite domain: 'English was and still is often learnt in the context of the other Indian languages; *only the very top level of the private-school elite know English outside the broader unstable vernacular matrix of India*' (Mee, 2001, emphasis added). Nonetheless, the use of English carries important status cues across social classes in India. As political scientist Paul Brass so aptly notes: 'English remains the pre-eminent language of prestige and opportunity in India' (Brass, 2004: 372).

The comments are drawn from important contributions to the debates about the politics of language in India, and of the place of English in those politics. These two statements were made almost as 'asides'. The ideas about the speakers of English were not challenged in these articles, they were offered as general understandings. Similar statements could be found in a large number of contributions, irrespective of the specifics of the debates. What they

---

[5] At breakfast in Calcutta on the day I was to present the paper on the topic of this essay at a seminar at Centre for Studies in Social Sciences, Calcutta (CSSSC), I had a conversation with a man who was moving from Delhi to Calcutta. He had come over early to look for a home, and for a school for his four-year-old son. He told me that he had handed over the responsibility for finding a home to his employer, and would spend all his time looking for an English-medium school that would suit his Montessori English-medium pre-school educated son.

all—Jon Mee, Aijaz Ahmed, Paul Brass and others—assume in a deep and profound way, without any critical comment or analysis, is the idea that knowledge of English, and especially fluency in that language, is the road to a position in the elites of Indian society. If you are fluent in English, then you are a member of the elite. The congruence is absolute.

To complicate matters further it should be noted that the doxic idea that I have referred to is also shared by some influential Anglo-Indians; for example, Frank Anthony, who at the time was president-in-chief of the AIAIA, claimed that 'the community is cent-per-cent literate' (Anthony, 1969: ix). Ann Lobo also said that all those she met while conducting her fieldwork were literate (Lobo, 1994: 456) and she went to some of the same *bustees* that I went to where I met illiterate Anglo-Indians. I am not surprised, however, that she missed it. If I had not witnessed thumbprint signatures, and asked about it, and then had discussions with people I had come to know well about their level of literacy I also would have missed it. I would have assumed, like others in India do, that they spoke English, therefore, they were literate. This, perhaps, illustrates well, the value of participant-observation.

The doxa (Bourdieu and Wacquant, 1992: 73–74), or the absolutely taken-for-granted idea that I am drawing attention to, is the fundamental assumption that all English speakers with any fluency in the English language in India belong to a highly privileged elite with access to power and wealth. In addition, above all else, they are literate. In other words, in India, the idea of an illiterate English speaker verges on the oxymoronic.

Clearly, what this shows is that in discussions of the English language in India, and particularly of English speakers in India, Anglo-Indians have been entirely overlooked. Why is this and what does this omission tell us about understandings of language, community and status in India? It shows that Anglo-Indians are invisible in the national imagination. Although clearly Indian, they have been completely ignored. Their very invisibility is expressed in the ideas about English that I have referred to. In what follows, in the spirit of public anthropology, I set out to challenge this invisibility through a direct challenge to the doxic notions themselves.

Case Studies

Peter, whose story I have included earlier in this work, epitomises what I frequently saw in Calcutta. The sense I had of him is that he is a man who assesses himself and finds that he lacks 'being', in the Bourdieuian sense of the word. In Bourdieu's view people's sense of their social worth, or *being*, is crucially important, as illustrated when he writes: 'It is not true that everything that people do or say is aimed at maximising social profit; but one can say that they do it to perpetuate or to augment their social being' (Bourdieu, 1993a: 274). This idea was elaborated upon by Ghassan Hage at a social anthropology seminar given at Massey University in 1998, where he said that when considering social aspiration (the desire to be more that what one is) 'the question is not "to be or not to be?" but "how much to be?"'

Peter's unfulfilled aspiration for himself is one that is of particular significance to Anglo-Indians, and relates to having an education. The way in which he articulates his experiences and aspirations indicates quite clearly that he believes that the best way for him to improve his family's future is through his children. Besides focusing his aspirations on his children he supports them in whatever ways he can. The story of Peter's life is a particularly vivid example of the social suffering[6] of an illiterate English speaker.

The examples I now turn to, though briefer, highlight other dimensions of this paradox of being an English speaker yet having none of the prestige that is thought to accompany it.

During one fieldwork trip I met an older Anglo-Indian who I subsequently found was a street-dweller and beggar. He fitted the description of the sort of man I would perhaps approach if I needed directions or local advice. It had been my experience (as a tourist in India and Nepal, and as a researcher) that someone who looked *educated* was more likely to speak English and was able to

---

[6] Social Suffering, following Bourdieu, is the suffering that results from the experience of structural violence. Thus, in a country where English speaking and literacy are doxically equivalent, English speakers experience their lives as inherently contradictory. Bourdieu discusses this in a way particularly apt for this case in his discussion of the 'contradictions of inheritance' (Bourdieu, 1993b: 507–513).

assist me. Right or wrong, even wearing spectacles seemed a sign to me of a person's education, as was Western clothing. This man fitted the description: he was wearing spectacles and neatly pressed clothes, and he spoke English well. Had I sought advice from him I would have thought I was right in my assumptions about his educational status. I discovered subsequently that in fact he is almost illiterate and had only rudimentary education. His impoverished circumstances were not so unforeseen once I knew this.

Other examples of illiterate English speakers were those older, very poor members of the community, who, as I noted at the beginning of this essay, I frequently observed receiving pensions distributed by an Anglo-Indian social service organisation. I was taken aback by the number of pension recipients who signed for their pension with a thumbprint. When I expressed this surprise I was told by committee members that the auditors were not very happy about it either—'But what to do?' was the helpless rhetorical question in response.

In fact, it was this fieldwork observation that first alerted me to the fact of Anglo-Indian illiteracy. Some years later, during the course of a presentation I gave at the Sixth World Reunion of Anglo-Indians held in Melbourne, in 2004, I showed a photo I had taken of pensioners signing with a thumbprint. I was told by others present that people had been shocked by the image. Diasporic Anglo-Indians also appear to be unaware of the existence of illiterate people in their community (see Photo 9.1).

My fieldwork observation here is corroborated by some scenes in the film *A Calcutta Christmas* (Delofski, 1998) which shows several scenes of elderly Anglo-Indian residents of the Tollygunge Home signing for their Christmas pension with a thumbprint. In addition to these elderly Anglo-Indians, there are also people in their early forties who cannot read or write, a fact evidenced by Peter's story. What was heartening was that in many cases of illiterate parents with school-aged children, the children were attending primary or secondary school, and in some cases were even receiving a tertiary education, as Peter's children did. An observation was made at the Calcutta Anglo-Indian Day panel discussion that I attended in 2003 to the effect that today's parents are better at parenting than their predecessors had been because they are actively encouraging

130 *Christmas in Calcutta*

Photo 9.1:
People Signing with Thumbprints

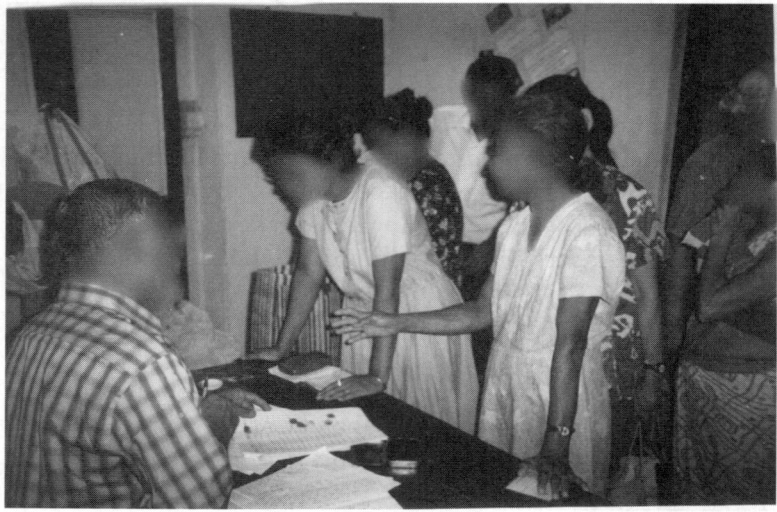

Source: Author.
Note: The faces in this photo have been blurred by the author to ensure privacy.

their children in their schooling even though they may not have the educational skills themselves.

Causes of Illiteracy and Poorly Educated Anglo-Indians

Though my general argument is not so concerned with the causes of Anglo-Indian illiteracy, but more with its effects and solutions, nevertheless it may be useful to consider the question briefly. How then, did the situation of Anglo-Indian illiteracy and poorly educated Anglo-Indians come about? One explanation grows out of reflection on the words of one of Laura Bear's[7] research participants, a man

---

[7] Laura Bear, an anthropologist and historian, carried out research with Anglo-Indians in Calcutta and Kharagpur in the mid-1990s.

from Kharagpur. In response to a question about why Anglo-Indians were employed on the railways, he responded:

> That's quite natural, that's the blood. The blood flows simple as that. That's why it's inborn in us, this culture, the British culture. We don't have to be educated. We don't have to have the least education even primary education. English is our mother-tongue, we talk English. So that's how we are brought up, our parents and our parent's parents. So even if we are not educated, but we still have that culture, must be because it's in our blood. (Bear, 1998: 163)

In other words, for this person, simply speaking English as a mother tongue guaranteed the inheritance of cultural capital, which obviated the need for educational capital. This attitude explains Anglo-Indians' lack of engagement with education in the past. But it is surprising that this view was still held as recently as when Bear carried out her fieldwork in the mid-1990s, given the changes in attitude to education that I observed less than 10 years later. In more recent years, Anglo-Indians have started to take their studies seriously and have realised that

> in the past they'd send their children to school but most of the children would become drop-outs, because the parents themselves were not interested too much. That was in the past. Now things have changed for the last, say decade. Things have changed because now they feel responsible and they feel that without an education, there is no future for the community and the children. But prior to 10 years back, from the time of 1947, 1947, nobody ever thought seriously about education and the children's future. Parents were always in a domestic struggle of making ends meet. They were not getting very good jobs. But somehow they managed to exist.
>
> So what is happening now is that we are trying very hard to educate the children so that the least they can do is be a graduate—because going as far as year 12 is not enough in today's world. (Personal communication from a Calcutta-based Anglo-Indian research participant, 2002)

Another contributing factor to Anglo-Indian illiteracy may have been the job-reservation system, which was in practice until the 1960s. As noted earlier, Anglo-Indians until then received preferential employment opportunities in central government services such as Railways, Customs, Posts and Telegraph, and the Defence Services. Hence, they may not have taken education so seriously, already being guaranteed work. This is implied in the words of Neil O'Brien, the current president-in-chief of the AIAIA: 'Now that the crutch of reservations has been thrown aside the next generation has come to realise that they need to get a good education' (Personal communication, 2002). In other words, job reservations were seen as an impediment to a focus on education. Reginald Maher, an Anglo-Indian journalist and scholar, had long before held the view that these reservations were of 'transitory and illusory benefit' and 'wrought on the other hand the greatest damage' (Maher, 1962: 41–42). The 'damage' that he writes of is the belief that Anglo-Indians became victims of prejudice, being seen by non-Anglo-Indians as 'the favored', as well as becoming increasingly reliant on the types of jobs their forefathers had held serving the government. The real damage, however, may have been a lack of engagement with maintaining literacy (Maher, 1962: 42).

Yet another reason, suggested to me by an Anglo-Indian schoolteacher who left India in the 1970s, was the structure of the linguistic requirement of the Indian examination system in the years after Independence. He said that when he was at school in the 1960s, in order to pass the final Indian School Certificate (ISC) exams in class 10, students were required to pass an exam in a language other than English. For most Indians this meant their native language—for example, Hindi or Bengali in the case of students in West Bengal. The very structure of the Indian examination system was based upon the premise that English could not be the vernacular or mother tongue of Indians. Combined with a certain amount of Anglo-Indian ethnocentrism towards Indian languages, and the lack of support from home (due to English being the only language spoken there) a pass in the second language was seldom achieved. Non-English-speaking Indians who study for the ISC, on the other hand, live a life of full immersion in two languages: of English at school and their mother tongue at home. Because English is their mother tongue, Anglo-Indians only ever have full immersion in one language and are, therefore, handicapped from the beginning in relation to the demands of the Indian examination system. They are, in other words, set up for failure. And, as Bourdieu has observed, people tend to adapt to the life chances they are likely to have.

It is ironic, then, that the very language that carries the greatest social capital in the wider arena of India's social scene offers a practical disadvantage at school for those who speak it as a first language. Having English as a first language should, one would think, offer Anglo-Indians an advantage in a social system that fetishises the English language, but instead it causes many to stumble within the education system. Although the special nature of Anglo-Indian schools has been protected by two Articles of the Constitution of India, 1950,[8] what has not been properly understood is the injustice of the requirement for Anglo-Indian children to pass other Indian language exams in order to be promoted into the next class. Therefore, one could ask why the requirements of the examination system of India should not be revised with the view to eliminating the discrimination that Anglo-Indians face in terms of the linguistic requirement, which in turn is based on the false idea that you cannot have an illiterate English speaker.

The observations presented in this essay, drawn from ethnographic fieldwork, show that there is a problem with the idea that in India the linguistic capital, associated with fluency in English, is transferable, or congruent with other types of capital—economic, social and cultural capital. The ethnographic examples indicate that there is *not* an automatic correspondence between being fluent in English and possessing these other forms of capital. We need to look again more closely and empirically at the species of capital at work in the field of language and to recognise perhaps the greater importance of, indeed the greater power of, other forms of capital. This is particularly apparent in the school setting where

---

[8] Article 29(1) states: 'Any section of citizens residing in any territory of India or any part thereof having a distinct language, script or culture of its own shall have the right to conserve that same. This protection extends to its right to administer its own schools where the community's Christian heritage is fostered and the English mother tongue is reinforced through its use as the medium of instruction.' Article 30(1) states: 'All minorities, whether based on religion or language, shall have the right to establish and administer educational institutions of their choice.' In addition, Article 337 offers protection provided enrolment conditions are met.

134 *Christmas in Calcutta*

Anglo-Indians are generally disadvantaged in comparison to others attending the same schools.

Although, in theory at least, they have open admission to some of Calcutta's best schools,[9] in many cases Anglo-Indians just do not possess the other types of capital to gain all they might from that attendance. Even when entry is achieved, their studies may be jeopardised by economic capital-related circumstances. In the family homes of very poor Anglo-Indians, for example, cramped living quarters with no adequate study space make studying at home difficult (as illustrated in Photos 9.2 and 9.3). What has even more negative impact on their study is their inability to afford the

Photo 9.2:
Young Anglo-Indian Boy Studying in His Home (2003)

Source: Author.

[9] Although Anglo-Indians may attend without paying an entrance fee, I was told, however, that on a number of occasions that entry is not guaranteed either, that when a school board has the choice of admitting an Anglo-Indian or a full fee-paying student then they are likely to select the fee-payer.

Photo 9.3:
Secondary School Student Studying at Her Desk (2003)

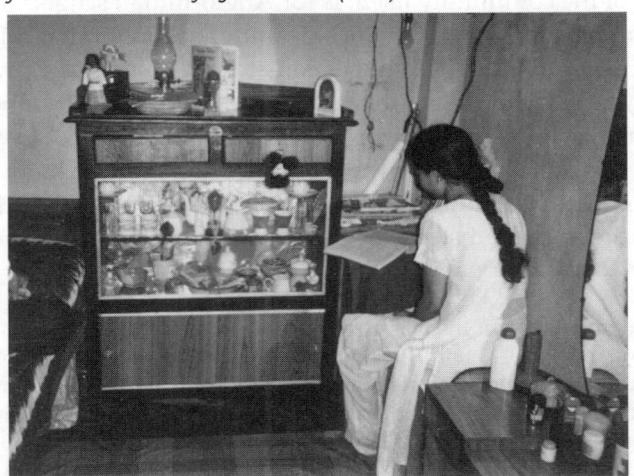

Source: Author.

seemingly essential out-of-school-hours tuitions.[10] Unlike other attendees at the schools who needed to have a certain amount of capital in order to have gained admission, Anglo-Indians are able to enter schools without that capital. Therefore, whereas non-Anglo-Indian Indians can easily afford such tuition, Anglo-Indians are not able to and, hence, are unable to reinforce their learning in the same ways.

It is my hope that through an increased understanding of the situation for Anglo-Indians they might gain access to resources that will promote their success. It is, after all, due in large part to the Anglo-Indians that Calcutta has the system of schools available that serves the elites, who in turn have been active in social change.

---

[10] A number of people in Calcutta, both Anglo-Indians and others, stated that one of the main problems with the Indian school system (as opposed to the Australasian school systems that I am familiar with) was that it was a two-tiered system—one tier comprising classroom teaching and another in the form of tuitions, which run simultaneously and complementarily, and are often offered by the classroom teacher. It seems that without the extra lessons the chances of passing sufficiently to be promoted into the next grade are severely diminished.

Another possible and alternative solution, which is within the scope of the community itself, is for Anglo-Indian schools to offer scholarships to help to pay for this out-of-school tuition. Michael Robertson has practical suggestions to offer, such as providing Anglo-Indian children with textbooks as well as the all-important special coaching. The Anglo-Indian School Boards could surely make this a priority. This would assist Anglo-Indian students in learning another Indian language, other than English, which may stand them in good stead for their place in the nation. Robertson makes this additional point:

> They must look at the classrooms and find out how many kids are going into 9, 10, 11 and 12. Now that is where your answer lies. And then look at what's happening in the interim. You can use the arguments that they don't want to study, but the kids are very sensitive people. You have to understand they're not studying in class because it's so difficult for them. Again there's prejudice by the teacher who thinks, 'Okay, an Anglo-Indian child—you'll never learn Hindi. Get out of the classroom.' Now my daughter learnt Hindi very successfully, but never at school. She had a private tutor who's very good and she did exceedingly well in Hindi.
>
> But she needed the tuitions, or she would not have survived. Teaching in classrooms is so bad.
>
> With so many children in the class how can they ever give any personal attention? And these children need focused attention in the language they don't know. And you take another child who speaks the language at home, and gets all the tuitions and what have you. It's unfair! Now that's got to be recognised by schools. (Interview, 2004)

Conclusion

If it were to become more widely known that there are English speakers in India who are illiterate, and if it was not simply assumed that all English speakers are members of the elite, then it might be the case that Frank Anthony's words at the time of Independence might be taken more seriously. He said, 'English is an Indian language because it is the language of a recognised Indian minority, the Anglo-Indians' (Anthony, 1969: xi). By a strange paradox, it may well be that by recognising that literacy and being able to speak English are not synonymous, Anthony's view may be more readily accepted—especially by those who automatically assume English's *elite* status. Another hope that one can have is that this paradoxical situation may be short-lived because of the efforts of the community itself to directly confront this kind of issue.

At the Sixth World Anglo-Indian Reunion held in Melbourne in 2004, the chairman of the AIAIA, who is also a member of the Inter State Board of Anglo-Indian Education, in his address on the current situation of Anglo-Indians in India, presented information that shows that Anglo-Indian students are now more successful than ever before in national school exams.

This essay addresses what may be a particular historical moment. It was written as a commentary on the effect of having English as a first language in India, based on compelling ethnographic evidence, which indicates the existence of a small, overlooked, number of illiterate English speakers. Although Anglo-Indians are a community of Indians whose native tongue is English, they display the same range of class distinctions as are to be found in any other community, as evidenced by the life stories in this book. They range from the extremely poor, living in desperate circumstances in *bustee*s on the edges of railway lines, to the very wealthy with multi-room apartments in wealthy areas of Calcutta. The variety of life opportunities available to them reflects the same variety that is to be found amongst other communities in India. Whilst they have a particular position vis-à-vis the English language and English-medium schools, in other ways they are just another Indian community. Like any community in India, they struggle against all sorts of odds to attain 100 per cent literacy. Rather than expecting these people to all be literate (which is not an expectation made of other Indian language speakers), English should be seen as an *ordinary* language (rather than only a language of prestige). If they do get to the point when they can accurately claim 100 per cent literacy then all credit should go to them; in the meantime, they should not be burdened with this inequitable expectation.

10

Philip: With Education Comes Success

I first met Philip when he was just a young lad who had come home from school for the winter holidays. I knew some of his life story. I caught up with him again recently, when he was 22 years old, and asked to interview him so I could fill in some gaps in his life. Philip is a slightly built, tall, fine-featured young man. With his dimples and bright intense eyes, he could fit in with many of India's ethnic groups. He comes from a good-looking family and he's no exception. The story he tells is very much about what it means to be a young Anglo-Indian man in Calcutta in post-2010. It also illustrates the idea that education can make an enormous difference to a person's life chances.

This life story, which was collected over two interview sessions, is written mostly as a first person narrative from interview excerpts. It was edited in places by Philip once I had written it up.

> As Mum always tells me, my life started before I was born into the family. I'm part of a family that existed before I arrived. She reminds me that I am the last child to come into the family, because prior to me there is Avril and Natasha. Natasha had a very hard life. Compared to me Natasha was a hundred times worse.

> By the time he was twelve Dad had dropped out of school. He says to an extent maybe he was responsible for not being educated, because he was too interested in going to the movies. But at the same time it's the mother's duty to push. Because no child wants to go to school, ever. So that's what his mum didn't do, in fact she got him married off at a really early age. Dad got married without even realising his own responsibilities in life. He got married off, maybe to bring another servant into the family, as Dad said he was. After they married, my mum took over the household duties; that means washing up, making rotis and things like that.

> Dad doesn't have much of a job. Okay, he used to sell black market tickets in movie halls. There's no longer a market for that because

tickets are available any time. He sells other things too but it's never worked out very well.

So that's where things started for us as a family. Dad was expecting that some job would just come up. Mum and Dad got married, and then Avril came along. Now Avril's life was actually very good, compared with ours. Avril's more attached to her Grandmum and Granddad because they brought Avril up for some time. Just before Natasha [the younger of Philip's two sisters] came along, Dad for the first time, revolted against his mother and left their home and moved into a small shanty, a house as small as, maybe as small as our bed. It was in the slums. Have you seen those small little shanties along the road near Tiljala? Natasha was born in a place like that, not in that location, but in a place similar to that. They had about a year there, during which time Natasha was surviving on biscuits and water. Daddy was going out and selling anything he could, but he didn't have a proper sense of business. Maybe he was getting the sales, but he would call on all the merchants (the people who he buys his products from) at the same time so have no money for us to live on. If you call on all the people at the same time you have to give out that entire money that you've collected on that same day. So your earnings have basically gone down to zero and you're just a charity. When you're in need of charity yourself!

Dad was laden with debt, at that point. So whatever he sold just went into that. Maybe Dad would give ₹2 at that time to Mum to manage the household. ₹2 is what? Nothing! All you have to do is drink water and maybe have some puffed rice or something, *moori*, as we call it in India. So that was it. Then Mum's sister came along one day to visit. She saw the scene and she didn't like it. So she helped them to move out from that place. The next place was where I was born. After I came one person ran off to Dad saying, 'You've got a son'. There we had an Anglo-Indian type neighbourhood where everyone knows each other.

Was he working on that day?

Yeah, Dad was working on that day. Dad couldn't afford to miss one day of work. But he spent everything he earned that day, instead of buying a bottle of milk or something, Dad landed up with rasogollas[1] for everyone in the area. He was actually so overjoyed.

[1] A milk-based sweet.

So anyway the neighbours got together and gave them gifts, which at that time helped us out.

School Life

So after that things went on. The best thing that happened was that Cedric, who's a sort of uncle, got us into school [Dr Graham's Homes]. Cedric paid for our uniform, he paid for the little tuck[2] that we took up there. So we went off, with Natasha protecting me all that she could.

So you both went at the same time.

Yeah, Natasha and I went at the same time.

You were how old?

I was two and a half. People asked my Mum how she managed to send me to school at that time. But she thought it was in my best interest and today I realise it. Mum had made up her mind that her children are going to be educated. Be it even to Bengali level, but Mum had it set in her mind.

Basically all I remember of Lucia King [where the very young boarders stay at Dr Graham's Homes] is rolling over the stiles and doing roly-poly on the field. It was my first time seeing such a big field, having swings. It's like you're taking a person living down there and actually giving him all the luxuries of life. I still thank Dr Graham's Homes for that. That is what gave me a childhood, without which I wouldn't have known it's a childhood.

As supported children though, we were treated differently by some people. I still remember that when something was robbed one time, from our cottage, the blind belief was that supported children were the people who robbed it. And this one matron just put us all out in our underwear and vests out in that Kalimpong cold until someone owned up.

But really I thank my sponsors. Sometimes they would buy us clothes or even maybe send money. They gave me that little bit of

---

[2] Snack food commonly taken as treats or between-meal nibbles to boarding schools.

dignity. And that's what I literally thank those people for. I thank them now, but sponsor letters were something I hated to write. You expect a class three child, an eight-year-old, to actually fill up a letter as long as two pages? What would I write? I would like to just make a little drawing and things like that. That's what you'd expect. My letters would be the same. 'I went to Victoria Memorial. I went to the racecourse. I went.... We had a Christmas party. I had a good time at home.' What else would I write? I don't even know these people. I know those people are sending me money but at that time, at that age, am I going to realise that people are sending me money and that I should be grateful? Not at that age. But now I thank the gods that I have, at every step in life, I've got someone caring. When I was at school if it wasn't my cottage aunty, it was my teacher.

I'm still really proud of my school. I once had such a lovely teacher. She was a Tibetan, and they're always soft at heart. She would give me little wafers and things like that. There were others who would help too, like one of our neighbours at home was pretty helpful, he even gave us a big bag of tucks one time, with cheese and a little jam. He sent it to Natasha and she'd bring the jam bottle to breakfast and just spread a little on my bread and give me two slices. I was a little shy with Natasha. I wouldn't like to talk to her much in school. I would run away from her every time I'd see her, until I learnt she had food for me, or she's going to take me to the canteen. Otherwise I didn't ever care. I would just literally run away at the first sight. 'Oh my God, she's a girl.'

Winters at Home

You'd go home for three months every winter?

Yes, but the first time I didn't want to. I was very happy and I knew home was about poverty and up there I'm getting everything. When a child is small only, I think he's just like an animal. Whichever side he gets, he goes that side. So I didn't want to go back home. When I was supposed to go back I was literally catching the house warden and crying and things like that. But then, yeah, I had to come back home and leave behind the luxuries of school.

I still remember the time at home when Mum gave me rice for dinner. I said, 'I don't want to have lunch I want to have dinner.' Because in school we got bread for dinner. That was all that they could afford. I didn't know that, I just said, 'I don't want lunch I want dinner.' And anyways Dad tried his best to persuade me; I didn't get persuaded. Mum tried her best to persuade me; I didn't get persuaded. I said, 'I won't eat that. I want dinner.' So the neighbours gave me a few chapattis. I was familiar with chapattis because we got chapattis once a week for dinner. So I said, 'Okay, yeah, chapattis will do. But I won't have rice because we don't have rice for dinner at school.'

We went to school with a cousin, Stanley. The three of us were very close. Stanley, myself and Natasha, we were very close. We were at school together and we got back home and we spent our holidays together. We'd go home but we would spend most of the time in their house as they had a bigger house and dad always would take us there. Mum never ever liked that. Mum was like, 'If there's just one slice of bread at home, my children have got to face the truth that there is just one slice of bread at home and not go ahead and eat at the people's places.' Mum was very strict on that. However, my dad was of the notion that as long as they're giving to eat anyway, let them eat. So both of them were correct in their own points of view.

We'd come down from school for three months, and we were more than two months in Stanley's house and maybe one month at home: maybe the first couple of weeks and the last week there. It was a godsend that they actually gave us something to eat. But Mum wasn't very comfortable with that. She didn't like it that her children were coming home but not staying with her.

At one stage, when we came and stayed for the winter holidays we'd be in a house that, looking back at it, I think it was a cattle house.

A cattle house?

Yeah. I'm sure cattle had lived there and they had evacuated the cattle then made a house out of it. Looking at the way the house was I'm sure it was a cattle house.

What was it about the house...? Mud walls and things like that?

No, brick walls, strong. And there were little rings, I remember, little rings against the walls. I'm sure they would have been used to keep the cattle tied up.

Okay. I see what you mean, yeah. So pretty small too? And a shared, a common toilet?

Yeah, a common toilet: a little house with a common toilet for about 20 families. We'd have to run to the tube well to get water which was at least 200 metres away. And the grocery store would always have a book full of debt. There was a person, a local moneylender around there. She would always have a book full of debt. And their house rent was usually not paid. Dad at that time ... I don't know what happened to him but business wasn't going very well and he was giving less money at home even than the little bit he used to give. After a while Dad even brought Mum to Stanley's house to stay. Mum wanted to leave but because of the rent we didn't have a house anymore.

After a while they moved off to the house that you first came to. That house was a little bigger, and even the common toilet was a little cleaner.

And it wasn't shared amongst so many was it?

Yeah, and the people were from an Islamic background. They are more about sharing. Those people can never see anyone go hungry. I think Dad got his major help from Muslim people, apart from Dr Graham's Homes and the Christian society helping us. The local help that we got was from Muslims. There Dad had a little shop it's like, just an outlet on the road. So anyway the dons said, 'Okay, you can put a shop there from now on.'

The dons? Are those are the people who control the area?

Yeah, and Dad didn't have to pay a penny to them. It was just in order to help Dad out. But then, of course, Dad was also in charge. He had to make sure that there was no robbery around there. And they said, 'anyone gets pick-pocketed I will hold you responsible', and things like that. That place worked out fine for Dad though. That was the only place that actually had a few little happy moments for Dad. Other than that, no other place....

Responsibilities of an Older Sister

With regards to Avril (Philip's older sister), she has done a lot for us. I still remember Avril going off for tuitions. Boys teasing the hell out her. But she still had to go to these tuitions. If she didn't go we wouldn't be able to pay the rent. She was around about 15 when she started her tuitions, just locally, to a local Muslim family. There were six brothers and sisters. That was a lottery house for us. They would give her ₹1,500 a month. And Avril would pick up another thousand from school. She actually got a job working at a school.

I think the reason why she got married a little early is that she was fed up of it. She was just a 16–17-year-old being stuck with everything in society. If she wanted to have an ice-cream for God's sake she would think, 'I must care whether other people have eaten at home'.

However, things are destined to happen, that's when Avril met her husband, Kumar. Yeah she's married 9 or 10 years now. They are married and they have a child now. She's very happy with him and there couldn't be anyone who could keep her happier, but then she always feels, because there is that little communication gap between them. That little thing about comparing the way her family lives, and his ways. They're still working on how to bring up [their son] so he has the little Anglo-Indian ways, that Avril wants, as well as the Bengali [Hindu] parts from his Dad's side.

Was he [Avril's husband] able to help with things at home?

He didn't directly, but by just taking on responsibility for Avril. Although when he came, he did help out by giving us maybe clothes at Christmas, by making us celebrate festivals once again, which we hadn't celebrated in some time. Maybe the last festival that I celebrated with Dad's money was one time when Dad came home and brought a lot of money back, ₹2,000. And basically Dad said, 'Go, use it for shopping.' Okay, well and good. We went ahead we used it for shopping and next day we realised that that money was supposed to be given to someone else. So again he went ahead and took out some loan from someone else and paid off that money. We'd rather we didn't celebrate a festival than be in more debt. So anyway things went on. Dad started getting a little more work. Before that it was like whatever Dad brought home was either given to cops, given to someone here, someone there. Things went on like that until Mum's operation. She had to have a big operation. Dad was just getting on top of things. Just trying to give it that little push and again you are thrown down there again.

Finishing School

When I came down from school after class 12, I still had my 12 exams to do. Avril was married by then and since her house was a better environment to study, cause she had two rooms, I'd study there. I came back in December, before Christmas, and then just studied for the exams. I studied the whole of winter and then I went back up.

Did you need tuitions at that stage?

No. I've never taken tuitions in my life. Even with regards to college I didn't require them. I really don't know how other people approach their studies. I just think it's there if you just give it a slight reading or something it's done. Or maybe just pay attention when the teacher is teaching.

So in March, after I sat for the exams, I came down here forever. At first I had a rollicking time with my friends for a month or so, all the Calcutta guys. But we soon realised that where a hundred bucks (₹100) was a big sum in school, out here it's like, it goes away on transport.

Tertiary Study and First Job

Soon after I came down to Cal the college enrolment process started: I had to get the forms, get this, get that. But in the end I just filled out one for St Xavier's College. I was kind of sure with my marks and things like that. I had scored an average of 87. In political science I scored a 92. But then in economics I scored 15 on 100. So otherwise my average would have been in the 90s. I just filled in for that college because I was just interested in going to that college, and also, I knew that others, like [named university], involved politics. And with regards to politics I am absent. My Dad is absent. I don't have anyone to run around with me so....

So you mean politics in that you need to know somebody? You need contacts?

Yeah, politics as in you need to know somebody. And then you need to run around to this party office, that party office. Then you need to run around to a student union to get you into the college. Then after doing all that you need to pay some down. However, I was not interested in all that. I got into St Xavier's pretty smooth, all rocking in fact. I got political science honours, the honours that I wanted.

My first semester got me a little down since that was my first time working as well. I wanted to get started working straightaway, as soon as I came down, but they said, 'You can't since we're waiting for your results. We only take 12 pass, and you are saying you are 12 pass but we don't know if you are 12 pass. You need to show your results.' So anyways I waited for them and then hit on this one company, but they denied me. The reason being I was studying in St Xavier's and they don't take in the regular students because they have rotational shifts.

Okay, so they don't want students who have to go to classes at regular times.

And with St Xavier's College, if you don't have a 75 per cent attendance you cannot sit your end of semester exams. So you have to have at least attended three out of four classes.

That makes sense.

But there are colleges in Calcutta where you only need to turn up for your exams. My girlfriend studies in one like that. You just enrol and then go for your exams.

But how do you get the material to study?

Basically with regards to the material there are some regular students around there.

So you pay them?

Yeah. Or maybe there's a teacher or someone who gets out their notes and tells them what they have to study.

But St Xavier's isn't into that?

St Xavier's, they won't even take a damn fine.[3] That's the reason I did six months more. I was willing to give them any fine they wanted.

What was the fine for?

In my third year there was one class that was on early in the morning, which I would somehow manage to miss. I would be rushing

---

[3] I realise now that he meant a bribe, rather than what is usually mean by the term 'fine'.

back from work but I was earning so much money at that side, so just to attend one class... 'Leave it', I thought. With the amount of money I was earning, even if I gave a small portion I thought I'd get through. But then that didn't quite work out. They weren't willing to take the money. Instead they said I needed to do an extra six months. So just for that one subject, which wasn't even a main subject for me, I had to do an extra six months in college. I just had to do it.

Tell me about your days at that time.

I literally don't know how to start. I don't know whether it started at night or started in the morning, because there were two starts to my day. It's kind of confusing cause from work I directly went to college and then went home. Yeah, so I would get up at 9 o'clock at night, have a bath, go off to work, and work the whole night. We had just small breaks, a half hour dinner break and things like that. I would take my tiffin along. The company would provide tiffin but Mum never let me eat from outside.

It was a very weird time that my work finished. I didn't have time to go home once my work finished. If I went home I couldn't come to college, so that meant I had to stay back in office. Maybe sleep an hour in office and then move on to college to get there by 9:15. My work would finish by 7:30. I would go to sleep by around about 8, after telling all the guys 'bye'. I would get up by 9, have a little wash or whatever, get a little freshened up and then go off with my red eyes. I'd go off to college until it finished at around about 4–4:30. Then after college I would walk down to the bazaar and catch a bus. A bus is cheap and could take me right to where I needed to go. But the problem with the bus is when you have a lot of traffic. So even though the normal route takes you an hour, at that time, with my college finishing at 4:30, I wouldn't land home until 6:30. And then I'd have work at 10:30, or 11:30. So at the most I slept four hours a day—three in the evening and one in the morning.

When Natasha saw my work schedule and my college schedule, she said, 'This guy's just a visitor'. I would stay just 3 hours at home and then I'd be out on the road. Office to college, college to office. For three years, no, three and a half years in the end, I just had to do that. My Dad obviously couldn't give me as much as I needed to go to college with. Dr Graham's homes would have given me my college fees, but there'd be nothing else. It's ₹725 for the regular tuition fee. That's for your regular classes. And then you have your exam fees and things like that. So it approximately came up to about ₹17,000[4] a year with exam fees, lab fees, site fees and library fees.

Dr Graham's continued my college fees for a little while, after which I dropped it because I didn't need it, and maybe someone else could use it. Actually, another reason for me leaving it was that I would need to go to Birkmyre every day and I didn't have time to waste there. Basically the requirement is that if you are doing your graduation from Birkmyre, from Dr Graham's homes, you cannot work, except a bit part time. Dr Graham's Homes basically gave me everything. Maybe I was not a child born with a golden spoon in my mouth, but Dr Graham's Homes, with aid from abroad from my sponsors, did manage to put a diamond spoon into my mouth. So maybe you don't have to be born with that golden spoon. Anglo-Indians are lucky.

You still have to work.

Yeah. You have to work at it. Like, for example, 24 Anglo-Indian boys all passed out of school together. Twenty-four Anglo-Indian boys got into college. Now this is going to give you a little glimpse of what Anglo-Indian life is in Calcutta, or anywhere in India. But since I've been to Calcutta I can only talk about Calcutta. Dr Graham's Homes was paying 24 Anglo-Indian boys to go to college. They are paying you to stay in Birkmyre hostel. You don't have to pay anything. You can eat three times a day. On top of that they give you ₹600 a month. I know that's very less but they also give you the liberty to do a small part-time job, as long as you do college as well. So I would say it's only advantages, there's no disadvantage, that Dr Graham's homes gives. Maybe according to my situation I needed that full-time job. But I think if I could go ahead and pass out graduation with a full-time job, by just putting a little extra hard work. But other Anglo-Indian boys are not willing to even put that.

So how did those 24 go?

Out of those 24 Anglo-Indian boys, round about only five or six went up to be graduates, only five or six completed. It's like, what do you expect in life? Someone's doing that for you for free. You're getting funds abroad and things like that. Staying away from your family as well. Just complete it for God's sake!

[4] Approximately US$350 when I interviewed him.

Work

I earn good money. Not boasting about it but, yeah, I was the best caller. I've been the best caller everywhere I go.

What makes a good caller?

What makes a good caller is conversation skills, and basically kind of hard work. With regards to conversation skills, I have a good command over English so being conversant in English has never been hard. The BPO sector, the Business Process Outsourcing, basically call centres, has proved to be a boon for me. There are rumours that America will take it back someday, but till then I have the money from them. And I think with the proper savings and utilising that kind of money properly....

And getting some assets?

Yeah. Basically for a person of my age I would consider myself pretty successful. None of my colleagues have managed to buy their own house; none of my colleagues give ₹11,000 a month at home. If I earn say 23 (₹23,000) at the end of the month I give a major chunk of it at home. Sometimes I get just my basic and no commission, maybe due to absence or due to an exam coming up and things like that. Or maybe just the season's bad.

About 18 months after working I just decided one day that I needed a better job, because my performance was good. I was willing to do the hard work and with regards to the BPO sector if you work hard, you get paid a lot. In the new company I was picking up round about 30 (₹30,000) to 35 (₹35,000) a month, with my incentives of course. My basic was 14 (₹14,000) but my commission's higher than my basic salary. There was a month I picked up 55 (₹55,000). With the commissions we managed to buy this house.

Getting the house was actually something that got us ahead. It was mine and Mum's plan. Even maybe now if I go to Delhi or Mumbai or maybe even get one of the best houses in Cal I would never sell that house. I actually saw Mum kissing the walls of that house, Dad literally stroking the walls of that house. So that house is just really special. It's very special for me since my Mum and Dad are extremely close to that house. The value of that house has actually already rocketed, cause when we bought it buildings were going up ₹400 a square feet around there. After we bought it, we waited a year, and now we want to buy that back lot. Mum wants to construct a little room of mine. So when we approached them they said it's ₹1,200 rupees a square feet. It had gone up three times. Cause all the malls are coming up that side. That's the reason.

Girlfriends

It was in St Xavier's College that I got my first girlfriend. It was a headache. She would require time, which I didn't have. I'm going to be working all night and then with 4:30 college finishing and then you expect me to talk for two hours? Even a five-minute visit would like literally drain my time out.

And was she Anglo-Indian? Bengali?

She was Bengali. She was a Christian Bengali. And after that I thought, let's not get into girls. So I just continued working, working, and then I kept on climbing, climbing, climbing. Till then I met this girl, Anjali, my new girlfriend. I met her at work so I didn't have to take out extra time for her. That was the best thing. However, I don't think things will last very long with her. The reason being is she's from a different clan: she's Marwari. Anglo-Indians, we welcome everyone with open hearts. Yeah, it doesn't really matter if we are going to get married to a Bengali or a Christian. But with regards to them, with regards to people of Indian descent, who follow Hinduism, they need to get married in the hierarchy.

How are you going to cope with that?

I say, 'Let's just carry on as long as this goes and maybe if we think that things are just getting a little bit weird there's always an option called "friends"'. And then maybe she'll get a better guy and I'll get a better girl.

What does she think of that? Have you said that to her?

Yeah, she tells me the same thing, so just as long as it lasts we can.... She feels much the same because it's pointless building castles in the air because we know that in the end I'm coming from one class background and she's of the upper middle-class, and she belongs to a joint family where one uncle needs to approve the other uncle's children's marriage and things like that.

What do they know about you?

They don't really know about me. They just know me as a very good friend of hers, but apart from that they don't know much. They know me as a name. If she wants to go ahead and tell them about it at home it's just going to be her problem. It's not going to be mine I feel.

So it gets kind of difficult out here. But in regards to arranged marriages then of course the whole thing is a business deal. But you have to be careful; you don't want to be messing around with big dads. You don't want to be messing around. There was this one girl who was a politician's daughter who liked me a lot in college. But I didn't dare to even look at her. But she would go ahead and try getting things for me and try to make me happy. I used to say, 'Okay, thanks' for whatever it was. 'But nothing can go on cause you belong up there and I'm just a normal guy and maybe if your Dad just flicked his fingers it would mean my entire life out here would get wrecked.'

What about Anglo-Indian girls? Do you know many Anglo-Indian girls?

I know many Anglo-Indian girls. Through school, through college.

Would your Mum be happy if you married an Anglo-Indian girl?

My Mum's going to be happy if I'm going to get married at all. Yeah, with me marrying an Anglo-Indian, maybe if I find someone right, but till date.... I've been trying; basically, I've been trying hard to find someone amongst my own class, amongst my own clan. But it's just that the moment you think that, okay, yeah that girl's good, that girl would be a good match. Or at least maybe that girl is of a decent character to at least approach as a friend. But everyone knows everyone, so then you have an entire history rolling around her and you think, that's the last thing that you want.

There was this one girl I liked in school, an Anglo-Indian. She went off to Delhi. Now she's become a model. She still looks as beautiful. Yeah, Dr Graham's Homes basically had a lot of very beautiful girls.

With regards to Mum I've never hidden anything from her. If I drink I tell Mum at home. If I'm smoking I tell Mum at home I'm smoking. So I don't keep Mum in the dark. With regards to girlfriends Mum always advises me. She says, 'I know you get very close. I know things happen, here and there, but just remember don't let things cross the limit. 'Because once things cross the limit you know we would not be able to handle it.' We don't have the backing to handle it.

That's something you feel quite strongly.

Yeah. I don't have family to back me. I have a timid dad, and maybe a very strong Mum but what can Mum do alone? Dad wouldn't want to get into all this cause Dad is petrified of society.

Saturdays

You were saying one time I came over what your typical Saturday was like, the Saturdays you have off. Can you tell me again?

Those Saturdays are golden to me. I just literally look forward to all of those Saturdays. Maybe if you had spent some more time in India, or maybe if your daughter comes down the next time, I will take her out for a Saturday outing. It's like, golden. My Saturdays have been something that I've been cherishing from, right from the first place where I worked, till where I'm working these days. Saturday is a place where I don't know Mum, I don't know Dad, I don't know family. I just know my friends and just have a hell of a good time.

The first Saturday is a blast. I have every first, third and fifth Saturday off. So the first Saturday is a blast. Everyone has girlfriends with them. We go out for a movie in the morning and then we go out for a lunch. Sometimes we take other friends out shopping and we all meet up for lunch, and go to some high-class place. After our lunch we have coffee, or hookahs, and we enjoy our conversation; mostly it's office gossip. We have fun staring at girls, and the best part of staring at girls is that you're with your girlfriend so you cannot get into trouble. For dinner most of the time we go to Chinatown. Restaurants love us in Chinatown when we come in a big group. After dinner then we maybe buy some DVDs. Sometimes we go to one of our friend's house, one who has a TV. We sit and have our beer bottles with us and we watch television and drink beer. The girls are in the room too, gossiping. Most of the time we are back home by 11 or 12 at night.

That's the programme for the first Saturday. The third Saturday is a little cool. And the fifth Saturday is dry. We'll be run out of money. We all stay at home, talk over the telephone, 'Yeah I'm watching this show actually. I don't want to come out. There's a very good show on TV and actually I want to catch up with that. I have got to take my Mum to the doctor's.' Or we go to English movies, not Hindi movies. Ever since I've been dating Anjali I've been starving to watch an English movie so on fifth Saturdays I watch some English movies.

I haven't been to church for basically, honestly, for the past three years. On Sunday Mum wakes me up and I'll say, 'I'll pray to God directly. I'll say my "Our Father" I swear.' Dad and Mum go and then I get up to watch National Geographic the whole day. When Mum comes back she's literally frustrated.

The Future

With regards to my future I'm very concerned about it, because I've seen the downside of life and I would never like to see that again. And neither would I like anyone in my descending family to see that ever again, never. It's been cruel. Maybe we overcame it but that doesn't mean someone else has to go through it.

I'm just mid-way to my dreams. I'm planning on getting Mum and Dad a car, planning on getting myself a car, getting myself a house. Mum basically says, 'I don't want you to stay with me after marriage.' The reason being is after marriage there comes differences. You start listening to your wife and then you don't listen to your mother. It's just worldwide: mothers and mothers-in-law, wives and mothers-in-law never get along.

So in Anglo-Indian families do most of them ...

Most of them are nuclear families. They don't live together. They move out when they marry. But even after marriage Mum and Dad are still my responsibility, not my sisters'. If they are giving, it's out of their goodwill, but at the end of the day I'm going to be carrying on the title so I'd rather give, pay patronage, to that title.

With regards to my future: Let's see, some realistic dreams that are going to happen.... When I passed out from school I wanted to go ahead and do something with political science and maybe become a teacher. I also thought I'd like to be a lawyer. That's another reason why I was studying political science. But basically I didn't have all that time to study. Law means quite some time studying and I didn't have that time. But then in college one guy said, 'Why don't you try linguistics?' Natasha was going ahead and getting started in life but there's Mum and Dad waiting as well. I would not be going in for higher studies because they would be costing a lot and I don't have the time. If I want to do an MBA it's in my dreams too. I'm not going to be able to afford to do an MBA. So I'm taking up languages because that's something that I can afford with my monthly income. I plan to do German, and after German I'm kind of thinking of going into Spanish. So let's hope those things work out.

Philip knows he has worked hard to be where he is and intends to continue doing so. I'll be interested in following his life. Perhaps in another edition I will be able to write 'part two' of his life.

This section, finishing as it does with Philip's story, highlights the impact of having, or not having, a formal education. Providing this to members of the community is a focus of most of the social service organisations in the city. In the next section, I look at the social services, some of their activities, and I discuss what I see as a superb side effect of the work they do.

PART FOUR

Community Care

This section builds upon the three previous parts of this work: those of identity, faith and education, and examines community care across a wide spectrum of social services. Educational support, the impact of which has been demonstrated, is just one of the ways in which the various service organisations work to assist members of the community who are in need of it. Other forms of aid include helping people into work, providing medical services, blankets and small home comfort items, as well as care for the elderly, which comes in a variety of forms—from the provision of rations and pensions through to care in Anglo-Indian rest homes. The argument I make in this section, particularly in the essay, is that all of this support does more than meet the very real physical needs of members of the community; it also acts to bring Anglo-Indians together in ways that enhance the sense they have that they are all members of one community by the provision of opportunities for beneficiaries to dance, to eat Anglo-Indian food, play housie and generally enjoy socialising with other Anglo-Indians, rather than just receive handouts of food and pensions.

In this section, there are three life stories, along with the essay. We begin with Philomena Eaton's story. She has already made several appearances in this work, beginning in the 'Calcutta Christmas' story. She is a founding member of the Anglo-Indian social service society, CAISS, and has been its convenor for the last

10 years. Although her story ends with this service-related period of her life it is an earlier, less-well-known time of her life that her account of her life is initially focused upon. She says it is in this period of her life that the seeds were sown for the social work that she is now so engaged with.

In the essay that follows I discuss what I have observed is achieved by the social work that many Anglo-Indians, and others, are engaged in. Following that is Barry O'Brien's story, West Bengal's MLA at the time I recorded my interview with him, and member of the very political and successful O'Brien family. His role at the time required him to facilitate Anglo-Indian social services, and his presence alone lifted the spirits of many he came into contact with.

Then finally, the last story in this work is Meryl's story. After a long career as a secretary she is at the end of her life in an all-Anglo-Indian environment, a residential home. Meryl's story brings us back to Christmas, finishing, as it does, on another Christmas day in Calcutta.

11
Philomena Eaton: Social Service Convenor Extraordinaire

Philomena's story has strong links to both the 'Faith' and 'Community Care' sections, but as convenor of a social service organisation I couldn't but place it in this section. I note though that it is her devout Christianity that provides a guiding light for all she does; in addition, what she has devoted her life to, in particular, is service to her community. Philomena's life and works have become a sub-theme of this book, which is appropriate as her life and works have touched so many Anglo-Indians in Calcutta, and she has such a positive profile within the community. Everyone I meet speaks about Philomena in terms of affection, awe and admiration. She is in her early 70s, has a sparkle of humorous mischief in her eyes and is always ready with compassionate and practical help.

Along with a team of other Anglo-Indians she runs CAISS, an organisation set up in 1976 to help the less fortunate of her community. I discuss this organisation and its work in the essay in this section. One of my enduring memories is of her at work distributing pensions and rations to elderly Anglo-Indians from a little office off a courtyard and adjacent to another Anglo-Indian institution. Her compassion for the people she works for is obvious, but she is also realistic about the tactics that desperate people may use to get a little extra money. I was interested to see the way these people related to Philomena. They greeted her in an openly friendly and respectful way. She responded in a friendly manner but would not hesitate to tackle them over any transgression she may suspect, such as having moved to live with a family member who ought to be supporting them. The combination of compassion and canniness makes her perfect for her role as convenor of the organisation.

In late 2002, I interviewed Philomena about her life. In what follows I have edited and organised the material retaining the interview style. While Philomena's life now is public and service oriented, it hasn't always been this way. The first part of her story here provides a glimpse of her early life, which she maintains made her the outgoing, confident and articulate person she is today. It depicts a life that Anglo-Indians were able to lead at one time, and which she describes as the happiest years of her life. I also include some interview segments in which she talks about CAISS's work and her philosophy, as convenor, behind the work of this social service society. Together I'm hopeful that these pieces convey a sense of her character—her talent, humour and strength of spiritual commitment—and her exceptional ability to live up to her own standards on a daily basis in a single minded yet humane way.

Part One: Assam Days[1]

Philomena told me about her early life over the course of several interviews at her home; the flat in central Calcutta that has been home to her grandparents, parents, three siblings and a retired uncle. At the time I interviewed her she also shared it with her 18-year-old German shepherd dog, a cat and a kitten, 'not to mention three other strays who present themselves at 8 pm with clockwork regularity'.

She said that as she grew up she had 'enjoyed the basic necessities of life but not much else'. And that the strength of her upbringing 'lay in strong family ties, finding leisure activities within the family or with a couple of special friends'. Her mother played the violin and her father the piano. Musical evenings on a Sunday were the highlight of the week, 'especially with the special dinner which followed'. She attended a local Loreto school for all of her schooling, travelling each day by hackney carriage, rickshaw or tram, never by a taxi, which was considered 'a luxury' that her family couldn't afford.

---

[1] A version of this part of her story has been published as 'Assam Days: An Interview with Philomena Eaton' in *The Way We Were* (Andrews, 2006a).

A couple of years after leaving school she left home to work in Assam. She attributes much of who she is today, and the way she works, to her six years there.

I went to Assam as a secretary when I was two months off 21. Before I went I felt that unless I spread my wings I was never going to make anything of my life. Because, you know, I used to come back from work, lie in bed and read a book. End of story. And I felt that life must have more to it than that. Even my mother would push me out to join a club and to go here or there but I wasn't interested. My sister used to have any amount of boyfriends. And she was very house proud and she would look after any visitors who came. She would make the tea and I would be in the bedroom reading a book. I couldn't care less.

But I felt that there must be more to life than just going to work and coming home and reading a book. And so what happened is this; my mother was a secretary and my father bought her a second hand typewriter as a gift. I came home from work and saw it and immediately put a bit of paper in to it, just to try it out. The newspaper was lying just beside it at the Situations Vacant column. And there was a job going in Assam wanting a secretary in the oilfields—Assam Oil Company. My eye fell on it and so I started to type an application, just because it was there.

And when I finished typing, I hadn't made any mistakes. It was a beautifully typed letter. I thought to myself, 'What a shame to destroy it'. I promptly put it in an envelope and sent if off and forgot all about it. I got a shock when the head girl there telephoned me. She asked me to come for an interview and I was offered the job.

When I came home and explained what had happened, my father said, 'You're not going anywhere! Why are you going to Assam? What do you want there? Our girls don't. It's out of the question!' And I said, 'Mummy, what to do? I've gone and made this big blunder. I've sent this application and it will look so bad now to refuse.' I said, 'Mummy please, I want to do something with my life. I really don't know where I'm going here and I want to be a good secretary. I feel that if I go there, I'll get a little experience, you know, and also of living on my own.' She only asked me one question. She said, 'Are you leaving home because you're unhappy?' I said, 'I've got nothing to be unhappy about. I'm not unhappy'. So she said, 'All right, you promise me one thing.

You go, and if even for one day you're not happy then you come home.' I said, 'I promise you I'll do that. I'll come right home.' I was so happy for six years. They were the happiest years of my life. I grew you know.

It Was a Very European Place

In those days it was a very European place with a lot of tea planters. And I was very dark, and not attractive. My sister was the attractive one, bless her heart. I had this terrible inferiority complex. My mother said, 'How are you going to feel when you are dark, in this community?' I said, 'Mummy, I'm going to prove myself. I am going prove to myself that I'm as good as anybody else.' And then when the new oil fields opened up they offered me the senior job there. So you know I felt that....

You had passed some sort of test?

No. Well. Not only that, but I, let's face it, even in the Anglo-Indian community.... I told you that story about going to Delhi; about the old man and these girls who wouldn't dance with him because they thought he was too dark. There was that same thing; if you're dark it can affect your opportunities. Maybe it happened in other communities but it certainly happened in the Anglo-Indian community.

There's a type of hierarchy of colour?

Yes. And that combined with being so shy because I wasn't attractive. And I was as thin as a rake and maybe I didn't have a personality so I'd just sit quietly at any party I went to. But when I went to Assam, I can't tell you how I blossomed because people accepted me for what I was, and I've never forgotten that.

The first day that I went the head girl said, 'You spend the night tonight in this bungalow and tomorrow you'll move in with Jeannie', who was the other Anglo-Indian girl there. She was descended from the French, and she had red hair and green eyes. Now we were both Anglo-Indians together and look at the difference between the two of us. I mean it just goes to show, and she was just as Anglo-Indian as I was.

Mummy Had Warned Me about These Tea Garden Types

That first night, the others wanted to go off somewhere but I was very tired and I wanted to write a letter home. I was sitting by myself and then this fellow came up. Now Mummy had warned me about these tea garden types. She had said, 'They are rather wild.'

The people that work on them do you mean, or who own the tea gardens?

The tea gardens' managers and assistants and all. But you know it was a great life. You don't get that life now. It was a beautiful life—very free, very easy. The boys would come out (generally from England). They would do three or four contracts, that's about 12 years. Then they would become managers, or superintendents. They'd get married and raise families, or if they didn't get married they'd have liaisons with tea garden women. That's why you've got Dr Graham's Homes in Kalimpong. It was a different kind of life, and Mummy warned me about them. So the minute a tea garden fellow came near me my antennas went ting, ting, ting. So this fellow came up to the bungalow and I said to myself, 'Oh, he's come to 'survey the land'. He must have seen Jeannie with the red hair and green eyes and now he's come to see the new secretary. Oh boy, what a shock he's going to get.' I was laughing to myself and I thought, 'I wonder what he's going to tell all his pals at the club about the new secretary'. Anyway he was a very nice chap. He came and spoke to me and said, 'Philly, I want to give you a bit of advice. If you want to enjoy your stay in Assam you do whatever you want to do as long as your conscience tells you you're not doing wrong. And don't bother to listen to everything people say, or you'll be miserable.' And I followed what he said and I enjoyed myself.

We would all start work at six in the morning, work till 10. We'd have our lunch, potter around the garden, have a snooze then go back to work. At three o'clock we used to finish for the day. The servants would have our tennis kits ready. We used to go either to tennis, swimming or play some golf, and then we'd go to the movies or we'd just sit and have a snack in the club, or we'd have dinner at the club in summertime. The servants used to bring our dinner down to the pool. We wouldn't come back till 10, not later than 10, because everybody began work early in the morning.

We Thought Nothing of Going 40 or 50 Miles to a Dance

Then on the weekends, we got Saturday and Sunday off, we used to go off, say to a dance, and think nothing of going 40 or 50 miles. We'd hear that a club was having a dance, so people from the whole surrounding area would come there. It was like that.

We would leave the dance floor at say two or three in the morning. So by the time we got back at about four, four thirty, what would we do? We'd have our swimsuits in the car, so we'd go straight to the pool. Everybody would have a good swim, come home by six thirty—hair wet—have a nice hot cup of coffee, have a bath and be at church at eight o'clock.

And then come back, have breakfast out on a picnic. We used to go up the river on picnics—rafting up the river. All day long we used to go, and come back in the evening, get dressed, go to the movie, come home. I used to write home and tell my mother and she would say, 'Such dissipation'. But we enjoyed ourselves.

I had a good group of friends, you know, and they accepted me for what I was.

We Had a Club, the British Had Their Own Club

Were your friends all Anglo-Indians?

No, not all, and they never said we were. We had a club called the Hilltop Club, which the Anglo-Indians would go to. The British had their own club. The Anglo-Indians were not the top people in the company, or in the country. They were in middle-level management. The British were at the top, and then came the Anglo-Indians.

I would go to both the clubs but I enjoyed the Hilltop Club because it was our type of music, our type of dancing. It wasn't a question of just standing at the bar having a drink. It was more fun, so we used to go over there and have regular Saturday evening dances. Sometimes the Europeans would come to the Hilltop Club. We would have Easter dances and they were free to come. There was no problem. When they would come they would say they're 'going slumming'. That's what they would say. Like that. But they came to have a good time. Because if they didn't, they wouldn't have come.

I celebrated my 21st birthday two months after I arrived. My mother sent a big parcel, and the cards were coming and all, and then the girl I worked with said, 'What's happening?' So I said 'Oh it's my birthday, my 21st coming up.'

And she asked, 'What are you going to do for your birthday?' I said, 'I don't know. I don't know anybody. What to do? I've just come and I'm still very new.' So this girl I worked with said, 'Okay, we're having a Valentine's dance at the Club so we'll have a little party at the bungalow; the covenanted staff bungalow. We'll have a little party, just a few drinks, and then we'll go to the Club. We'll celebrate your birthday like that.' So I said, 'Fine'. I landed up there; the house was ablaze with lights. There was a cake, a 21 pound cake in the shape of a key. These tea garden boys had made it from the factory for me. Now I was so touched.

And then after that we went to the Club. I had to cut the cake and give everybody a piece, and everybody wished me and wanted to dance with me. You know I've never forgotten that day. They made me feel important. I said to myself, 'If people treat me like this why should I feel awkward?' and, you know, I really blossomed. I became self-assured.

I Learnt a Lot Over There

I learnt a lot over there, a great deal. I learnt so many things, which I never had a chance to learn here. I mean, like tennis. Where do we ever learn to play tennis here? There's no clubs to go to. I mean we've got to be well placed in life to go to the clubs in Cal, and we were not well placed at that time, with four of us in school. Mummy and Daddy were struggling to give us a good education.

I remember one Sunday when I came home, I put my shorts on and Mother said, 'What on earth have you got on?' I said, 'Mummy I've got my shorts on. Today's Sunday, it's a relaxing day.' But she wouldn't have it. 'You've got no self-respect. The cook is coming and going and you're wearing these shorts. Go and take them off.' And that was the end of my shorts.

So you'd worn them in Assam, which was fine for there?

That was fine. The culture was different in the two places. In Assam, we used to go sunbathing in the garden. You know, in swimsuits, and nobody would turn a hair, but I couldn't do that here. After I came back I never swam again. I never played tennis again. But then I found other avenues. Like doing all this social work.

Yes. When did you start that?

I came back when I was 27. And then Percy Jones, who was in the Anglo-Indian Association at that time, came to me one day and told about work that was being done for Anglo-Indians.

At this point she joined the AIAIA but after a few years a group of association members, including Philomena, broke away from the national association and in 1976 formed CAISS. One AIAIA member who I interviewed who didn't break away, out of a sense of loyalty to the local AIAIA office holders, who were personal friends, offered this explanation for the breakaway:

[The people who left to form] CAISS felt that if they were with the Anglo-Indian Association they'll be in straight-jackets. You know, whatever money they get they have to pass it on to the Centre, they can't use it in the way they want it; they'd have to pass it on to Delhi. They can't use it in the way they want too. There's too much accountability and hardly any performance, you know. So they formed their own little group and believe me they are doing a fantastic job. You know they've got a night shelter.

Philomena explains that the society was formed in Calcutta in 1976 for the 'upliftment of the less fortunate members of the community'. It is important to her that they operate in a transparent and non-partisan fashion, and that no member (as opposed to beneficiary) has any privileges due to that membership.

The people in CAISS, they give their time very generously. They don't look for anything in return. Nothing in return. Even for the shows that we have, we all pay our full tickets. We don't take anything, you know, like because we're on the committee and so on and so on.

No perks?

No, nothing. We all take our full tickets. We went on a picnic recently and the ladies, four or five ladies, decided we were going to make *aloo chaat*.[2] You must have seen these men on the road selling *aloo chaat*? So we decided we were going to do this for the picnic, so each one of us boiled our potatoes and we brought it, and we made ₹460 on the little stall—that we did. We didn't know how it was going to come out, but they sold like hotcakes. What we put in, the costs, we never took out for it. We didn't say, 'Oh yes, we spent ten rupees, or twenty or thirty or whatever.' It was part of what we gave and on the contrary, when we ate ourselves, we paid for the plate that we ate. That's what we did. So it was like that, I mean even in this night shelter, one of us gave the crucifixes, another one gave the framing of the pictures. You know, each one did something. Now for Christmas two of the girls gave them [night shelter residents] the breakfast, Christmas breakfast. Two of us gave them the dinner. Then on New Year's Day two others gave the breakfast, two others gave the dinner. Like that, you know, we do it as a joint effort.

In our interview she was clear about her philosophy on the social work she does:

I always say, 'When you do the work we are doing, you never sit in judgement.' I don't care whether you have been married or not married, whether you've had children out of wedlock, in wedlock, where your husband is, who your husband is. I am not concerned with your moral issues. I am concerned with the fact that you are hungry. You need food or your child needs education, full stop. I'm not concerned whether you've lived a rake's life and now that you've come to the age of 60 you've got no house any more. Perhaps it is your own fault but I'm not here to judge you. I'm here to say that you are living on the pavement *today*. This is your situation *now*. What can I do about it? Full stop. I couldn't care less about your past.

[2] An Indian snack made with potato, herbs and spices.

I always say if you live in those circumstances, say in a slum area, you would be in the same predicament as those young girls are today. You would be, because of the force of circumstances, and not for any other reason.

So, you know, I always tell people, don't begrudge what you do for the poor, because God gives his gratitude in so many, many different ways. And don't do it because you want praise. Just do it. Maybe because it's part of your religion and you've grown up like that. I've always felt that whatever talents you have, you've got to share them. I've always believed that. If you've got something, give it to somebody. Don't keep it.

But you know I've always said that whatever little I have done for Him, for His people, He has given me so much more 'pressed down and running over'.

Philomena has now been the convenor of CAISS for 10 years. Before she took on this responsibility, she had served terms in various positions: as secretary, on the education and other panels and as joint convenor. Until she was convenor they hadn't had a woman in the role and she said that initially she wasn't very confident about how she would manage. There is no question that she is extremely able in the role and everyone looks to her for guidance. The community is extremely fortunate to have her expertise, care and wisdom.

Philomena makes regular appearances in this book, which is fitting, as I see her and the work she does as a constant theme of my research experience. As well as spending the best parts of three Christmas days with her, there have been numerous other occasions to get to know her, including four World Anglo-Indian Reunions (Photo 11.1). In 2008, she finally retired for good from the excellent job she did for a profession. Busy as ever with CAISS and other organisations she continues to centralise the welfare of Anglo-Indians in her life.

Philomena Eaton: Social Service Convenor Extraordinaire 167

Photo 11.1:
Robyn with Philomena Eaton at the World Anglo-Indian Reunion in Melbourne (2004)

Source: Author.

12

Essay: Community Care and Consolidation

Introduction

When I made a trip back to Calcutta in November 2009 I gave the life stories in this book that I had written by then back to the people whose stories they are.[1] I also gave them a mock-up of the table of contents so that they could see where their story fitted, and what else was covered in this book. When I gave it to Irene she looked closely at the table of contents, questioned me about the other people and commented on the essay titles. She seemed happy enough with what she read until she got to the fourth essay: this essay. At this point she stopped, looked up at me with a critically quizzical expression and asked, 'So what have you said here?' I told her that this was a chapter that I was still working on but it would be about the ways in which Anglo-Indians help each other and how this strengthens the community. She replied, with a distinctly sceptical tone, 'I'll be interested to read that because I don't think we do that at all well, and we aren't much of a community.' This response was a version of what I've heard throughout the time I've been involved with the community. Other variations are: 'We don't look after each other like the Parsees do' or 'Even those who have done well forget us when they leave the country. They don't even send money home.' The verbalising of such sentiments is frequently followed by the pessimistic prognosis that their community is dying.

Yet I've observed Calcutta's Anglo-Indians doing plenty to assist each other, and I'm aware of the global population—both individuals and organisations—assisting in numerous ways. Calcutta's

---

[1] Meryl had passed away by this time so I gave a copy of her story to someone else to check for accuracy and potentially sensitive areas. This person knew Meryl well and I know that Meryl had great respect for her judgement in all matters.

Anglo-Indians also appear to be a reasonably cohesive social group who have plenty in common with each other. Although they are far from socially or economically homogenous, within the variations they share fundamental worldviews, including their spirituality and sociability, as well as aspirations for themselves and their children. I was constantly surprised by how many networks there are that link these people to each other; for example, they attend many of the same schools, churches and Anglo-Indian organisations and they seem to know the same key figures in the city through one connection or another. Through connections established by their service organisations, many of these Anglo-Indians who are engaged with their community also interact regularly. The philanthropic work that is carried out forms donor and recipient communities of care—or what Caplan refers to as the Anglo-Indian *moral community* (1998).

In this essay I will describe the actors and activities involved in some philanthropic enterprises and argue that the existence of these forms of sociality and the social services that involve people from a range of social positions is crucial for the cohesion and ongoing health of the community—not just for the services they provide to individuals, but also for the social networks they facilitate. Christmas is the peak time for activities organised around Anglo-Indian poverty alleviation, with social services organisations, the schools, churches, clubs all involved. Caplan (1998: 423) has made the same observation in Madras; that this is the time that '(Anglo-Indian) organisations organise treats, parties and special meals for children, old people and other "deserving" poor in their constituency'.

It is also the time when overseas Anglo-Indians are most likely to be back in Calcutta and get involved in the various events that are scheduled. This book, with Christmas as its calendrical focus, is ideally situated to describe and analyse the events occurring at this time of the year and what they achieve. What I hope to achieve through this essay, again from the perspective of public anthropology, is to affirm and encourage what is being done already. From what I have observed I contend that social services are delivered in a way that benefits the community on more than one level: in addition to meeting the immediate physical needs of impoverished Anglo-Indians, it serves the purpose of bringing people together to take part in quintessential Anglo-Indian activities. The participants' enjoyment and sense of pride in the gatherings contribute to a strong sense of community and this can only enhance its longevity.[2]

Caplan (1998: 423) observed that in Madras, '[m]uch competitive giving seems to focus on the Christmas season'. He also argues that such philanthropy is required to achieve (political) stature within the community. Although Caplan highlights a different impetus, or perspective, than I do in this essay, the similarities in ethnographic detail indicate that Anglo-Indians in Calcutta and Madras share similar experiences in their relationships of giving and receiving at this time of the year. In his argument, Caplan stresses the need to look from both the givers' and receivers' perspectives; I add to this the need to look at the community formation and reproduction that takes place. What does it mean for that entity?

I begin by describing the work of one of the many Anglo-Indian social service organisations in the city—CAISS—which epitomises the style of charity that Anglo-Indians can find in the city. It is the organisation that I have had the most interaction with over the years and it is highly effective in the care it provides and the social networks it contributes to, both in and out of India.

CAISS was established in 1976 and has a reputation of humanity and integrity—so much so that a number of overseas organisations have chosen to work exclusively through CAISS to distribute their

---

[2] I use the term *community* in three subtly different ways in this essay: first, it occurs as an emic concept (i.e., one that is close to the way that the people, Anglo-Indians in this case, themselves interpret and describe the world. So it is *an insider's* perspective as opposed to an etic, or *outsider's*, perspective), which is the way that my ethnographic materials indicate that it is being used by Anglo-Indians themselves. It is also the way that Western, non-Anglo-Indians are most likely to use the term. Second, it has another emic usage that derives from its *Indian* setting, and is closer in meaning to *communal*—a term widely used in the subcontinent to understand the critical social relationships in the wider society. This usage is close to how social scientists might think about *ethnic groups*. The third way the term is used is in an etic way as I, an anthropologist, seek to understand what I have observed. The term appears in this form most strongly when I talk about the social and cultural production and reproduction of Anglo-Indians.

donations. The first time I met the current convenor Philomena Eaton, in early 2002, I was invited by her to visit their night shelter and to come to the ration distribution. I took her up on both offers. The night shelter in central Calcutta's S. N. Banerjee Road is a two-storied building that has its top floor converted into one bunkroom for women, one for men, a bedroom for the resident superintendent, two bathrooms, a kitchen and a dining room. I was told about the establishment of the night shelter in terms of being something of a miracle: Philomena told me that she had always wanted to do something for the elderly Anglo-Indians who lived as street-dwellers. She said she could hardly sleep on rainy nights when she thought of these people: she imagined them unable to find a large enough dry spot to lie down upon and unable to get any sleep themselves. She knew of night shelters in other cities and saw this as the best way to address this problem. CAISS management committee fully supported this idea, so they began looking for a building that would be suitable: central enough for street dwellers to walk to and from each day, and large enough to house a number of adults in separately gendered space. They soon became disheartened by the choice they had for what they could afford. It was then that two events occurred simultaneously. The first was that Philomena heard about a place that she was sure would be perfect; it was large enough to divide into the areas they needed, and it even had a veranda looking over the street, which would be good for ventilation, as well as offering a view. The second event was the arrival of a letter from an Anglo-Indian man now settled in Canada with an offer of a large sum of money for CAISS to spend on whatever they liked. The money was enough to cover the building they'd just found, with enough left over to complete the alterations for its new function as a night shelter. Within a few months the night shelter was up and running, providing dinner and breakfast, as well as a clean, dry, safe place to sleep, use of a bathroom, some company and clean clothes if the nightly residents needed them. More than 10 years on, the shelter is still in good use, as is the downstairs area, which serves as a vocational training room, a meeting place for CAISS's various subcommittees and as a small storehouse.

The night shelter has become a central focus of the organisation, with this space bringing various people together in addition to the officers of CAISS, the nightly residents and the superintendent. Other visitors to the venue include applicants for educational assistance who are interviewed in the downstairs offices, the youth group that meets regularly and Anglo-Indians taking advantage of the vocational courses that are run for training in computer and sewing machine use. It is also used as the venue for entertaining overseas visitors (mostly Anglo-Indians) with a meal and the opportunity to talk with those who are currently using the shelter for its primary purpose. Visitors are also invited to help with another key activity of CAISS, their ration distributions, as I had been.

On the Sunday after visiting the night shelter, I walked through relatively quiet and cool Sunday morning streets to reach the ration dispersal point by 8am. Although the distribution was not to begin for some time there was already a line-up of elderly men and women carrying empty off-white bags stamped with CAISS logo. Several hours later, after the hundreds of rations (one kilogram each of potatoes, *atta*, rice; half a kilogram each of onions, daal, lentils and milk powder) had been distributed, the fortnightly job was completed. I was told that every second fortnight was pension day, where money was distributed along with the rations. Eye clinics and other medical assistance are also organised on these mornings.

In 2008, they streamlined this process with a move to monthly distributions (thus doubling the quantities), saving themselves and the recipients, some of whom had to take long hot journeys on public transport to and from the distribution point, many hours each fortnight.

Over the six weeks leading up to Christmas and New Year, there are numerous additional events held by CAISS: by the end of November they will already have held their jumble (as they call this distribution of second-hand clothing and household soft furnishings) and have organised the forthcoming events, which include a fund-raising fete on the first Sunday of December, a fund-raising stall at a diocesan fair held at St Paul's Cathedral grounds, their 'Christmas tree' — an all-day Christmas party for about 900 less fortunate Anglo-Indians — the Boxing Day dance for CAISS members, a lunchtime party for Anglo-Indian seniors between Christmas and New Year, a picnic early in the New Year for members, as well as the continuation of monthly ration and pension distributions, educational assistance, vocational training and medical assistance and the night shelter throughout this time. At this time of the year, these events alone involve the interaction of many hundreds of Calcutta's Anglo-Indians in one way or another, either as recipients or as providers and/or distributers of goods and services.

The work carried out by CAISS (and other Anglo-Indian social service organisations) link those from different class and socioeconomic positions, conditionally, and far from universally, as givers and receivers of assistance. There are many ways in which this occurs but one way in which those who give and those who receive interact was demonstrated effectively on a day that I assisted CAISS members with one of their annual pre-Christmas *jumbles*. Local Anglo-Indians had been very generous in giving their used but still good soft furnishings and clothing for distribution. Of the couple of truckloads of donated goods, the articles of clothing in biggest supply were women's skirts, tops, dresses and trousers. What was most in demand, however, was not this type of clothing; rather it was the less plentiful *salwar kameez* suits and saris. This class, or socio-economic, aspect to women's clothing—demonstrated by the givers wearing more Western clothing and the recipients' more Indian-styled clothes—meant that saris in particular were a scarce resource at the jumble. A local Anglo-Indian woman and I were looking after a table that dispensed saris, among other garments, which were in hot demand. The system we were advised to use to distribute these items was based upon our judgement, or perception, of the likelihood of them actually wearing the clothing (as opposed to selling it the first chance they got). This was determined by a combination of factors: the clothing they wore on the day or an indication from one of CAISS's members that this person often wore a sari (or that their wife did) and the rationale a person offered explaining why they should be given one. One young woman wearing Western clothes, for example, explained that she was starting work at a bank the following day and would be expected to wear a sari. I had recently spoken to an older Anglo-Indian woman who worked in an office for a large company who told me that nowadays the most acceptable *work clothing* for women in West Bengal was a Western-styled business suit of a skirt and jacket, or a sari. Therefore, we handed this young woman her choice of the saris we had. If this is a recent change for Anglo-Indians then perhaps there will be a few more second-hand saris to distribute in future jumbles.

What Else Is on Offer at Christmastime in Calcutta?

There are numerous other events that are held in the city at this time, which also involve Anglo-Indians in some way. An overview, roughly chronological, of some of these events include: the Children's City Choir (which Anglo-Indians know as Dr Graham's schools' choir, and is referred to in Michael Robertson's story), which performs at the Calcutta Racecourse on the first Sunday of December, then at St Paul's Cathedral the following day, and at the Tollygunge club a day or two later. Hundreds, perhaps thousands, of Anglo-Indians have links to Dr Graham's school in Kalimpong through their own education, their children's or family or friends who have been educated there. Other school-based Christmas activities are the St Joseph's evening concert in mid-December, St Thomas's Kidderpore and Middleton Row's Loreto schools daytime parties for Anglo-Indians in rest homes. The clubs, such as Dalhousie, Rangers and the Grail Club, run a series of evening events for members and guests, and host Christmas trees as part of their service to the community. The AIAIA runs a party for their seniors at the Frank Anthony School. Birkmyre Hostel (the home of the administrative offices of Dr Graham's Homes) hosts a Christmas tree for children before Christmas and a lunch for seniors after Christmas. I heard from some rest home residents that they get enough toiletries, new blankets and shawls, jams and biscuits at the Christmas parties to last them well into the following year.

Bow Barracks' parties are another set of annual Christmas-time events that will be held for as long as the Barracks remain standing:[3] during the week before Christmas the Bow Barracks' organising committee runs a housie and tea afternoon for seniors, a Christmas tree for children where Father Christmas arrives on a cycle rickshaw and distributes gifts, as well as setting up a stage and showcasing their most talented singers and other entertainers in an outdoor evening concert, which attracts people from all over Calcutta.

What Are the Incentives?

Each one of these events takes an enormous amount of organising by small groups of people, many of whom are also in paid employment and have family commitments. What motivates so much philanthropic activity within a relatively small community? An answer that many would give is that they are simply performing their Christian duty in caring for their poor. Anglo-Indians live their spirituality on a day-to-day basis and the members of the various Anglo-Indian associations are no exception. Their practical expressions of faith were demonstrated to me very early on in my interaction with the community; for example, when I made a trip with some of CAISS's members to Anglo-Indian homes in the slum, or *bustee* of Tiljala. This is a quarter where people are forced to make do with the most minimal of amenities in high-density housing situations: it is not unusual for six or seven people to be living in one room, with no running water, and sharing a single toilet and cramped washing facilities with a number of other families. This poses real physical risks for girls and young women especially. Besides these day-to-day physical hardships, the Anglo-Indians I have visited endure further burdens and afflictions, such as blindness, heart problems, a son paralysed and needing 24-hour care, a

---

[3] The Bow Barracks have been threatened with demolition for longer than I've been involved with the community. The film *Bow Barracks Forever* (Dutt, 2007) focuses on this particular situation.

daughter with 'a worm in her brain', women abandoned through the death or desertion of their husbands. CAISS officers take all of this in, and draw on the belief systems they share with the people they visit to find appropriate comments to offer in a way that preserves the dignity of the recipient. Some examples include one CAISS member's response to a woman who was distressed about her son who had died recently. She comforted her with, 'He's with God now and he's happy—think like that'; to a blind man she said, 'Your blindness helps you to be close to Him. It's His plan. If you could see you wouldn't be so close'; to a bedridden woman, 'Your work now is to smile and pray. There is plenty to pray about in this world'. And in response to a grateful recipient who was singing CAISS's praises, 'It's not CAISS's work but God's'. In addition to Christianity, there are other models of philanthropy in India, such as the Parsees who are renowned for their philanthropy, and Sikhs, who through their belief of *sewa* are 'taught to serve and care for people' as a way of 'worshipping and becoming closer to God' (Ganeri, 2003: 18).

Michael Robertson, in his life story, talks about becoming interested in working with a community organisation for several reasons, one of which is the fact that his father had encouraged him to get involved. In addition, he was just beginning to re-identify as Anglo-Indian and wanted to do something to assist his community. He felt that it was important, especially with the changed national political situation in the 1970s, for Anglo-Indians to re-establish their identity. He had clear ideas about what the most effective way to build a positive identity would be: believing then as he still does, that education and employment offer the best solutions for a brighter future for the community. Remarkably, when he joined the community he had no idea of the plight of the poorest of Anglo-Indians such as those in Tiljala. Philomena, on the other hand, said that she joined the social service organisation because it was suggested to her by others who shared her distress at the situation some in her community faced. Another elderly Anglo-Indian woman, who I met early on in my first visit to Calcutta, helps with many different groups: orphans, street children and their families, church groups, and is unceasingly supportive of Anglo-Indian youth. While she cares for and feeds many people out of her fridge every day, she commented on the fact that it is so much easier to assist more extensively if you have an organisation behind you, than it is to do it on your own. Her means are minimal but whatever she has she gives away, and in the most discreet manner, which draws little attention to her or her actions.

Caplan (1998) suggests another possible rationale for taking on certain types of social work, arguing that much philanthropy (in Madras) is undertaken as it is required in order to gain the type of status in the community, which can lead to leadership roles. This is a discourse that I have also heard in Calcutta, mainly from would-be beneficiaries of such philanthropic action. One family in prominent political positions is regularly criticised for 'doing nothing' to help the poor. By way of contrast, I was frequently told that if the hard-working leader of one of the social service organisations decided to stand for office then everyone would vote for them. There is, however, generally no facility to *vote* for representatives.[4]

Networks

In my visits to the city, I came to see the community as being made up of a complex web of connections. There seem to me to be a set of key players in 21st century Calcutta—some are individuals, others are organisations. The people who seem to have the widest influence were well known and include leaders of the various organisations, and present and past MLAs. The organisations include CAISS, the AIAIA, the Dr Graham's Homes establishment (including Birkmyre Hostel) and the East India Charitable Trust (EICT). There are numerous other important players too—the schools, the

[4] I am reminded of Ghassan Hage's essay, 'On Worrying: The Lost Art of the Well-administered National Cuddle' (2004) in which he discusses what he sees as a central role of the state or nation: to be the mechanism for the distribution of hope to its citizens. However, what happens when a community does not have a state, or when the state does not take that role? This, I believe, is closer to the situation for Anglo-Indians.

churches, the clubs (in particular the Rangers, Dalhousie Institute and the Grail) and the rest homes. It was evident that the work all of these people and organisations do is significant in maintaining and enhancing the social structures within the community.

Clubs and associations who run Christmas (and other) programmes distribute many of their services in a way that involves the provision of entertainment and recreation for their recipients, rather than just giving them alms and other assistance. In this way, members of the organisations become engaged with and get to know other local Anglo-Indian recipients of services, and thus expand the networks of recipients and providers. Importantly, what the associations also do is model Anglo-Indian sociality and norms of behaviour, that is, they reproduce and augment their Anglo-Indian cultural capital.

For diasporic Anglo-Indians, the social service organisations serve a purpose too—they provide a focus for their charity and a connection back to India. There are a number of projects that not only offer care for those who need it, but also provide networks for the community. For example, a Canadian association's *Adopt a Gran* project sponsors several of the residents of one of the rest homes I spent time in. The Internet is used effectively to promote various fun-raising projects, which also enable members of this diaspora to be in close contact with each other. I was made particularly aware of this when I was in Calcutta in December 2007: one woman I used to visit in the Homes, who was part of the *Adopt a Gran* scheme, died while I was there after her health deteriorated suddenly. The next day I attended her burial service, then came back to my flat to find an email to my New Zealand address from someone in Canada telling me the news of her death.

The various residential homes for elderly Anglo-Indians also offer an opportunity for Anglo-Indians—diasporic and local— who may not often come into contact with each other, to do so. Christmastime in particular is a time of increased activity for the home's residents as they receive numerous invitations to attend Christmas parties, particularly those held by Church and Anglo-Indian schools, and Anglo-Indian clubs, and visits from schools and other groups who decorate the homes, sing Christmas carols and distribute gifts. The last story in this work includes a description of one home at Christmastime.

Benedict Anderson (1991) wrote about *imagined communities*, which referred to particular types of social groups who share certain commonalities but are imagined in that they are unlikely to meet all the members of the group. Anglo-Indians fit this description in terms of them being a diasporic community, but within Calcutta, because of their small population and the shared networks they have established through their social service organisations, many have in fact met others in their community.

Conclusion

The argument central to this essay is that a significant contribution to the mechanism by which Anglo-Indians maintain and augment their sense of community is achieved through enacting the practices involved in offering services to their *less fortunate*. These services can be (and are) carried out individually, but the most effective way of achieving this is through the various organisations. Although this community enhancement may be a side effect resulting from the organisations' primary objective of poverty alleviation, they are contributing to something larger and even more sustaining.

13

Barry O'Brien: Charismatic Politician

For as long as I've been involved in research with Calcutta's Anglo-Indian community I've heard of the O'Brien family. It's not only Anglo-Indians who know of the O'Briens but often in conversation I'd mention the family to other local Indians and they would know of them too. The O'Briens are entitled to being called a dynasty: they've generations of successful family members, especially in the knowledge realm—they currently feature in textbook publishing and quizzing, and they're leaders in politics. Barry has recently completed a five-year term as an MLA representing West Bengal's Anglo-Indians; his father, Neil, has also served as an MLA and is the long-time president-in-chief of the AIAIA, and Barry's older brother, Derek, has been appointed an MP for Mamata Banerjee's Trinamool Congress Party, which achieved a landslide victory in 2011, bringing to an end the 34-year governance of the Communist Party of India (Marxist). Clearly this family is in a position to make a positive impact on Anglo-Indians in Calcutta.

As an MLA, Barry's responsibilities involved keeping in touch with and working for his community. The railway towns such as Kharagpur and Asansol seemed a particular focus of his energies in this regard. In a recent visit I made to Asansol, it was clear that Anglo-Indians there hold Barry in high regard. They described him as charismatic, and they indicated that they felt he'd done a lot for them. I was shown a number of new concrete roads in areas that Anglo-Indians lived in higher numbers that were attributed to his MLA funding. In Calcutta too there is evidence of his MLA-related spending, for example the two bus shelters in Lower Circular Road: one commemorating Frank Anthony, opposite the Frank Anthony School, and one commemorating Derozio, opposite St James and Pratt Memorial schools, being two such examples. He was also very interested in running a census of the Anglo-Indians in West Bengal that would provide statistics to assist with planning the work he wanted to be able to do. As he said,

> So if we'd had this idea a few years ago it would have really helped me in my work. So for the future MLA as well as social service organisations, like the Association and CAISS etc., plus the Government, we can give them a clear idea of what the problems in the community are, in numbers. And I'll go one step further, the fact remains that a significant part of the help for the community still comes from a lot of Anglo-Indians who have migrated and moved out. I'm not saying that they don't trust and believe people who are doing the work here, but there's much more concrete evidence now that there are so many people who need help with getting a home, or there are so many people who are doing really well. We're talking in numbers now, in statistics.

Until late 2010, I had had little opportunity to get to know Barry but after spending time on a project with him over the Christmas season I came to some understanding and appreciation of the energy and charm of this particular O'Brien. On one of my last days in Calcutta he made time for an interview, as we travelled in a car together to the same event. I was interested in hearing his story for two reasons: one was his family's prominence; the other was that he struck me as being unusual for an Anglo-Indian in being completely comfortable in an Anglo-Indian or in a Bengali world. When I had made this observation to him earlier, he explained that it was the result of his family history and the environment he was brought up in, so this is where I asked him to begin his account.

> Okay, it basically started with my great-grandfather, Daniel O'Brien, who was of Irish descent. Either he or his father came out here, and we think he had a government job. He was stationed somewhere in the tea gardens area [in the foothills of the Himalayas] or thereabouts and he had a very good Bengali Indian friend. And anyway he must have been in about his early 40s and unmarried, and this friend of his had three nieces who had lost their parents, and their parents had owned some tea gardens. They were very wealthy Bengalis. And the story goes that the uncle decided to get these three girls married. And the story also goes that the tea gardens disappeared so whether the uncle sort of swallowed it all up, or whatever, these girls saw no part of it. The eldest one, her name was Nellie, was married to

this much older Irishman or, of Irish decent (my great-grandfather), when she was just about 15.

He was a very good man and they had two sons and two daughters together. It was when she was expecting another that her husband Daniel went for a *shikaar*, or hunt. In those days they would go on these *shikaar*s over the weekend or for a few days. But while he was away he got tin poisoning and he died. They must have been having tinned foodstuffs and got it from them. So he died leaving her with her two daughters, two sons and another on the way. Sadly the two daughters died early in their teens, of tuberculosis. In those days it wasn't curable.

So Nellie was quite alone, but she was an incredible woman, a great fighter and she decided to study medicine. And this is, I mean we're talking a hundred years ago. And she did that with the third boy on one lap, and books of medicine and a lantern in front of her. And she studied to become a doctor.

They were by then in a city in, what's now, Bangladesh. She saw very difficult days. Then as the kids grew up a bit they then went to Agra. I don't know why they went there but anyway they went to Agra. And finally she decided to settle down in Calcutta. She couldn't educate all her children so the eldest one made the sacrifice; his name was Pat, Patrick. He was a teenager when he started working, leaving the second one, who is my grandfather, Amos Peter, to do his studies because he was academically inclined and very intelligent; he got himself qualified. He got a postgraduate in English and taught English everywhere from Kashmir to Kanyakumari and ended up as the head of the Benares University's English Department. So that is the second one, my grandfather. Now the eldest went away finally and was posted in Pakistan and lived on in Pakistan after Independence and then migrated to Canada. The other two, my grandfather and the youngest, Eric, stayed back in India. Their mother was earning well as a doctor and she started saving money to build her own home. She bought some property in a place called Ballygunge. Now that's right in the heart of the city, a residential part of the city, but those days it was far flung. It was certainly far away from where any Anglo-Indians lived. I don't think there were even any Christians in the vicinity. In those days you could safely say that all Anglo-Indians lived in Wellesley, Ripon Street and Elliott Road: the central Calcutta parts. She bought this property obviously because she could afford it and she started building one floor at a time.

She became a gynaecologist. In those days, particularly the Muslim community, people were looking for lady doctors, who were few and far between. So she was in great demand and they would pay her lots of money, even more than she asked. These were middle-class Muslim families, who were maybe having small businesses. So anyway they would leave the money in little sort of sacks. They would pay her well, and that's how she had a car, she had a telephone and she'd built her home. We're talking about the late 1930s and early 1940s. All this was done single-handedly.

My father remembers (because my father was brought up by his grandmother, which I'll come to a little later) sitting on the balcony at the back of our home where Dr Mrs N. B. O'Brien had built her home. He remembers waiting for hours to see his grandmother coming back. This was when there was rioting and Calcutta was going through a blood bath. Then he would see quite a few Muslim menfolk with sticks, lathis in hand escorting her home. This lady with the flower dress. Yeah, and she wasn't Anglo-Indian, she was Bengali, but she always wore dresses.

So the eldest son Patrick, he went on to Pakistan and then to Canada. The second one, Amos Peter, my grandfather, he was having a great time all over the country as a much sought-after professor and she suddenly told him, 'Why don't you get married?' So he said, 'Well, I don't have the time. I certainly don't have the time to look for a girl. So you want to get me married, you find the girl.' So she went to St Vincent's. It's St Katherine's home now but it was called St Vincent's then. There were a lot of orphans and girls who had nobody to care for them and she went and picked out the most beautiful young girl over there whose name was Edna. I spent a lot of time with her later on when we grew up but I saw some photographs of when my grandfather must have met her and married her. She looked like a Hollywood star. I mean really beautiful. And I think both her parents were British. Or maybe her father was British and her mother was Anglo-Indian. But she didn't just look very Indian at all. And so she was the selected girl and then they got married and moved to my great-grandmother's home in Ballygunge. Unfortunately she couldn't adjust. It was really the wilderness there then. Apparently you could hear the jackals, and she couldn't adjust to that. And I presume that they couldn't adjust as people either, so the marriage didn't last and when my father was four they split. Then my great-grandmother told her son, 'You carry on because your job is taking you here and there. You don't worry about your son. I'll look after him.' She had been through everything so to look after a little boy, her grandson, was no big deal for her. So she took the entire responsibility and looked after him; so my father's grandmother was virtually a mother to him.

Ours was one of the first few buildings, if not the first, in this area. And gradually it sort of mushroomed and grew into a very traditional middle-class Bengali locality, a safe secure typical Bengali locality. This is where my father grew up. My father had a pretty good relationship with his neighbours but he didn't spend a lot of time with them because he was really into his books. He was into school and spending time with his grandmother. My grandfather married several years later and settled down in a place called Cuttack in Orissa, not far from Puri, and he had three sons. But over here it was just my great-grandmother and my father, and the youngest uncle, Eric. The youngest uncle lived here with his mother and wife and children but he died very early. So his family was here but then even they moved on till finally it was just my father and his grandmother. And after some time my father got married to an Anglo-Indian lady, Joyce Jordan.

Yes, who I heard was very beautiful.

Oh yes, she was considered the stunner of Calcutta in the 1960s and 1970s. She would drive her red Herald car. She had this incredible figure and she was very beautiful and she was an absolutely railway colony Anglo-Indian. She's from all over because they moved around. My grandfather Bunny Jordan, he picked up many languages, including Bengali. When he was posted at Garden Reach he picked up Bengali, then Telegu when he was posted in Andhra Pradesh. So she had, you know, a varied experience as she was growing up. I mean varied as in sometimes they were living just outside a jungle, sometimes they were in a big, or a smallish town. Anyway, it was a very different upbringing from my father. And there were 11 brothers and sisters in her family so they were poles apart as it were. When they got married they lived with my great-grandmother and that's where we were born. And we were the only non-Bengali family.

Family Life

There are three of us. Derek is the eldest, then Andy, then myself. All born one after the other in 1961, 1962 and 1963 and we were the only non-Bengali family. Forget about anything else—there were only

Bengalis. After a while a few others came in, but we were certainly the only Christian family, and the only Anglo-Indian family. So we grew up there in that neighbourhood, we literally grew up playing cricket on the streets, playing football on the streets, participating in everything that the local boys did. And we never held back, and neither did our parents hold us back. They allowed us to participate in everything. I mean it was a social participation. So we were back from school by four o'clock and immediately we were out on the road playing because we didn't have a park. So we would play all these games with these boys. We interacted with them for a couple of hours every day and therefore learnt to speak good Bengali.

In India we have the great blessing of many people who need to be employed in homes, so we always had two or three domestic help, as they're called here, and they were Bengalis so we were spending even more time interacting in Bengali. And that's the best way to learn a language. I studied Hindi in school. I studied a bit of Bengali, but not seriously, but I speak very fluent Bengali and I think a language breaks down many barriers and puts people at ease. So I think more and more Anglo-Indians have and should know one language besides English really well.

Well that's something else that a survey would be able to tell us about.

Yes, absolutely. I've noticed that Anglo-Indians in India who have known the regional language or Hindi fluently, whichever is the most widely spoken language in that state, have gone much further in many ways than the Anglo-Indian who hasn't. It's a bit of a generalisation but I have seen that happen. And also, whenever we had a function, Christmas Day or whatever, my mother would go round with cakes and whatever else to every single home in the area. And our neighbours would actually see priests coming for a family prayer, and they would see the huge Christmas celebrations. We're the only ones here; so would we underplay it? No way, no way. We're the only ones here, so we didn't want to underplay it. No way, no way. We used to put up our little nativity scene for the Christmas season and they all come to see it. My mother, as she's getting older, wants to compete with them as it were, and the nativity scene she puts up is getting bigger and bigger each year. There are lights on our family home for three or four weeks. She's trying to match their Puja lights. When they're on there's a lot of lights over here.

When they used to have their Pujas, to organise Kali Pujas, which is really like a community event, we would be involved. We'd be sitting down with them, near the pandal, the structure near their statue. Obviously, as very staunch Christians and Catholics, for us it was just a social thing. But just the fact that we were with them, it just made us one of them and, you know, we were always treated well. In fact, for many years, I was in charge of organising things for it. After the Puja the statues, the images of goddesses, would be immersed in the river. It takes a lot of organising to do that: you've got to organise the transport, the permissions etc., and for many years I was in charge of it. And I remember once actually, you know getting everything organised and saying, 'Okay, bye, see you guys. I'm going to Mass now.'

I think what was special about our family is we were able to live right in the midst of everything non-Anglo-Indian and enjoy it, be part of it, not in a superficial way, and yet really, really be Anglo-Indians. We would go to the DI, the Dalhousie Institute, which in the 1960s and 1970s was very Anglo-Indian, and it still is in many ways, but more so in the 1960s and 1970s. The majority of the members are Anglo-Indian. The functions are Anglo-Indian. All our friends were Anglo-Indian, so we didn't miss out. There are many Anglo-Indians who would end up being with people who speak another language or have a different culture and end up one of them. So they were one or the other, but we had this great blessing and it was our good fortune that we had both.

Education

We all went to St Xavier's right through school except for two years when my father was transferred to Delhi in the early 1970s. There we studied at the Christian Brothers School, St Columbus. Then I came back to St Xavier's, and then in (class) 11 and 12 I went to La Martinere. The time at a Christian Brothers school had a huge impact on me, even though I was there only for two years. I had many years of Jesuit education in India, and then two years in an Anglican school, La Martiniere, where a lot of different things happened. There was a girls' school, so there was a lot of interaction with them. That was a totally different atmosphere. And then I went on to Jadavpur University where, again I was the only Anglo-Indian. And over there it was very traditional; this was in the early 1980s. There were 33 girls in my class and only seven boys and out of the 33 girls I would say at least 20 or 22 of them would come with a whole lot of oil in their hair and plaited very traditionally, and wearing saris.

They were from very conservative Bengali families. I think many of them may have fallen in love with me and maybe I was also attracted to many of them. I was so at ease because of the language and the culture and everything. We used to go to films together and yet we knew nothing else would happen because, well, we just knew it. So at Jadavpur University I studied International Relations. We have a very good department but unfortunately I didn't study as hard as I should have studied. I was very much into theatre actually and was already regretting not going to the National School of Drama, which is the centrepiece of theatre in Delhi. But I just didn't get down to it and I should have. I mean I was interested in international relations and political science but it wasn't the first thing that I wanted to do. Anyway by the time I finished I decided that I wanted to be a teacher.

Fortunately for me in my very first year of college I got one and then two or three other part-time teaching jobs. So while going to college I was already earning some money by teaching at schools. One was a Marwari school for girls, it was owned by the Birlas, a big Marwari family here. This was a very conservative Bengali English-medium school, and then I worked in another, a girl's school, which was not Marwari but had very traditional girls from Gujarat and other backgrounds going there. I think this whole mix has really been my education, you know, having the good fortune of having this huge mix, this background of St Columbus, St Xavier's, La Martiniere, Jadavpur University, growing up in Ballygunge, going to the DI, then these schools that I taught at were all very conservative Bengali schools.

But after that I planned to study further of course, and then suddenly a friend of mine, David McMahon, says, 'Hey you, before you do your masters, why don't you just come and work for us? I'm looking for a guy, and you write well. So why don't you come and just work in our sports magazine for a year?' I said, 'Yes' and that was the best mistake I ever made. The one year went on to become two and then to three and four. I saw lots of the world. I went to the Wimbledon; I covered the World Cup Cricket and World Cup Table Tennis. So I saw a lot of India and a little bit abroad, though not much, it was mostly India. But through that travelling I met so many people. I travelled by train and by bus and by air. I joined in November of 1985 and in May, for one of my first solo assignments, I was sent to cover the funeral of Tenzing Norgay in Darjeeling. And one of the first interviews I ever did was a one-and-a-half to two hour interview with Sir Edmund Hillary at Windermere, a wonderful heritage hotel in Darjeeling. And we just chatted and chatted and chatted. One of my finest moments was when Sir Edmund, the great Sir Edmund Hillary, made my tea and stirred my tea and gave it to me. And I found what an incredible man he was. Besides the fact that, I mean everyone knows what he did [he was the first man to climb Mt Everest] but the amount of work that he has done in Nepal.... He's an incredible man.

During the four years when I worked as a journalist, I worked in producing an English sports magazine, but the group I worked for is Bengali. It was like the equivalent, in a Bengali sense, of working for *Time Magazine* or the *Sunday Times* in England, because they have the largest Bengali circulation here. And once again except for us blokes, within the office, amongst our friends we all spoke in English, but we'd speak in Bengali with the other departments, the computer department or the art department.

Anyway, so I was earning a fairly decent amount of money by my young standards. And I did the good Anglo-Indian thing, you know, roaming around, zooming around on my bike, and going to the DI, having a few beers, going to this party, that party. Forgetting about who I dated yesterday. So I did all that, which was also important to do, not just being a goody-goody boy.

But after that I said it's time to get back to studies now and time to be a teacher. Unfortunately for me the school where I was a part-time teacher asked me to join up, they said, 'We need you immediately.' So I joined South Point School as a teacher. It's not an ICSE [Indian Certificate of Secondary Education] school so they didn't need more degrees than I had. I then became the assistant principal of the school at a very young age. I never ever got down to completing my studies, which is a huge regret. I intend to remedy that now. So I am planning on getting myself educated rather late in my life. I'm going to study subjects that I want to study.

South Point at that time was the largest school in the world with 14,500 students. Guess what? No Anglo-Indians. Guess what? No Christians. They had 14,500 students with a teaching staff of 450. So once again I was the only one, and I was in charge of discipline, and extra-curricular activities, so I was interacting a lot with parents. And, therefore, to make myself understood and to drive the point home I would speak to them in Bengali.

So, you know, I've reached a stage, I hope nobody misunderstands, where when I speak in Bengali, I think in Bengali. To be good in a language I think is the ultimate. I mean when I speak Hindi I don't think in Hindi. I translate. Fortunately for me my Hindi is pretty good also but it's not as good as my Bengali, and all this has stood me in good stead. Now as an MLA obviously I speak in English when I speak in the Assembly, but that doesn't stop me from occasionally giving an anecdote or a punch line, or something which I can't translate, giving it in Bengali. And they all sort of like that.

So we're obviously a combination of the two sides, but most Anglo-Indians don't know the other side. Anglo-Indians should be very proud of their Indian heritage. Many of them would be but they don't know much about it. And in most cases the mother is not Indian, in many cases she'd be Anglo-Indian. We're the same: from my mother's side we don't know our Indian heritage. We only know the French Bouché and the Jordans, but my mother could never tell us what the Indian connection is. But from my father's side it's quite clear.

And on a personal, you're married 20 years now?

Yes, Denise and I are married for 20 years now. We knew each other for about two years, so 22 years together. We have three daughters who are in their teens. Denise comes from a solid Anglo-Indian family, very different from mine. Once again she will not be able to tell you about her Indian side; obviously there's an Indian side in her judging by her looks and her complexion. But her family on both sides is Anglo-Indian through and through. Her father Terrance Port was the secretary of the AIAIA after he retired. Before that he was a very typical sort of a shippie. He didn't work on the ships but he worked at the port of Calcutta, and he was a legendary person over there. You know, the Anglo-Indian who would sort of wear his shorts and go out early in the morning, go to Mass, you know pick up his *bakakhannies*[1] or his *dhal puries*, come back, have a little snooze, work really hard. When he's having a drink enjoy his drink, party hard. Very good jiver, you know, was my father-in-law. Unfortunately he's passed away.

I think Denise and I were supposed to meet. We should have met at a party or somewhere, but guess where we met? We met at an Anglo-Indian sort of a discussion or seminar early on a Sunday morning, organised by CAISS. She had a friend and a colleague who told her that he was going to this session, so she might like

---

[1] This is a Calcutta speciality food, a savoury fried pastry round which is eaten hot.

to come along. And he told me too. So both of us landed up in his home in Royd Street early on Sunday morning and he wasn't ready, of course. He's a very laid back chap. Anyway, so we chatted and then we went to this all-day seminar where she didn't say much but I said a lot, because that's my way, my verbal diarrhoea they call it. And she's a very quiet person. So that's where we met. Then we didn't meet for a while and then I think our next date was Easter. We sort of met at Easter, at the DI, and then well then we fell in love and I proposed to her on the 31st of December at midnight at the DI, on the dance floor. And that's the good news. The bad news is I was drinking glucose water because I had just recovered from jaundice and couldn't drink alcohol. So I was in my senses, or not in my senses, depending on which way you look at it. And I proposed to her without any engagement ring. I couldn't afford one actually. I didn't go down on my knee but we've had, like everybody else, our ups and downs, but most importantly I think because we share a commonality of looking in the same direction, wanting the same things out of life, you know our faith, our religion, our community, our eating habits, the clothes that we wear. I think all this made it much easier. So hats off to the people who marry outside their community and their religion because I think it's much more difficult, so all credit to them.

While Barry didn't dwell on his time as an MLA in telling me his story, it is that period of his life that has seen him most involved in serving his community. In the times I spent with him, I saw considerable energy and state money put into brightening the lives of community members—whether it was by distributing blankets during the month or two of winter, taking a role on various Anglo-Indian committees, running housie games in rest homes or conducting personal visits such as calling in on an elderly Anglo-Indian woman on the occasion of her 89th birthday—making her day! His term as an MLA is now over but he is putting his energies into other Anglo-Indian projects such as the EICT and I expect we will see him take on other Anglo-Indian-related responsibilities in the near future.

14

Meryl: Life, Last Days and Care

Writing this life story was tough because Meryl had recently and unexpectedly passed away. She became ill within a few months of my returning to New Zealand after interviewing her—suddenly developing slurred speech and loss of fine motor skills. Her condition deteriorated so quickly that I was not able to call and speak to her before she passed away. My impulse after hearing from Philomena Eaton that she had died was to immediately write up her life story, interrupting other work I was involved in, to be in touch with her in some way. I had always expected to see her again because, although she was close to 80 years old, she was so full of life.

I had been told about Meryl before I met her. Members of the Homes' management committee had told me of her background of being 'head girl with a tea company for years' and her 'ability to run things', explaining that this was why she had been offered the position of resident superintendent. They also indicated that I might need to tread carefully with her in order to maintain easy access to the Homes and its residents.

When I first met Meryl, with her shock of flowing white hair, she was hurrying off to feed Prince, the Home's guard dog, and barely acknowledged my presence. Prince had been aptly named; Meryl adored him. I had my camera with me so I followed, offering to take a photo of the two of them together, which she agreed to immediately. I took the photo—through a set of bars with the sleek-coated pale brown Prince behind them showing all his teeth as he snarled terrifyingly at me. Meryl looked unperturbed, adjusting her knee-length shirt and smoothing her blouse as she stood beside the crouching growling creature and smiled happily for the photo. Prince, a smallish Labrador or similar breed, I was later told, had never been outside the Home's grounds since Meryl and another resident had bought him as a puppy from the market. He was tied up during the day and released for guard duty in the evening. He was friendly and protective towards everybody whom he had known from the beginning of his time at the Home; anyone else risked being mauled, seriously.

As resident superintendent Meryl had moved downstairs, primarily, she told me, to sleep closer to Prince. She had responsibility for the Home's day-to-day operations, which included liaising between the hands-on management committee and the residents, and with the staff of two cooks, a sweeper and a night watchman. She needed to be aware of any special requirements (medical, dietary, transportation) of the residents; she kept a close eye on all comings and goings from the Home; and the cook had to be given instructions for the meals. She was the person entrusted with the day-to-day finances to cover marketing for the day's food, replacing gas bottles and for bread and other deliveries. It was the constant locking away and unlocking of dry food supplies, butter and jam, coffee and tea, linen, and so on that she found the most demanding and the cause of most interruptions to anything else she tried to do. She told me that her duties included making tea in the mornings for each of the residents but because she had never learned to make tea (or cook a thing), this task had been delegated to the night watchman at the end of his duty. She was also given extra responsibilities as they arose, such as meeting tradesmen if any repairs or maintenance was required.

With so many duties, it was difficult to schedule an interview time but after I'd given her an information sheet about the research I was doing she expressed an interest in being involved. She saw that I was also doing some research in Melbourne and had asked if I had come across her cousin. I didn't expect that I would have, given the large population of Anglo-Indians in Melbourne, but asked the cousin's name all the same. I had indeed met her and was able to make arrangements for them to talk a few days later, on Christmas day. This perhaps provided a catalyst for us quickly working out an easy convivial relationship. I enjoyed her wicked sense of humour and could appreciate how hard she tried to keep everyone happy. Finally, after a couple of weeks, we managed to organise an interview time one evening, with only a few brief interruptions as we proceeded.

Night falls early in Calcutta in December, so though it wasn't much after 7 pm, when we sat down, it was dark. Although the Home was a bit dingy with age and the effect of Calcutta's dust and pollution, on that evening any shabbiness was brightened by the coloured streamers twisting and swinging from wall to picture frame to light fitting, and the banners and decorations around the walls. They'd been put up by students from St Xavier's School who'd come to sing carols and festoon the place earlier that day. The manger set, and Christmas cards on the sideboard also added festive highlights.

We began our interview, which I have drawn upon here. I begin with a brief introduction to Meryl's early life but the key foci of this narrative are two major events: her experience of the time around Indian Independence and then of her coming to the Home. Meryl provided me good insights into why her move was needed, so I include the context of her pre-institutional home life in order to convey that here too.

Meryl was born and brought up in Calcutta. Her father was a sergeant in the Calcutta Police Force, one of a number of Anglo-Indian and British men who made up the force at that time. Her parents and her brother (who was older than her by 11 years) lived in the police quarters in what was known then as Central Avenue (now Chittaranjan Avenue). The British officers could afford to send their children to the hill schools of Darjeeling and Kurseong. Meryl recalled she was the only Calcutta-educated student these officers would allow their children to play with during their school holiday breaks. She attributes this to a fear that their children would otherwise lose the good manners that had been drummed into them at school, and she was known as the best mannered child in the building.

Meryl went to Calcutta Girls' High School where she finished her Senior Cambridge year with final examinations in December 1944. Meryl insisted that she wasn't studious (preferring movies and going to dances, especially with a slightly older cousin from South India and his friends who were all in the Air Force) but she had obtained a first division, the highest pass possible.

Following her schooling she took a nine-month secretarial course run by the Young Women's Christian Association (YWCA) and was then sent to a British company, which owned 13 tea gardens in Assam. She began in this position in 1945 working with almost exclusively British staff. This was just two years before Indian Independence, which brought tumultuous times to India, affecting everyone but especially the British. Once the Raj was over, British citizens began to feel pressurised to leave the country as well. In her 40 years with the company, she saw changes in personnel, in politics as well as several changes in company ownership and name.

She was perhaps the most constant and certainly a highly valued employee throughout that time, as she worked her way from stenographer to the managing director's personal assistant—the top administrative job. She was told that she was the 'first lady to have reached the top'; up until then only men had held this position. She was unusual in not moving companies with the boss when he did, preferring instead to stay on and learn to work with the next one. She said that a new boss usually chose his own secretary, 'but I adjusted to each of them'. She told me a little about working for one early in her career:

> The one I worked for longest was Sir Richard Duckworth. He was an English baronet. And a very difficult man. Very impatient and all that. You know he had done war service, and he had lost his right arm, his right hand, but still he excelled in everything. He was a very handsome man.
>
> He was born in Burma because his parents, they were then in Burma. But he had to retire from India, although he was still not retiring age, because then the change was taking place, you know. Only one British director was allowed.

Quit India and Personal Repercussions

I asked Meryl what she remembered about *the change* and particularly of times around Independence and Partition. She would have been 19 or 20 years old at that time.

> One day I was at office and they got news that the stretch of road near Loreto Day School, where we were staying then, was under curfew. There was lot of this 'Quit India' business, you know, for the British

to quit India. And so my boss, the manager of the department, said, 'I'll give you a lift home.' But when he came to the head of Dharamtala Esplanade he wasn't allowed to enter. They said, 'There's a curfew.' So he said, 'I have to leave you here. Will you be alright?'

Were you worried?

No I, when you're young you don't think of danger and all this. And I got out and I was walking down with not a soul on the road.

This curfew was in force. And that was about 3 o'clock in the afternoon. So I was walking, then one young man, a Muslim, he must have been, he had that lungi on. He came out from the side street and he told me to hurry up and go. He said, 'There's going to be a lot of trouble.' So I put on speed and all and I came to the gate, and the guard at the gate opened it quickly. I came in and we closed the gate, and then all hell broke loose! They came running out from the side lanes and they were throwing brickbats and bottles and all this, and the British trucks were passing with the troops on board.

Who were throwing all those things?

All these, all these Indians.

Muslims, Hindus?

Muslims I think. Muslims. Yes. It was the Muslims. And the trucks were passing with these soldiers and they were throwing these at the truck.

Then another day I was standing on the veranda; it's a low veranda and I was standing, only one floor up, because there was a procession going. And the British troops they stopped them. They were going to the governor's house.

So the procession: was it the Muslims again, or Hindus?

I think mixed. And they were making their way there.

What were they protesting...?

They wanted the British to leave. All this Quit India movement against the British. So they were making their way to the governor's house. So the police, all British police, they stopped them at the head of Dharamtala, and wouldn't let them go further. So they squatted on the road in front of our house. I spotted them so I went out to see what was happening. I was standing there and one of them threw a brick at me! It just whizzed past my face, and this British sergeant saw it, and he gave the order to fire. And they fired. And then afterwards he came to our house.

The British soldier did?

Yeah, he came the next day or so and he asked my father. Because he was being asked, 'Why did you give orders?' They had tried to avoid firing and all. So he was being asked, 'Why did you give the order to fire?' So he asked my father whether he would allow me to come to the court and say what happened. My father said, 'Yes.' But he said, 'I'll try to avoid it' so I wouldn't have to go. And they didn't call me.

So when the police fired, did he hurt the man who ...?

I think there was an injury, I think somebody....

An injury, he didn't kill him?

He didn't kill.... Maybe he did kill him and that's why they wanted a court enquiry and all. Anyway it was passed over. I didn't have to go.

How did you feel about this protest, and the idea that the British were being forced to leave?

At that age I didn't feel anything. I really didn't feel anything. Because we had Indians working in our office and they were very nice people: they all spoke English, they all took a delight in writing a good English letter and all. They picked up all the good things, you know, from the British.

Did you feel as though you identified more with the Indians or more with the British? Can you remember?

Yes. I was more with the British. I was working with them and all that. Then gradually the Indians came in and they were very Westernised. They'd picked up a lot from the British and I didn't feel any great change, you know because they were much like the British in their mannerisms and their culture.

Once, once all this, the Partition took place and after the dust settled, you know, then there were no problems. In fact, the Indians would treat us with respect, they would treat us well, wherever we went.

Okay, I see. And had the British treated you well too?

Oh yes, very well. For the British, ladies came first. They gave us a fantastic lunch and first the ladies had to have lunch, then the British bosses, then the managers, then the assistants, you know, the British assistants would have lunch, then the Anglo-Indian boys. They treated us with a lot of respect. And if they saw us leaving office and one of them was leaving, they'd always offer us a lift.

They looked after you. And did the Indians do that too?

The Indians, they would never, like, offer us a lift, because their minds are rather narrow. Because somebody may see them with a lady you see, and then they'll tell the wife and the family or something. So if you are working late he will send you home with the driver.

Okay, so he'd look after you too but he wouldn't be seen with you.

Yes. Yes. But there were those who were educated in England and all this, they were not so bad. They were different. There was one young man in the second company I worked for, he was born in England and at the age of eight (his parents were doctors) they came away. He was very nice. He'd bring me home many a time and all, and he was so knowledgeable about everything, you know, and all up-to-date with things. He used to play the guitar and sing. He was a chartered accountant. He was very clever. Then when he left our company, this was a small company, and he joined a bigger company. He still came to see us though and he'd tell me, he used to call me Miss M, 'Miss M, I miss you.' He'd say that. So, my working life has been very happy.

It seems that it was some years until Indianisation processes began to affect the company that she worked for. In the 1960s, there was a range of law changes that affected foreign-owned companies operating in India. One was that from then through the 1970s the number of foreign directors permitted in any company was drastically reduced. The changes in regulations resulted in the closure of a large number of British and other international companies in the main centres where many Anglo-Indians had employment. These companies packing up and leaving the subcontinent provided further impetus for Anglo-Indians to leave. The company Meryl worked for became owned by Marwaris, but as she said,

> The people are very Westernised. One of the owners was born and brought up in England. So he was very cultured. Then it went on into the 1970s, this change came and English directors have to leave India. It ended up with only one English director, and then that even was over.
>
> Then the businesses had to be run by Indians, but they had picked up a lot from the British, you know, their ways of managing and everything. It was very easy adjusting to them.
>
> I had learnt such a lot from Sir Richard, because his English was perfect and he was very particular, and all that. So they looked to me to type the correct English. And then gradually, whereas my first bosses were older than me, and they would be in a position to tell me off and all, latterly I was older than my bosses. They were younger so I could dictate to them. So like that, 40 years I worked there.
>
> I stayed there, right through. I think I must have been the only secretary in Calcutta who has stayed in one company. Because as I said when the boss leaves, the secretary leaves. But I went right through. Yes, I was happy in my work, that's why I was there, you know.
>
> And then after I retired they called me back for a smaller company with six gardens in Darjeeling. So they called me back and there I worked part-time. Just helping out in the same group, with the same owners. I worked there another 11 years.
>
> Then in August 1999 I retired from this smaller company and I came here in December 1999.

The one significant immediate effect that those turbulent times of the Independence Movement had on Meryl's family was how they felt about where they lived. Her brother, who was about 30 years old at this time, insisted that the family move house. He thought they were in for an extended period of political rallies passing their home. Meryl's mother didn't want to move; she, like Meryl, was reluctant to make changes unless they were really needed. She said to her son that she was settled, got on well with her neighbours and so saw no good reason to go. But over a short space of time, just a couple of years later, both of Meryl's parents died, and then they moved house—Meryl, her brother and Syd, her young cousin from South India who was living with them by then too. A centrally located Wellesley Street flat became their new home, and this is where Meryl lived for 40 years until she came to the Home. She described their new address as being a very comfortable and spacious flat with one large room, a smaller room, a bathroom, kitchen and a veranda. She recalled proudly the intricately patterned marble flooring, crediting this as one of the flat's features, which made it attractive enough to have been requisitioned by the Royal Army Force during the war years. When they moved into the flat it was well-maintained and well-serviced with power and running water. However, like so many stately colonial buildings in Calcutta, it was poorly maintained in the post-Independence years. It wasn't long before water was no longer able to be pumped up; instead they had to buy water daily from the waterman. The landlord refused to carry out any maintenance, so in the end any costs outlaid for essential maintenance were covered by Meryl.

Family

Meryl recalled that one of the happiest periods of her life were the years spent living in the Wellesley Street home with her brother and her two cousins from South India: the one who'd been living with her family for a while, and his slightly older brother who'd come to live with his cousins after their parents died. They settled into their new home and enjoyed getting to know their new neighbours, whom Meryl described as 'partying types' of Anglo-Indians, in contrast to the 'simple, quiet-living' Anglo-Indian neighbours of their last home, that her mother had got on so well with. The change in address represented a change in class of the neighbourhood too: they moved from a wealthier and more conservative

Anglo-Indian neighbourhood to a less affluent but more epicurean Anglo-Indian neighbourhood. Wellesley Street was at the hub of a group of central city streets whose Anglo-Indian residents gave the community a reputation for being a fun-loving carefree people. Meryl certainly found her new neighbours to be exciting company, but after a while, as he came to know them better, her brother didn't approve of them at all. She was aware of their faults explaining to me, somewhat regretfully, that 'These people, they didn't have any regular jobs and they'd dress up and you'd think they are very well off, but actually, they would try to extract from others to meet their living expenses and all, you know?' Her cousin became besotted by one of the neighbours: a divorced, single mother who lived in the flat next door. Her brother was appalled by this development, and threatened to leave if the person concerned continued to visit. Meryl didn't take his threats seriously, and the cousin didn't want to, and so the visits continued. But one day Meryl came home from work to find that her brother had packed all of his belongings and moved out to a flat in Park Circus, quite a distance from them. Meryl was stunned that he would do that, but confided to me that she herself had been so taken with the young woman that her concern about her brother's sudden departure soon dissipated. She described her, and the times, in this way:

> She was from a railway colony. Somewhere up north. She had left her husband, and had come to Calcutta with two children. She was very glamorous and so this was an attraction, you know. That generation of Anglo-Indians, they were very nice looking and very smart and all that. And we were quite attracted by her talk. She talked very freely. We never heard all this talk before, you know. So Syd got ... he was about 20 years younger than her. And he fell for her and my brother didn't like all this at all. He, of course, was staying separate by then. But she was one of those people; she'd have a boyfriend for two years then change. As she's getting tired of this boyfriend, she'd have another one lined up, like that. That type of person. So then there was trouble between her, and Syd and his mother, and all that. So Syd and his brother went to live elsewhere.

Meryl seemed to have found the situation a lot of fun while it lasted. However, after the cousins' mother found out about the company they were keeping she came up to Calcutta to sort them all out. The upshot was that both of her boys were packed off to England and Meryl was left in the flat with her cousin's paramour and her children. By this time Meryl's view of the woman was changing, 'Her lifestyle was not nice at all. It had to come to an end, so she left, and then I was alone.' She said that her other neighbours had also gone by then. Her experience here is mirrored by so many Anglo-Indians who remained in Calcutta—most of their Anglo-Indians friends and neighbours disappeared, migrating from India to Britain and other countries.

I asked her how she managed once she was on her own in the flat and she explained:

> The servant who used to work for us, he stayed on, and he would be there all day. I had my pet dogs, you know. He was very fond of animals and he'd look after the dogs and then I'd come home from work, and he'd cook for me. He did everything. Like a man-Friday, he did everything. I didn't have to do a thing.

She seems to have entered a very settled time in her life, which she didn't elaborate on in our talks. She obviously enjoyed her job, and did very well there. Jumping forward a number of decades, I asked how she had come to be a resident in the Homes. She responded that it was down to her brothers' sudden death, but added that it was a good thing she was there, and another story ensued.

She told me that her brother spent time overseas serving as a warrant officer. He had come back and joined a British tea company, which had large tea warehouses, and was also involved in construction. After a number of years there, when he'd saved enough money, he left and started up his own business, which sent guards to accompany heavy consignments by rail. After setting himself up in business, her brother married later in life and a new set of problems began—for Meryl at least. According to Meryl, he married only on the advice of friends who thought he should take a wife to look after him in his old age. Her new sister-in-law was from the hills, not an Anglo-Indian but a Christian whose father had recently retired from service with the British Gurkhas. Meryl didn't think much of her brother's choice, describing her sister-in-law's social background as 'farmer types, you know, they live off the produce of the land. And they don't educate their girls'. At the time they married her brother's business was doing very well. Meryl believed that these assets and his earning potential were the main attraction for this woman who was half his age—so she was probably in her late 20s or early 30s when they married, although, according to Meryl, even in her later years she would never admit to being older than 48. For the first few years, his business continued to allow them a comfortable lifestyle, but that situation was not to remain, as Meryl explains:

> He was doing well but then as time went on, everything was changing. The Marwaris and the Sindhis and Punjabis, they were all ... they are business people, they don't serve, you know? So then these small operators they get pushed out.
>
> So he was not doing too well and this girl was very sharp and very pretty and all that. She had a sharp mind. She was a good person, but ambitious. His wife is very nice if you met her. You'd say she's a very nice person, but she's very possessive and very jealous and was wanting more and more. The more you gave the more she wanted. She saw anything on TV, advertised on TV, she wanted it. Now the time came when my brother couldn't give her all of that, so their attention turned towards me. Both of them, they thought that I had lots of money, all well hidden. And that was the start of the trouble.

'The trouble', as Meryl referred to it, alluded to the plans they made for Meryl's funds once they found their own were dwindling. They seemed to have expected Meryl to provide them the lifestyle they wanted. It wasn't long before she was paying all the costs involved in the running of both households. As if that wasn't enough, they then asked Meryl to move out of her flat and move into theirs with them. Meryl felt that this seemingly charitable, or at least economically sound suggestion, was selfishly motivated. In Calcutta, there are several different rental payment options: one is to pay a small deposit to the landlord upon moving in and then a higher monthly rental, the other is to pay the landlord a *salami* (a large inflation-adjusted deposit) and a small monthly rent. The amount paid as *salami* can be the equivalent of a deposit to purchase a house and is regarded by tenants as an asset as it's repaid upon moving out, when the next tenant pays the going rate. Meryl held her ground against moving out of her flat; instead her brother and sister-in-law moved in with her.

While the three of them had gotten along well enough, the situation deteriorated for Meryl when her brother suddenly died after a very brief illness. Like Meryl, he'd been 'hale and hearty' all his life. However, within three days of developing some sort of congestion, and then a fever, he died. He would have been over 80 years old by this time, Meryl was over 70 (at the time of this interview), and his wife was still 48 'ish'. Meryl said that her sister-in-law persisted in 'wanting things and thinking I've got money and just not spending it'. Understandably, she said, 'It was not at all nice to live like that. It was terrible.' Her church friends advised her to leave and move into a home. She didn't want to leave her dogs behind but after a lot of deliberation, and discussion with Philomena she was convinced to take them to a shelter where she'd still be able to visit them.

'Home' Life

Meryl surprised herself by very quickly adjusting to living at the Home:

> I'd never visited an old age home. I'd never dreamt of being in an old age home and in fact I told my brother I would never let him go to one. I thought an old age home is some place you go and you languish till you die. But it's almost like your own home: there's lots of flexibility and it's really as if you were in your own home. Really I feel much happier here than if I was staying with my sister-in-law. I wouldn't be able to stay with her.
>
> My relation, you know, that other cousin in Australia was phoning and asking, 'What's happened?' She told me that they have kept a room for me there. They were ready for me to go over there.

> *Did you want to go overseas, ever?*

> No, I never cared, as I told you, if I'm happy in one situation, I don't like to change.

Yet this was a big change to come here.

What a big change! I never thought I would ever come to an old age home. I never even visited an old age home. I told you what my idea of it was, of an old age home. I just came in a daze, you know, my footsteps were just directed over here. I just came in a daze and I found I was very glad that I came. I never missed my home at all. Forty years I'd lived in that flat. Now I don't ever go back to that house.

Over the month or so that I visited the Home, Meryl seemed very well and happy, despite being kept busy with her new responsibilities. At close to 80 years old she was active and able to walk down to the local market regularly, mostly to buy CDs to listen to. She loved watching TV programmes such as *The Bold and the Beautiful* and Agatha Christie reruns in particular. I knew not to bother her when either was on. Other residents seemed to respect this too.

Meryl still had a good appetite, especially for any sweet or savoury treats that came to the Homes. She had a great sense of humour and of fair play. She took her responsibilities seriously, agonising with me, for example, about a new rule imposed by the Home's management about giving treats to the Home's staff whenever residents received them. She was told that the staff was not to be given any extras because they'd got into the habit of expecting that whenever anything came into the Homes they would get something too. This rule was short-lived, to Meryl's relief, with committee members themselves breaking it after just a few days.

One Christmas day we — Keith, my brother and sister-in-law and two young friends of my daughter Rochelle — spent a few hours in the afternoon at the Home. We'd taken gifts and made good our promise to play bingo with them. I noticed that Daisy, one of the residents who had periods of depression when she refused to come downstairs, was missing from the lounge. I went up to her room and sure enough she was lying on her bed feigning sleep. I gently cajoled her into coming down, telling her it was the only way she'd get to meet Keith who she'd asked about on my earlier visits — male visitors are prohibited from going upstairs. She tidied herself up, even applying some lipstick and I took her down. She and Keith then spent time chatting and laughing. I was pleased to see her looking so happy, especially with it being Christmas day. Meryl had been watching too and made an excuse to call me into her office. I was bewildered when she began to warn me, 'You'd better keep an eye on Keith because Daisy can be a bit of a flirt'. My amusement at this caution was mixed with an appreciation of her concern for me. This wasn't the first time she'd gone out of her way to look after me. On the evening of our late-night interview, she'd insisted that the night watchman accompany me in a taxi back to my flat. I'd been aware that it was getting pretty late but the opportunity to interview Meryl was so valuable that I'd put that concern to the back of my mind. As a last resort, I could always have just stayed over. I was also made aware of some careful and diplomatic negotiations that were going on so that I could go with the Home residents to a Christmas party at Loreto House. In the end I didn't go, because Meryl couldn't leave the Home to attend it, but she'd been arranging with staff at the school for me to be specially invited. She said, 'One of the managers said this would be nice for you to see, to experience. But he also thought it might be a bit like gate crashing'. So they were trying to avoid, on my behalf, a bad impression being created.

For Christmas, we gave all of the residents a money gift (at Meryl's suggestion when I had asked her advice) and a copy of a group photo I had taken of them. For Meryl I added an extra photo—the one I had taken of her and Prince on the first day we met. She was delighted and exclaimed at how wild he looked, 'Ohhh, he looks like a wolf'. Also on that Christmas day, she was able to call her cousin from my mobile phone: this may have been the last time they talked.

Final Words: Reflections on Research and the Community

This book is the result of my research with Anglo-Indians in Calcutta over more than a decade. During that passage of time the city changed its name from Calcutta to Kolkata, Mother Teresa has been beatified and the Marxist government of over three decades had given way to Mamata Banerjee's Trinamool Congress Party. Theories about the imminent demise of the Anglo-Indian community always abounded. Contrary to this I have found, during my visits, a contesting story about Anglo-Indians, one of prominence in the national imagination. Anglo-Indian Derek O'Brien was nominated to the central government via the Trinamool Congress Party, the world Anglo-Indian Reunion was held in Calcutta and promenaded in the daily press, the Derozio Collection—literature on Anglo-Indians—was established in the Calcutta University library. All of this is in counterpoint to predictions of demise. Through all the vagaries of time and fortune, Anglo-Indians in Calcutta have gone about living their lives in diverse ways. I hope in my book to have captured the complexity of these lives, and the issues they face, not only at the time of the year when Anglo-Indians are most visible—Christmas time—but throughout the year, and into the future. Through their life stories, very often presented in their own voices, the range of ways of being Anglo-Indian will be apparent.

Each of the essays serves a particular purpose and while my arguments may not always find favour with all Anglo-Indians (e.g., the argument for modification, at least in implementation, of the constitutional definition), I hope that those who disagree with one aspect of my arguments will yet find ideas in this work that resonate with their own views and projects.

Although, technically an outsider to the community and Calcutta, I take seriously an oft-expressed concern by Anglo-Indians about the fragility of their future and I've looked for ideas that might provide some longevity.

Education is seen by most Anglo-Indians as the way forward, but there are practical changes within the educational institutional structures that can be enacted that would make this more effective for more students in the future; for example, making available books, uniforms, free tuitions and more scholarships to those who would benefit from them. It has always been a surprise to note that no Anglo-Indian history seems to be taught in Anglo-Indian schools. Surely they need to take a justified and realistic pride in being knowledgeable about their own history. Fortuitously, as I write, there is a move to establish, at a tertiary level, a centre for Anglo-Indian Studies, likely to be hosted by Calcutta University. Such an initiative could very well prompt their schools to provide appropriate courses in Anglo-Indian studies.

The solution to any alienation felt by Anglo-Indians because of the changes in the practice of Christianity, Catholicism in particular, may need to be pursued. As with any such issue, the first step in finding a solution is to identify the problem. What might go part way to solving this particular problem could involve scheduling local masses with more Westernised practices (not just English language). For example, in my New Zealand parish, *Indian* Masses are celebrated every month for the local Indian population. Hence, there is no reason why this practice cannot work in reverse in Calcutta. As I complete this book I am collaborating with Brent H. Otto S. J. on a project investigating the role religion has played, and continues to play, in forming Anglo-Indian culture and identity. Perhaps some further ideas will emerge from that research.

In the final section of my book, my aim has been to affirm what is being done so well by Anglo-Indian social service organisations. What they do is vital for Anglo-Indian sustenance—at both the individual and community level. As this book is being completed, CAISS, with Philomena Eaton as the reunion convenor, has just hosted the World Anglo-Indian Reunion in Calcutta. What could demonstrate more clearly that the social service organisations are at the helm of the community as it goes forward into the 21st century?

Just as I began on a personal note, I will finish by reflecting on the impact of my research with Anglo-Indians on my personal life, which has been in ways I would never have expected.

Anthropologists have had varied experiences when living amongst their research participants. Experiencing hardships, far away from home, is certainly not unknown. In the case of my work amongst Anglo-Indians, I was very fortunate to thoroughly enjoy experiencing their lifestyle highlighted by their love of socialising, dances and hospitality, and I have made many lifelong friends.

In the early years of my PhD research, after my marriage broke down, it was my involvement and commitment to Anglo-Indian research and my family and friends that saw me through this difficult phase. Later, through an Anglo-Indian symposium, I met and some years later partnered with Keith Butler, an Anglo-Indian writer originally from Delhi but whose school days and early years of working were in Calcutta. Through Keith and his publications I have had access to a particular period and phase of the Anglo-Indian experience. We have travelled back to India regularly over the years since. Going back to Calcutta these days is always an enjoyable time in which I am able to catch up with friends, as much as work on one project or another. Thankfully, the community offers multiple research opportunities; so I look forward to spending many more Christmas seasons in Calcutta.

Bibliography

Abu Lughod, L. (1993). *Writing Women's Words: Bedouin Stories*. Berkeley: University of California Press.
Anderson, B. (1991). *Imagined Communities: Reflections on the Origin and Spread of Nationalism*. London: Verso.
Andrews, R. (2005). *Being Anglo-Indian: Practices and Stories from Calcutta*. PhD Thesis. Massey University, Palmerston North.
———. (2006a). Assam Days: An Interview with Philomena Eaton, in M. Deefholts and G. Deefholts (eds), *The Way We Were*. New Jersey: CTR Inc.
———. (2006b). English in India: Reflections Based on Fieldwork among Anglo-Indians in Kolkata. *India Review*, 5(3–4): 499–518.
———. (2009). Living and working in Calcutta: Jane's Story, in F. Patal and K. Naidoo (eds), *Working Women: Stories of Strife, Struggle and Survival*. New Delhi: SAGE Publications.
———. (2010). Christianity as an Indian Religion: The Anglo-Indian Experience [Research]. *Journal of Contemporary Religion*, 25(2): 173–188.
Angrosino, M. V. (1994). The Culture Concept and the Mission of the Roman Catholic Church. *American Anthropologist*, 96(4): 824–832. Retrieved from http://www.jstor.org/stable/682446.
Anthony, F. (1969). *Britain's Betrayal in India*. Bombay: Allied Publishers.
Ashcroft, B. (2001). *On Post-colonial Futures: Transformations of Colonial Culture*. London, New York: Continuum.
Barone, T (2001) *Touching Eternity: The Enduring Outcomes of Teaching*. New York: Teachers' College Press of Columbia University.
Barth, F. (1969). *Ethnic Groups and Ethnic Boundaries: The Social Organisation of Culture difference*. London: George Allen and Unwin.
Bayly, S. (1989). *Saints, Goddesses, and Kings: Muslims and Christians in South Indian Society, 1700–1900*. Cambridge: Cambridge University Press.
Bear, L. (1998). *Traveling Modernity: Capitalism, Community and the Nation in the Colonial Governance of the Indian railways*. Michigan: University of Michigan.
———. (2007). *Lines of the Nation: Indian Railway Workers, Bureaucracy, and the Intimate Historical Self*. New York: Columbia University Press.
Blunt, A. (2002). 'Land of Our Mothers: Home, Identity, and Nationality for Anglo-Indians in British India 1919–1947'. *History Workshop Journal*, 54: 49–72.
———. (2005). *Domicile and Diaspora: Anglo-Indian Women and the Spatial Politics of Home*. Oxford: Blackwell.
Borofsky, R. (2006). Conceptualising Public Anthropology. Retrieved from www.publicanthropology.org/Definingpa.html, accessed on 13 May 2012.
———. (2007). Defining Public Anthropology: A Personal Perspective. Retrieved from http://www.publicanthropology.org/public-anthropology/, accessed on 8 March 2013.

Bourdieu, P. (1993a). Concluding Remarks: For a Sociological Understanding on Intellectual Works, in C. Calhoun, E. LiPuma and M. Postone (eds), *Critical Perspectives*. Cambridge: Polity.

———. (1993b). *The Weight of the World: Social Suffering in Contemporary Society*. Stanford: Stanford University Press.

Bourdieu, P. and L. Wacquant. (1992). *An Introduction to Reflexive Sociology*. Chicago: University of Chicago Press.

Bourgois, P. (1996). *In Search of Respect: Selling Crack in El Barrio*. Cambridge: Cambridge University Press.

Brass, P. (2004). Elite Interests, Popular Passions, and Social Power in the Language Politics of India. *Ethnic and Racial Studies*, 27(3): 353–375.

Caplan, L. (1995). Creole World, Purist Rhetoric: Anglo-Indian Cultural Debates in Colonial and Contemporary Madras. *Journal of the Royal Anthropological Institute*, 1(4): 743–762.

———. (1996). Dimensions of Urban Poverty: Anglo-Indian Poor and Their Guardians in Madras. *Urban Anthropology*, 25(4): 311–346.

———. (1998). Gifting and Receiving: Anglo-Indian Charity and Its Beneficiaries in Madras. *Contributions to Indian Sociology*, 32(2): 409–431.

———. (2001). *Children of Colonialism: Anglo-Indians in a Post-Colonial World*. Oxford: Berg.

Chaudhuri, N. C. (1967). *The Continent of Circe: Being an Essay on the Peoples of India*. London: Chatto and Windus.

Council, E. (1963). Constitution on the Sacred Liturgy *Sacrosanctum Concilium*: Vatican 2.

D'Cruz, G. (2006). *Midnight's Orphans: Anglo-Indians in Post-Colonial Literature* (Vol. 1). Bern: Peter Lang.

Delofski, M. (1998). *A Calcutta Christmas: Stories of Friendship and Hope*. Australia Limited. Retrieved from www.filmaust.com.au.

Dempsey, C. (2001). *Kerala Christian Sainthood: Collisions of Culture and Worldview in South India*. Oxford: Oxford University Press.

Dempsey, C. and S. J. Raj. (eds). (2002). *Popular Christianity: Riting between the Lines*. New York: State University of New York Press.

D'Souza, A. A. (1976). *Anglo-Indian Education; A Study of Its Origins and Growth in Bengal up to 1960*. New Delhi: Oxford University Press.

Dumont, L. (1971). *Religion, Politics and History in India; Collected Papers in Indian Sociology*. Paris: Mouton.

Durkheim, E. (1965). *The Elementary Forms of the Religious Life, a Study in Religious Sociology*. (J. W. Swain, Trans.). London: Allen and Unwin.

Dutt, A. (2007). *Bow Barracks Forever*: Pritish Nandy Communications. Duration time: 118 minutes.

Frykenberg, R. E. (2008). *Christianity in India: From Beginnings to the Present*. Oxford: Oxford University Press.

Fuller, C. (1992). *The Camphor Flame; Popular Hinduism and Society in India*. Priceton: University Press.

Ganeri, A. (2003). *The Guru Granth Sahib and Sikhism*. London: Evans Brothers Limited.

Geertz, C. (1998). Deep Hanging Out. *The New York Review of Books*, 45(16): 69–72.

Gilbert, A. (1996). *The Anglo-Indians in Australia, from Unsuccessful Caste Members to Attaining Immigrants: An Examination of Anglo-Indian Labour Force Performance and their life Perceptions*. PhD Thesis. Monash University.

Green, J. (1998). Language: English in India: The Grandmother Tongue. *Critical Quarterly* 40(1): 107–111.
Hage, G. (2004). *Against Paranoid Nationalism*. Annandale N.S.W.: Pluto press.
Hawes, C. (1993). *Eurasians in British India, 1773–1833: The Making of a Reluctant Community*. PhD Thesis. University of London, London.
———. (1996). *Poor Relations: The Making of a Eurasian Community in British India 1773–1833*. Surrey: Curzon Press.
Lobo, A. (1994). *A Comparative Study of Educational Disadvantage in India within the Anglo-Indian Community: a Historical and Contemporary Analysis*. PhD Thesis. Institute of Education, London.
———. (1996a). Anglo-Indian Schools and Anglo-Indian Educational Disadvantage Part 2. *The International Journal of Anglo-Indian Studies*. Retrieved from http://www.alphalink.com.au/~agilbert/cover1.html.
———. (1996b). Anglo-Indian Schools and Anglo-Indian Educational Disadvantage Part 1. *The International Journal of Anglo-Indian Studies*. Retrieved from http://www.alphalink.com.au/~agilbert/cover1.html.
Maher, R. (1962). *These Are the Anglo-Indians*. Calcutta: Sona Printers.
Massey, D., S. Joaquin Arango, Graeme Hugo, Ali Kouaouci, Adela Pellegrino and J. Edward Taylor. (1998). *Worlds in Motion: Understanding International Migration at the End of the Millennium*. Oxford: Claredon Press.
McCourt, F. (1996). *Angela's Ashes: A Memoir*. London: HarperCollins.
McMenamin, D. (2001). Identifying Domiciled Europeans in Colonial India: Poor Whites or Privileged Community. *The International Journal of Anglo-Indian Studies*, 6(1). Retrieved from http://www.alphalink.com.au/~agilbert/identi~1.html.
———. (2006). Anglo-Indian Experiences during Partition and Its Impact upon Their Lives. *New Zealand Journal of Asian Studies*, 8(1): 69–95.
Mee, J. (2001). Not at Home in English? India's Foreign Returned Fictions. *The Round Table*, 366: 711–720.
Merchant, I. (1999). *Cotton Mary*: Universal Studios. Duration time: 124 minutes.
Mills, M. (1996). Some Comments on Stereotypes of the Anglo-Indians. *The International Journal of Anglo-Indian Studies*, 1(1). Retrieved from http://www.alphalink.com.au/~agilbert/jmills1.html.
———. (1998). *Ethnic Myth and Ethnic Survival: The Case of India's Anglo-Indian (Eurasian) Minority*. PhD Thesis. Toronto. York University.
Mishra, P. K. (2000). English Language, Postcolonial Subjectivity and Globalisation in India. *A Review of International English Literature*, 31(1 and 2): 383–410.
Moch, L. P. (2005). Gender and Migration Research, in M. Bommes and E. T. Morawska (eds), *International Migration Research*, pp. 95–110. Hampshire: Ashgate.
Mundadan, A. M. (1984). *Indian Christians: Search for Identity and Struggle for Autonomy*. Bangalore: Dharmaram Publications.
Myerhoff, B. (1978). *Number Our Days*. New York: Simon and Schuster.
Nagel, J. (1998). Constructing Ethnicity: Creating and Recreating Ethnic Identity and Culture, in M. W. Hughey (ed.), *New Tribalisms: The Resurgence of Race and Ethnicity*. New York: New York Press.
Narayanan, V. (2002). Afterword: Diverse Hindu Responses to Diverse Christianities in India, in S. J. Raj and C. Dempsey (eds), *Popular Christianity in India: Riting Between the Lines*. New York: State University of New York Press.

Raman, A. S. (1996). The Future of English in India. *Contemporary Review*, 268(1560): 16–22.

Robinson, R. (2003a). *Christians of India*. New Delhi: SAGE Publications.

——— . (2003b). Fluid Boundaries: Christian Communities in India, in B. Charkrabarty (ed.), *Communal Identity in India*, pp. 287–305. Oxford: Oxford University Press.

Roychowdhury, L. (2001). *The Jadu House: Travels in Anglo-India*. London: Black Swan.

Sahlins, M. (1993). Goodbye to Tristes Tropes: Ethnohistory in the Context of Modern World History. *Journal of Modern History*, 65: 1–25.

Sankar. (2007). *Chowringhee* (A. Sinha, Trans. First in English ed.). New Delhi: Penguin.

Sealy, A. I. (1988). *Trotter-Nama*. New York: Knopf.

——— . (2007). The Anglo-Indians, in D. Prakash (ed.), *The Anglo-Indians*. New Delhi: Photoink.

Sen, J. (1988). Marriage among the Catholic Anglo-Indians in Calcutta *Marriage in India (Tribes, Muslims and Anglo-Indians)*. Calcutta: Anthropological Survey of India.

Shostak, M. (1990). *Nisa: The Life and Words of a Kung Woman*. London: Earthscan Publications limited.

Stark, H. (1926). *Hostages in India: Or the Life Story of the Anglo-Indian Race*. Calcutta: Fine Arts Cottage Press.

Trlin, A. D. (1997). For the Promotion of Economic Growth and Prosperity: New Zealand's Immigration Policy, 1991–1995, in A. D. Trlin and P. Spoonley (eds), *New Zealand and International Migration: A Digest and Bibliography, Number 3*, pp. 1–27. Palmerston North: Massey University.

Tully, M. and Gillian Wright. (2002). *India in Slow Motion*. New Delhi: Viking, Penguin.

Turner, E. (1996). *The Hands Feel It: Healing and Spirit Presence among a Northern Alaskan Poeple*. Illinois: Northern Illinois University Press.

Turner, J. (1997). Continuity and Constraint: Reconstructing the Concept of Tradition from a Pacific Perspective. *The Contemporary Pacific*, 9(2): 345–381.

Young, G. M. (1952). *Macaulay: Prose and Poetry*. London: Rupert Hart-Davis.

Younger, C. (1987). *Anglo-Indians: Neglected Children of the Raj*. Delhi: B.R. Publishing Corporation.

——— . (2003). *Wicked Women of the Raj: European Women Who Broke Society's Rules and Married Indian Princes*. New Delhi: HarperCollins.

Entries from Vatican Documents

Culture, P. C. f. (1995). Congregation for Divine Worship and the Discipline of the Sacraments, Instr. IV 'for the Right Implementation of the Second Vatican Council's Constitution on the Sacred Liturgy.' *Varietates Legitimate*: AAS 87 (1994/5): 294–295.

Vatican. (1994). *Inculturation and the Roman Liturgy*. Vatican City.

Index

Adivasi, 81
Adopt a Gran project, by Canada's association, 178
agarbatti (Indian incense), 74–75
All India Anglo-Indian Association (AIAIA), 16, 18, 29, 56, 125, 137, 164, 180
Anderson, Benedict, 179
Angeline, lifestory of, 1, 3–6
  professional training of, 6–7
  schooling of, 6–7
Anglo-Banglos, 19
Anglo-Indian Nisa, 3
Anglo-Indian Rest Home management committee, 27
Anglo-Indian School Boards, 136
Anglo-Indians, in Calcutta, 1–2, 206
  changes after Independence, 8–12
  and Christians/Christianity community, 68, 78
  practices followed by, 69–75
  cultural characteristics of, 17–23
  definition under Section 366, Article 2 of Indian Constitution, 13, 30
  official definition and its implications, 23–25
  illiteracy and poor education among, reasons, 130–136
  origin of, 13–17
  reunion in Toronto (2007), 25–26
  schools in Indian education system, 97, 124
  week, 114
Anthony, Frank, 97, 136
Aunty, 85

Banerjee, Mamata, 206
Barry O'Brien, interview with, 180–190
  educational qualification, 186–190
  family life, 184–186
  working for Anglo-Indian community, 180
Bear, Laura, 130
bhajjies, 62
bicultural society, 30
big *dechki*, 58
boundaries, formation of, 29
Bourgois, 102
Bow Barracks Forever movie, 17
Boxind Day dance, 172–173
British Gurkhas, 201
British Raj, in India, 13, 194
  attitude towards Anglo-Indians, 14
  elite system of schools during, 123
bustee (slum), 20, 22
Butler, Keith, 208

Calcutta Anglo Indian Service Society (CAISS), 26–28, 63, 155, 157, 164–166

establishment of, 170–171
Philomena Eaton's appointed as convenor of, 171
traditional events held by, 172
Calcutta Girls' High School, 193
Calcuttan Anglo-Indian woman, 28–29
Calcutta's Anglo-Indians, 19, 67, 108, 168, 173
Calcutta Tiljala Relief Incorporated (CTR), 22–23, 26
caste professions, 8
Catholic Christians, 25, 48–49
Catholic churches, 71, 79
Catholicism practice, 67, 207
Catholic masses, 71
central business district (CBD), 17, 21
Centre of Studies in the Social Sciences, Calcutta (CSSSC), 26
chauffeur, meaning of, 102
children of Anglo-Indians, protection to, 112–113
36 Chowringhee Lane film, 1
Christian community/Christianity, 49, 66
   Anglo-Indians practices, 78
   house altars and holy pictures, 69–71
   impact on Christianity, 82–83
   namaste practice, 71
   rosary and procession at barracks, 72–75
   Calcutta's Anglo-Indians, 67
   Hinduised, 69
   Holy Day obligation on Sunday, 68
   place in India, 75–78
Christian missionaries, views about Anglo-Indian population, 124

Christmas carols, 178
Christmas in Calcutta, 174–175
Christmas tree, 172–173
Church of North India (CNI) services, 71
Colonial administrators, 10
colonial period, Anglo-Indians origin during, 13–17
commercial jobs, 9
Communist Party of India (Marxist), 180
community care, 155–156
community cultural values, Anglo-Indian, 81

dalpuris, 57
dearness allowance scheme, 15
Derozio, Henry, 114
diasporic Anglo-Indians community, 178–179
Domiciled Europeans, definition of, 24
Dulcie, interview with, 51–54
   day-to-day assistance from local people, 63–65
   early working life, 55–63
   school work, 54–55
Dutt, Anjan, 17

East India Charitable Trust (EICT), 12, 177
East India Company, establishment in 17th century, 13
education/education system
   Anglo-Indians and, 123–125, 207
   for community survival put first, 115–116
   makes people life better, 116–117
   in modern India, 97

elderly Anglo-Indians, residential homes for, 178
elite system of schools, 123
Elliott Road (Calcutta), 21
employment reservations, for Anglo-Indians, 15
English language
   Anthony's views on, 136
   as language of prestige, 125–127
   as mother tongue of Anglo-Indians, 122
   recognition as another language of land, 122
English medium faith-based schools, 97
English-medium schools, 124
English speaking ability, of Anglo-Indians, 9
ethnicity, 29
ethnocentrism, Anglo-Indian, 132
Eurasians, 14. *See also* Anglo-Indians, in Calcutta
European preference, to Anglo-Indians before Independence, 9
European missionaries, in India, 97

faith practice, 49–50
family reunion wave, 16
Feast of Christ the King, celebration on Sunday, 66
Federation of Anglo-Indian Associations, 68
first War of Independence, 14
Frank Anthony Schools, 97, 180

Gandhi, Sonia, 27–28
Goa, Christianity in, 77, 84
Government of India Act, 14
grants allocation, for Anglo-Indian schools, 15

half-caste, 14. *See also* Eurasians
Hawes, Christopher, 14
Hicks, Clifford, 98
hierarchy of colour, 160
Hilltop Club, 162–163
Hindi as national language, concern for Anglo-Indians, 15
Hindu influence, on Christianity, 74
Hinduised Christians, 69
Hinduism, 67
Hindu priests, 69
Holy Day obligation, 68
holy pictures, 69–71
Homes, Graham, 38, 99, 107–108, 113, 115–117, 120, 140, 143, 147–148, 151, 161, 174, 177
House altars, 69–71
House of the People (Lok Sabha), 15
Howrah Jute Mills, 41
hybrid community, 14

illitarcy among Anglo-Indians, causes for, 130–136
illiterate English speaker, in Indian context, 121
   paradoxical situation of, 122
   Peter's case study, 128–130
imagined communities, 178
inculturation
   areas of liturgical, 80
   definition of, 79–80
   methods of, 80
   significance of, 79
Independence
   Anglo-Indians life, 8–12
   movement, 194, 198
Indian Cricket League, 76
Indian Red Cross Society, 56
Indian School Certificate (ISC), 132

individual migration, 16–17
inter-marriage by Anglo-Indians, with Indians, 10
internet, used to promote fund-raising projects, 178
Inter State Board of Anglo-Indian Education, 137
Irene, interview with, 32–33
  husband profile, 41–45
  involvement with son's father, 46–47
  life of
    early working life, 38–39
    married life, 40–41
    relationships, 39–40
  qualified as Anglo-Indian identity, 33–37
Islam, 74–75
iwi (tribal) involvement, New Zealand, 30

The Jadu House, 19
Jane, interview with, 93–94
  belief in god, 88–90
  courage to fight with polio, 90
  difficulties for parents to take care, 87
  disadvantage to be born as a girl, 87–88
  educational qualification, 91
  optimistic attitude, 95
  struck by polio during childhood days, 86
job reservation system, for Anglo-Indians, 9, 131

Kali puja, 72
Kerala, Christianity in
  contemporary Christianity in, 77
  Saint Thomas arrival in, 76–77

spreading by Belgium Priest, 75
kofta balls, 58

life of Anglo-Indians, since Independence, 8–12
Little Australia, 17, 22. *See also* Picnic Garden, Calcutta
Lobo, Ann, 124
local Anglo-Indian, 173, 178

Madras, Anglo-Indians in, 16, 170
marriage patterns, among Anglo-Indians, 19
Marwaris, 60, 198, 202
Marxist government, 206
Massey University, 128
Meryl, interview with
  family life, 199–203
  home life, 203–205
  Quit India and personal repercussions, 194–199
Methodist school, 7
Michael Robertson, interview with, 107–120
migration among Anglo-Indians, after British Raj, 15–16
Mills, Megan, 14
minority, Indians, 136–137
Minute recommendations, by Macauley for English-medium schools establishments, 124
Mitra, Amit, 98
mixed marriages, 27
moral community, Anglo-Indians, 169
Mother Teresa, 206
mother tongue, 123
Muslim *bustee*s and shacks, 20, 22
Mutiny, 14. *See also* first War of Independence

namaste practice, by Anglo-Indian Christian community, 71
national census (1911), 28
native rites, Christian, 77
nehari, 57
New Year, 63, 66, 165, 172–173
night shelter, 171
non-Anglo-Indians, 15, 48, 67
non-catholics, 78
non-governmental organizations (NGOs), 92

oxymoron, 121

Partition of India, 6, 194, 197
Peter, interview with, 99–100
 case study, 128–130
 early career, 101–102
 marriage life, 103, 106
 mode of earning, 104
Philip, interview with, 138–139
 finishing of school, 144–145
 girlfriends, 150–152
 golden Saturdays, 152–153
 planning about future, 153–154
 responsibilities of an older sister, 143–144
 school life, 140–141
 tertiary study and first job, 145–150
 winters at home, 141–143
 at World Anglo-Indian Reunion (2004) Melbourne, 167
Philomena Eaton, interview with
 Assam days, 158–160
 convenor of CAISS, 166
 meeting with friends at Hilltop Club, 162–163
 mother warning on tea garden types, 161

Picnic Garden, Calcutta, 17, 22
pious land, 68
poorly educated among Anglo-Indians, causes for, 130–136
Popular Christianity (C. Dempsey and S. J. Raj), 78
Post-Vatican II inculturation, 79–82
pre-Christmas jumbles, 173
procession practice, at barracks by Christians, 72–75
public anthropology, 122

Quit India movement, 194–199
quotas in government jobs, for Anglo-Indians, 15

Ramnee Convent, 7
religion, in India, 68, 76
religious, 72
Roman Catholic, 46
rosary practice, at barracks by Christians, 72–75

sacred, 68
saree, 32
scenes, 1
schools, in modern India, 97
secularism, 67
settler community, 30
S. N. Banerjee Road, Calcutta, 171
social change, 122
social service organisation, Anglo-Indian, 121
social suffering, 128
Sunday. *See* Holy Day obligation

Tagore, Rabindranath, 81
Teachers Training Certificate (TTC), 98, 106

tea garden, 161
Toronto's world Anglo-Indian
    reunion (2007), 25–26
Trinamool Congress Party, 206

Urdu coaching, by Angeline, 7
Urdu language, 6

West Bengal's Anglo-Indians, 180
Western forms of Christianity, 84
whites-only policy, Australia, 16

Williams, Blair, 26
Williams, Ellen, 26
women, Anglo-Indian, 18–19,
    26–27
World Anglo-Indian Reunion
    in Calcutta, 98, 206–207
    in Melbourne, 137, 166–167
    in Toronto, 25, 137, 167

Young Women's Christian
    Association (YWCA), 193

About the Author

Robyn Andrews is a Senior Lecturer in the Social Anthropology Programme at Massey University, New Zealand. She completed her PhD in 2005 which was based on ethnographic research of Calcutta's Anglo-Indian community. The author's main research interest is in Anglo-Indian studies. She is a recipient of several grants from the University towards this area of research. She continues in her research involvement with the community with a focus on the diaspora, life-story collection and ageing in particular. She was awarded a Massey University Women's Award in 2009. Andrews has published numerous articles in prominent journals and has several published articles in edited volumes.

SAS-APP-124
14/6/69